READING *between the* RECIPES

READING
between the
RECIPES

A year's worth of inspired, innovative, often outrageous ideas on New England food and cooking

By Leslie Land

YANKEE BOOKS
A division of
Yankee Publishing Incorporated
Dublin, New Hampshire

Designed by Jill Shaffer
Illustrated by Tamar Haber-Schaim

Yankee Publishing Incorporated
Dublin, New Hampshire 03444
First Edition
Copyright 1987 by Leslie Land
Printed in the United States of America.

Library of Congress Cataloging-in-Publication Data

Land, Leslie.
    Reading between the recipes.

    Includes index.
    1. Cookery, American — New England style.
I. Title.
TX715.L239   1987   641.5974   87-11883
ISBN 0-89909-143-1

CONTENTS

 **Spring**

 **Summer**

 **Winter**

*I*NTRODUCTION

THOUGH I started cooking as a child in rural Pennsylvania and started writing about it as a chef in urban California, the two didn't come together in earnest until shortly after I moved to Maine. Ironically, I came to Maine because it was beautiful, because the intellectual and social temperament of the place seemed likely to suit, because farms were cheap. Like so many who came here before me, I didn't stop to think about the food situation at all.

This was, for one so strongly gastronomically inclined, a nearly disastrous omission, because ever since the Pilgrims landed and promptly almost starved to death, moving to New England from Somewhere Else has been tough on people who like to eat. Mangoes will not grow here, for instance, and neither will anything else except alfalfa sprouts for a good part of the year. Four centuries of comparative ethnic homogeneity have effectively driven everything but meat and potatoes into the category of exotic foreign cuisine, and the legacy, foodwise, of those Pilgrims is not one of sensual indulgence.

Things have changed enormously in the years that followed my arrival, but at that time the state of Maine was rich in exactly those culinary resources that had greeted the first European settlers: lobsters (though these were no longer lying around on the beaches in windrows, waiting to be picked up), mussels (which *were* lying around on the beaches in windrows, etc.), clams and fish, an abundance of wild fruit — blueberries, raspberries, strawberries, mushrooms — and game. Furthermore, it was easy to get next to a piece of land, land which, though justly famous for growing stones, was fertile enough if encouraged.

I gathered the mussels, picked the fruits, made friends with hunters and fishermen. I planted my garden, mail-ordered and imported, learned to do without the vast array of comestibles California had taught me to expect unquestioningly. As I had in the Golden State, I cooked to make my living, catering parties, teaching small classes, consulting for the "new style" restaurants that began arriving just about when I did. As I had all my life, I cooked for pleasure, for my friends, for myself, for the sensual gratification inherent in feeling and handling and making and tasting, and for the deep satisfaction that comes with providing nourishment.

Reading Between the Recipes is a sort of informal chronicle of that life in food, a "greatest hits" collection — with some expansion and embellishment — of the newspaper columns I began writing for the *Camden* (Maine) *Herald* in 1974. These columns have always been very personal, essentially a series of chatty letters from a dedicated cook and gardener who also happens to love reading, talking, and the rhythms of the English language — fundamental affections developed almost as early as an appreciation of good things to eat.

The house I grew up in was rich with books, and I think I read them all. There's no doubt my voracity included the shelves full of "cookbooks" that contained not only classic instruction manuals — *Joy of Cooking*, etc. — but also literary works by such authors as M.F.K. Fisher and Ludwig Bemelmans. Thus I learned, well before I learned to cook, that reading about food was (almost) as much fun as eating it, that food writing could mean a lot more than simple recipe transmission. This being the case, my columns have always been written as much to entertain as to inform, as much (or more) to inspire as to instruct.

They have also been written with the assumption that anyone who decides to use the recipes they offer knows at least the rudiments of ordinary cooking. If my experience as a teacher is any indication, this is almost everybody, although almost everybody is inclined to be overly modest about it. The truth is that anyone who has spent at least a little time preparing food knows a great deal more about the basics than they think.

They also know (as does *anyone* who enjoys the stuff) that all good cooking starts with the freshest and finest of raw materials. Since I live on the northern New England coast, my version of good cooking naturally features quite a bit of seafood, lamb, pork, and cream, while including lots of ol' reliable potatoes, carrots, and cabbage among the asparagus, squash blossoms, and wild raspberries.

Still, I did develop as a cook in Berkeley, California, where ethnic restaurants abound and all sorts of experimentation is not only encouraged but expected, so in my kitchen these classic Down East staples are fired with chilies, lightened with herbs and wine, prepared with the world-tour of techniques and flavors that has come to be called (albeit not, as a rule, by me) the "New American Style." The cooking described in this book is a hybrid of urban sensibility and rural resources, a best-of-both-worlds cuisine. It evolved in response to Snowbelt conditions but is philosophically applicable wherever people can still taste the difference between what is truly fresh and what is merely uncooked.

Here in New England, the seasons make themselves felt with special intensity, not just in the weather but in the constraints that weather (and our place at the end of the line) put on what's good to eat and when. Winter is seriously deficient in fresh produce; summer's gorgeous bounty is an ever heart-renewing miracle. Cold weather calls for hearty meals, and elaborate recipes hold few terrors when hanging out in the warm fragrant kitchen is such a pleasant way to spend the time. We probably cook more here in all seasons since there is only a short time in high summer when it's just plain too hot to want to. When that time does come, we cherish our salads with an ardor those who enjoy year-round gardening cannot imagine.

It may well be we're more closely tied to the seasonal procession of holidays, as well. Christmas *is* white on the evergreens; Independence Day *is* long, long, blue-skied perfect picnic time; pure summer all the more poignant for being so brief. A harvest festival like Thanksgiving has deep resonance when the next things on the agenda are the root cellar, freezer, and produce aisle.

So, being written from life, this can't help being a New England seasonal cookbook. It is divided into forty-eight chapters, which are tidily (if somewhat arbitrarily) assigned to spring, summer, autumn, and winter — four per month, in other words, which allows one week in every season for eating out. Though most are closely tied to the calendar, the nature of Nature is such that the timing and order of chapters cannot always be exactly accurate.

Spring, for instance, covers the months of March, April, and May, and the chapter on asparagus (spear of spring, sweet sword of newness) will be found in a May chapter. This is, however, in large part a matter of convenience. Spring is always asparagus, all right, but just *where* in spring asparagus actually appears will differ depending on what kind of year we've had, in the narrow sense, and, more generally, on whether the asparagus is growing in Massachusetts or Michigan, California or Colorado. Furthermore, the asparagus season, though brief, does last more than a single week. The reader is therefore advised to consult the indexes when dealing with seasonal produce. Checking out the tables of contents for adjacent seasons probably wouldn't hurt either. Now that modern vegetable marketing has so muted true seasonal progression, some foods may show up in places other than the obvious.

Christmas, on the other hand, can be expected to fall in the fourth week of December no matter where you live, though since cookies have no season for them as loves them, a general index is also provided. Finally, it must be confessed that there are a few chapters that fall every bit as randomly as life does. My chocoholic friend Ann-Marie is addicted in *all* seasons; she just happened to land in spring.

In other words, this book is not a complete guide to seasonal cooking, nor is it a historical overview of New England cuisine. It is instead a sampling of the ways I've found to share delight, rail against the shoddy, and speak out as a committed cook on some subjects that are important. It is meant to be read for pleasure as much as to be cooked from, to inspire the creation of new recipes and the cherishing of old ones while providing a small collection of my own and my friends' favorites from over the years.

A Note about the Recipes

This is by no means a balanced overview of the parts of the meal. There are far fewer fish recipes than one might expect, for instance, because I usually cook fish simply. There are, on the other hand, lots of vegetables in both starring and supporting roles. I like vegetables fancy, as well as plain. In the manner of all general cookbooks since time out of mind (or at least since Gutenberg), there is a definite tilt in the direction of dessert. Of all parts of the menu, desserts require the most specific instructions.

The recipes are to a large extent written out conversationally, as approximate transcriptions of what you'd get if I were sitting at the kitchen table and Holding Forth. They contain a lot more words than the telegraphic recipes in general circulation, but they are not really any longer when it comes to the execution. In fact, by using hints, asides, and warnings to clarify many small points most standard recipes ignore, they should, after the first reading, speed things up.

A Note about the Numbers

These are, of course, highly problematical. A teaspoon of paprika from a fresh, newly opened can has a lot more seasoning power than twice that amount of ancient dust that has been sitting on a shelf above the stove for months. Four ravenous people just in from a hard day's skiing will easily consume "six portions" of almost anything and still have room for seconds, even if you did give them hors d'oeuvres to start with. Except in places such as pastry making, where strict accuracy is obviously essential, the numbers provided in recipes should be seen through the eyes of common sense. Where two measurements are given — 2 cups beans, about 1 pound; or 1 large onion, about 1½ cups — the first takes precedence; the second is for clarification.

Acknowledgments

Most of the pieces in this book are compilations, knitting together in one place the best of several years' musings and recipes on their particular subjects. It is hoped that putting them together will obviate the need for drawers full of yellowing, brittle newspaper clippings, and I have tried to include readers' favorites as requested over the years. Most of the material comes from the "Good Food" column, but a few pieces or parts thereof are from my writing in other publications: *Maine Times, Cuisine, Yankee* Magazine, and the *New York Times*.

SPRING

EQUINOCTIAL LAMENT
Chased by the Lamb of Spring

I *HATE* SPRING, loathe and abominate the very sound of the word, young love and lilacs notwithstanding, regardless of the swallow's location (I don't care if the wretched birds are in Capistrano or Keokuk, as long as nobody mentions them).

According to the timeworn joke, my northern New England home knows only two seasons — winter and the Fourth of July. Would it were true. I know I'd miss lilies of the valley, rhubarb, sorrel, and the first green peas, but I could learn to live without them if it meant a true change in the order of things, because what we really have here is winter, the Fourth of July, and Mudtime.

Mud, of the purest ray serene, mud as far as the eye can see and the foot make tracks, from the middle of March through April and most of May, to say nothing of June in bad years. Oh, the grass does indeed green up. The peepers chirp. First tulips, then apples, then peonies bloom. But these are only minor motifs, scarcely seen through the incessant screen of mist and rain, a melody pretty but far too faint, drowned out by the loud crying of the year's most awesome chore list and the loud lip-smackings of legions of bloodsucking bugs.

So sing me no song of the sweet equinox; seek not to beguile me with folk tales of blossoms and birds. I say it's spinach and I say the hell with it.

Spinach, its actual especially-delicious-in-springtime self, of course, is another matter entirely. Those first tender plants — as few as five dark crinkled leaves and two or three paler ones, all joined by their pearly stems to that tender thread of root — make a bouquet as welcome as violets to the winter weary. Good for you, too, just loaded with phosphorus, iron, and pro-vitamin A. There was a while when it looked like Popeye was going to be debunked, as nutritionists pointed out that the oxalates in spinach tied up the calcium, making it unavailable to the body, and that these might even, in large doses, be harmful in themselves.

Fortunately, it's not that bad. Spinach isn't as great an iron source as previously supposed, but you'd have to eat a few pounds a day before the oxalates would be a problem. When it comes right down to it, this is something I could almost do, when the first garden spinach comes in, except that I have to leave plenty of room for the lamb.

Finding the actual lamb of spring is sometimes a bit of a trick, since "genuine spring lamb" can be slaughtered anytime from March first through early October. Current USDA regulations distinguish only between lamb, yearling mutton, and mutton, basing the distinctions on such things as the fragility and size of the animals' bones and the color and texture of the meat. Generally speaking, the smaller the cut for its type, the younger the animal from which the meat comes; in other words, a four-pound whole leg of lamb will be from a more lamblike creature than an eight pounder.

Baby lamb, though it has no legal definition, is generally accepted to be an animal less than six weeks old. But unless you are a person of Mediterranean heritage seeking a traditional Easter roast, there's not much point in purchasing these expensive, tender creatures because that's all they have to recommend them — tenderness. Being too young to have had the chance to run around much, they have a flavor so delicate the indelicate might call it bland.

Ordinary lamb of the supermarket sort is less subtle than the spring lamb of former days, less robust than the flavorful dark red mutton that is, alas, all but unknown here. Nevertheless, this is one place where "middle of the road" really does mean "all-purpose," and the lamb we can most easily buy has much to recommend it.

Among its other virtues is its position as one of the least messed-around-with of modern meats. Even agribusiness sheep lead relatively tranquil lives, neither intolerably overcrowded nor heavily drugged. And because sheep do so well on small farms, many "natural" and "organic" growers are entering the marketplace, offering locally grown lamb that is both fresh and delicious.

Whether locally grown, shipped from the Midwest, or imported frozen from New Zealand, just about all the lamb sold in this country is young enough to be nicely tender yet old enough to have at least a modicum of distinctive, meaty flavor without being unpleasantly strong.

It's great roasted, grilled, sautéed, stewed, and baked; it goes splendidly with all sorts of vegetables, grains, and seasonings; and why on earth it isn't more popular has always been a mystery to me. (I'd blame it on the gray meat syndrome, since lamb in America is almost invariably horribly overcooked. But people have been ruining pork for years without affecting *its* popularity much, so there must be some other reason.)

Spinach-Stuffed Mushrooms (and everything else)

For 4 appetizer or 2 main dish servings

¼ cup butter
1 small onion, chopped fine, about ¾ cup
12 ounces large mushrooms, as uniform in size as possible
1½ pounds fresh spinach, thoroughly washed, drip-dried, and coarsely
   chopped
½ cup coarse dry bread crumbs
½ cup coarsely chopped toasted almonds or hazelnuts
1 egg
Pinch each of salt, white pepper, and nutmeg
Knife point's worth of crushed garlic
2 ounces Parmesan cheese, grated fine
2 ounces Gruyère cheese, shredded on the small holes of the grater
Olive oil for the baking sheet

Melt the butter in a skillet over medium heat. When it foams, add the onion and cook, stirring frequently, until it is golden. While the onion is cooking, wipe off the mushrooms with a piece of damp paper towel. (Washing them removes flavor and harms texture and is hence to be avoided unless they're absolutely filthy.)

Cut off and discard the bottoms of the mushroom stems, then remove stems from caps and set them aside. Use a melon-baller or the sharp edge of an old spoon to scrape out some of the mushroom meat, making room for more filling. Combine scrapings and stems and chop coarsely.

When the onions are ready, raise the heat slightly and add the chopped mushrooms. Cook, stirring often, until the mushroom juice has evaporated and the mixture is starting to brown. Stir in the spinach and cook, stirring, just until the greenery is wilted. Take the pan from the heat and let the mixture cool.

Combine the spinach mixture with the bread crumbs and nuts, then blend in the egg, seasonings, and garlic. If the mixture is dry, add a tablespoon or two of cream, rich milk, sour cream, or dry sherry. The filling should be soft and creamy but not runny.

Fill the mushroom caps, piling the mixture lightly and first mounding, then slightly flattening, the tops. Mix the cheeses, then sprinkle the mixture on the mushrooms. Caps may be prepared up to this point several hours in advance, then chilled, tightly covered with plastic wrap. Let them return to room temperature before proceeding.

Move a rack to the upper third of the oven and preheat to 425°F. Lightly oil a flat baking sheet, set the mushrooms thereon, and pop 'em in. Bake 6 to 10 minutes, depending on size, just until the cheese is lightly browned and everything is hot through.

This stuffing is also good rolled into plain crêpes, thin slices of ham, sole fillets, or pounded chicken breasts. You'll have to adjust cooking time and temperature to suit the chosen envelope; the thicker and rawer, the longer and slower. The stuffed item also may be either steamed in a bit of broth or sautéed in some flavorful fat. Whatever the cooking method, hollandaise sauce makes an excellent accompaniment.

Lambsteak

This is my favorite way to eat lamb, charcoal-broiled when possible, pan-broiled when not. Either way you get juicy, flavorful meat much tastier than any but the very finest beef. Inconveniently, the recipe makes just enough for three, but there's nothing for it, given the size of lambs. Leftovers are terrific, however, so when necessary, simply double the meat and increase the marinade as described.

For 3 servings*

1 lambsteak, 2½ inches thick (see directions)
½ cup olive oil
Finely shredded zest (thin, colored outer rind) of 1 lemon
¼ cup lemon juice
1 teaspoon each crushed oregano, mustard seed, and sugar
1 or 2 large cloves garlic (optional)

---

*To increase for a double recipe, use 1 cup oil, ⅓ cup lemon juice, 2 teaspoons each oregano and mustard, and the same amount of lemon zest and sugar.

Have the butcher cut the steak from the wide end of a shank end leg of lamb, leaving the bone in. This cut is now widely marketed precut, but it's almost never thick enough.

Mix together everything except the garlic and the lamb, put it in a flat, noncorrodible dish such as a glass pie plate, and put the steak in the dish. Swish the marinade around and turn the steak over so all surfaces are covered, then cover the dish tightly with plastic wrap and marinate the steak in the refrigerator, turning occasionally, at least 5 hours; overnight is fine.

Take the meat out of the refrigerator long enough ahead of cooking that it will be room temperature. Remove it from the marinade and wipe it dry with paper towels (leftover marinade can be saved for about a week and used for another bath).

If you want, cut the garlic into thin slivers and stud the meat with it. It's certainly tasty, but the flavor of lamb without the flavor of garlic deserves to be remembered, too. Pare off all but a thin rim of fat and cut a few times around the edge, just through the membrane, not the meat, so the steak won't curl as it cooks. Broil by one of the methods below to the degree of rareness you usually accord steak. Serve carved against the grain in wide diagonal slices, the way you would carve London broil. I might add here that rare — somewhere between magenta and rose — is the only way to eat steak, and the same goes for the lamb.

TO BROIL OVER COALS: Use a bit of the pared-off fat to grease the thoroughly preheated grill. Lay on the lambsteak and sear about an inch above very hot coals for about a minute. Turn with tongs, sear the other side, then raise the grill to 3 to 4 inches above the heat and cook without turning again for 8 minutes or more, until the desired doneness is reached.

TO PAN-BROIL: This does create a bit of smoke but also gives much better results than the broilers that come with most stoves. Use a heavy cast-iron skillet big enough to give the meat a bit of breathing room. Put the pan over medium heat and get it good and hot. Rub lightly with a piece of the pared-off fat, raise heat to medium-high, and after a minute, start testing. When a drop of water dances, lay in the lambsteak. Sear about 2 minutes, turn with a flat pancake turner, and sear the other side. Pour off any accumulated fat, lower the heat, and continue cooking 8 more minutes, until the desired doneness is reached.

🌸 Shepherd's Pie

The delicate touch of cinnamon in the filling, the flaky filo dough crust, and the beauty of the presentation make this a company-special dish of leftovers. You might, in fact, want to make it from scratch. To do so, just use a little bit more meat and cook it longer at the initial stewing stage.

For 4 generous servings

1½ cups chopped onions, about 1 large
1 tablespoon olive oil
2½ to 3 cups cooked lamb, cut into ½-inch cubes
2-inch cinnamon stick
½ bay leaf, about a ½-inch piece
2 large cloves garlic, minced
⅓ cup finely minced parsley
½ cup water
½ teaspoon salt, or to taste
Enough baking potatoes to equal 2 cups prepared
4 tablespoons melted butter and olive oil in any combination
8 leaves frozen filo dough, thawed (see Note)

In a heavy skillet with a tight lid, slowly cook the onions uncovered in the olive oil until they are completely cooked, a nice warm medium brown. This will take quite a while, but you don't have to pay much attention. Stir occasionally. When the onions are browned, add the meat, cinnamon stick, bay leaf, garlic, parsley, and water. Stir well, then cover the pan and simmer over very low heat until the meat is almost tender, about 40 minutes. Uncover and stir every now and then. When the meat is ready, uncover the pan, raise the heat to medium-high, and cook, stirring constantly, until almost all the moisture has evaporated and the meat is covered with a very thick glaze of sauce. Stir in the salt and allow to cool. Remove cinnamon and bay.

While meat is cooking, peel potatoes, shred on coarse holes of the grater, and cover with a generous amount of cold water. Preheat the oven to 400°F. Lightly brush a deep 10-inch pie pan with the melted butter mixture (henceforth referred to as mixture). Set a sheet of filo on the work surface and brush it lightly with the mixture. It needn't be completely covered; a combination sprinkling/stroking motion that dots the entire surface will do. Lay the sheet in the pan, with most of the overlap to one side. Tuck the liner against the inside of the pan so it conforms to the shape. Repeat with the remaining sheets, distributing the overlaps so they are equidistant, like petals, around the outside of the dish. There should be only a small amount of mixture left when you finish.

Working quickly now, drain the potatoes, then roll 'em up in a tea towel and squeeze. You want them as dry as you can get them. Brush most of the mixture evenly over the inside of the lining, up as far as the edge of the pan, then use about two-thirds of the potato shreds to line the bottom and sides of the crust. Carefully add the meat and its bit of sauce. Center the remaining potatoes in a mound on top, then spread them by pinches into a 4-inch circle. The idea is to leave the surface as spiky as possible. Fold the filo edges so they overlap and reach about halfway to the center, leaving a bull's eye of potato shreds. By this time the filo will be very dry and brittle; the crust ring you are forming *already* mighty flaky. S'okay, just keep turning and folding. The finished product will look rather bird's-nesty, which is very pretty once it's browned. Sprinkle the remaining mixture over the surface, paying special attention to the potatoes, cut several slits in the filo so steam can escape, and bake the pie 10 minutes. Reduce heat to 375°F. and bake 30 minutes more, or until it is richly brown all over.

Let it cool a minute or two so it will cut neatly and be less likely to burn your tongue. This can be served plain, but a bowl of yogurt is an ideal partner. If you aren't a yogurt fan, serve the pie with a pitcher of classic Greek avgelemono sauce, which is simply rich broth seasoned with lemon juice and thickened with egg yolk.

A NOTE *about Filo Dough:* Also known as fillo, philo, and strudel. The frozen product, formerly available only in specialty stores, is more and more widely available at supermarkets. Most packages come with fairly complete instructions, the more important of which are: (1) *Do* thaw slowly; it helps keep the sheets from sticking together. (2) Be sure to keep the unused portion covered to prevent drying; the stuff is so thin it desiccates almost instantly. (3) Don't get fussed. Sheets often tear or stick together (or both) in spite of your best efforts. As most packages contain about two dozen sheets, while recipes seldom call for more than half that, you've got plenty of room to make mistakes. If one sheet gets botched, just toss it. Working with filo is very easy if you keep a lightsome attitude.

MELT SEASON

THE NAME comes from the Anglo-Saxon *smoelt*, meaning smooth or shining, a tribute echoed in the French name *éperlan*, or pearly, and the Spanish *eperlano* — all of which refer to the fish's silvery, scaleless skin. Its fragrance, when fresh, is strongly of cucumbers (some say violets). The flesh is tender and very sweet, and it has been a New England favorite since pre-Colonial times.

Smelt, like salmon, are anadromous fish, spending part of their lives in the ocean and part in fresh water. The great spawning runs of early spring yield the biggest catches, though smelting starts in late fall, as the fish come inshore. Smelt are also one of the ice fisherman's most dependable quarries.

My own single smelt-fishing experience occurred in the late fall, at daybreak, on dry land at the mouth of a stream, with cold feet and a Coleman lantern and a beautiful bamboo pole like something the Shakers might have made. There was none of this casting and reeling business, just a lowering of the bobbin-marked hooks and lots of hopeful waiting — the lines layered thick with ice, raised wet into the freezing air then dipped in the river again.

There was a flask, and an agreeable air of conviviality and (comparative) physical warmth, but no fire, no heater, no stove, no snug little smelt shack with pinups on the walls in which to sit comfortably and while away the expectant hours. Between about 3:30 and 6:00 A.M., the three of us caught twelve smelt, or maybe fourteen. The largest was a monster, perhaps ten inches long; the smallest was a Fabergé toy, a perfect four-inch-scale model fish, all silver and pearlshell.

We ate them for breakfast, fried in butter, with creamy scrambled eggs for sauce and little lemon zest–flecked cakes made from some left-over mashed potatoes, and they were quite possibly the best fish I've ever eaten, including the numberless smelt that have gone down my gullet since. Pride of the fisher may have had something to do with it, of course, but I have no doubt it was primarily because they were *fresh*, which makes, if possible, even more of a difference with smelt than it does with fish in general.

Fortunately, with smelt, as with asparagus, there is a sort of secondary freshness that's still pretty darn good. And a good thing, too, because when one goes to the fish market in New England in March, smelt is about it for finfish, unless you are not yet tired of halibut steaks or have somehow managed to retain your taste for badly processed cod.

Actually the last decade has seen some mighty encouraging changes when it comes to fresh fish and fish markets. What was once a hell of frozen haddock, relieved only by shellfish, has become a place where an ever-increasing variety of fresh fish is more and more widely available. More markets are opening and more of them are selling things like farm-raised catfish from down south and formerly scorned monkfish from right here in New England.

Nevertheless, the cold months remain the off-season for fish, when going after them is most dangerous and the fish themselves are out in deep water, trying, like everybody else, to keep warm. Improvements at the fresh-fish counter notwithstanding, this is still the time of year to enjoy fish that's been preserved — preferably that which has been preserved in some more interesting way than in the freezer.

No longer a necessity (thanks to fast transport, refrigeration, and freezing), salt cod is still enjoyed for its distinct and appealing flavor, much the same way salt pork products have held their own. Many traditional dishes simply wouldn't be possible without it, and for those who love it, like A.J. McClane, author of *The Encyclopedia of Fish Cookery*, "the agonies of withdrawal when left in a codless land are never dispelled."

It is generally conceded that salt codfish has worked its way most deeply into the cuisines of Spain, Portugal, and southern France. France's most famous treatment is probably *brandade de morue*, a rich, garlicky purée of the fish, lightened (if that's the word) with olive oil and milk. The best known Spanish classic is *bacalao à la vizcaína*, a preparation of the fish in an intense, sweet pepper–based piquant sauce that's appealing in the extreme, while Portugal's "favorite" entries are so numerous it's impossible to pick a front-runner. My vote goes to Cod in Green Sauce, the green of which comes from an abundance of parsley.

Still, delightful as these preparations are, they do not hold a candle, in my opinion, to codfish cakes, an old-fashioned New England breakfast staple that has never been surpassed. Crisp and golden without, tender yet chewy within, delicious served on their own or accompanied by scrambled eggs, they are a Sunday morning delight of long standing. Spiced up, made small, and served with any one of an assortment of appropriate dips, they also make an elegant nibble for the cocktail hour.

Buying Salt Cod

The addicted Mr. McClane is scornful of "supermarket salt cod exhumed from little wooden coffins (that) offers only a provocative memory of the past," but that is what's most readily available, and the truth is it's really pretty tasty. It is, however, milder than the whole split fish, cured with the skin on, that is still to be found in ethnic markets in large cities. Whatever sort you buy should be a nice white color, evenly but not heavily crusted with salt, fragrant only pleasantly.

HISTORICAL NOTE: Salt cod's great popularity in the Caribbean and parts of West Africa, though sometimes attributed to its good keeping qualities and robust flavor compared to the mildness of most tropical fish, is in fact an ironic legacy of the slave trade. Salt cod, America's first major commercial export, was shipped from New England to Spain and Portugal. The profits were then used to buy people in Africa, and these in turn were taken to the West Indies (being fed leftover salt cod along the way). There they were exchanged for sugar and the molasses that became New England rum. This tidy arrangement, the Golden Triangle, provided the basis of many Massachusetts fortunes and gave birth to what became known as "the codfish aristocracy."

Fried Smelt

While they can, of course, be deep-fried in batter or crumbs, and that is the way they are most often presented around here, their delicate taste and texture are better served by a short pass through a bit of butter. The starch coating may be seasoned flour, cornmeal, or some mixture of the two, but when the smelt are fresh, simplicity, in the form of plain flour, is once again recommended.

There is no recipe as such. Clean the fish; old-timers do it by twisting off the heads and drawing the entrails out as they do so, but I generally proceed in a more conventional manner. Wipe out the insides with paper towel or rinse them in milk. (Discard the rinse milk or give it to the cat.)

Dip the fish in milk, shake off all excess, then coat lightly with flour. Film a heavy skillet with a generous layer of butter and add about 1 teaspoon of oil to keep the butter from scorching. Heat until the fats are foaming, then fry the fish, uncrowded, until each side is brown and crisp — from 2 to 4 minutes a side depending on the size of the fish. Turn with a pancake turner so they don't bust and serve as soon as they come out of the pan.

Some people pour the scrambled eggs right onto the smelt and finish the two together, but this treatment diminishes the crispness of the smelt, while making the eggs absorb an untoward amount of butter. It is not, therefore, a course I recommend.

Lime wedges make a nice change from lemon, and coarse salt and the pepper grinder ought both to be handy. Theoretically, a half pound or so of fish per serving, weighed after beheading, will be plenty. In my experience, this is only a theory. Crisply fried fresh smelt don't seem to register in the stomach until you've eaten about twenty.

Fried Smelt, Part Two

The above remarks about deep-frying do not apply if you deep-fry the fish in very light, extra-virgin olive oil — an expensive indulgence compared to Crisco but cheap as indulgences go. Make sure the oil is at least 1½ inches deep, heat it to 365°F. to 370°F., prepare the smelt as described above, and expect them to take about 4 minutes. Don't crowd the pan. Paradise.

Codfish Cakes

For about 10 breakfast patties or 3 dozen cocktail sized

1 large carrot, cut in 1-inch chunks
1 medium onion, quartered
1 celery stalk with leaves, chopped coarse
1 bay leaf
1 whole dried red pepper (optional)
1 pound salt codfish, freshened according to the instructions on page 25
    but not precooked
3½ cups plain mashed potatoes, about 4 medium-sized potatoes
1 teaspoon grated nutmeg
1 teaspoon finely grated lemon zest (thin, colored outer rind)
2 tablespoons grated onion
1 egg
1 egg yolk
Fat for frying
Salt (may not be needed)
Milk (may not be needed)

Combine the carrot, quartered onion, celery, bay leaf, and red pepper with enough water to cover the fish generously in a stainless steel, glass, or enamel pan. Bring the liquid (without the fish) to a boil, lower heat slightly, and cook at a rolling simmer for about 15 minutes. Add the fish, turn the heat to low, and simmer gently 5 to 15 minutes, depending on size and thickness of the pieces. Turn off the heat, cover the pan, and let the mixture sit about 5 minutes.

Drain the fish and spread it out on paper towels to dry even further. Remove any skin and bones and measure; you should have 2½ to 3 cups. Put the fish in a bowl and use two forks to shred it. These shreds are what produce that famous chewy texture. For a smoother product, purée the fish in a blender or processor.

Combine the prepared fish with the potatoes, nutmeg, lemon zest, and grated onion, beating vigorously. Then beat in the egg and the yolk. For codfish balls, plan to deep-fry; for cakes, simply sauté. Lard, butter, and bacon fat all produce wonderful flavors; olive oil isn't very New England but is tasty nevertheless. Heat an amount of fat appropriate for your chosen cooking method — medium-hot for sautéing, 375°F. for deep-frying. Test fry about a tablespoon of the mixture and correct the seasoning. If you were efficient in the initial soaking, you might want to add some salt.

Form the remaining mixture into patties or balls (adding a bit of milk if the mixture is too dry to hold together) and cook, allowing 3 to 4 minutes a side for the cakes, 3 minutes all together for the fritters. Drain well and serve at once. Catsup is the traditional sauce, along with lemon wedges and a garnish of parsley sprigs, but sour cream, hot mustard, and tartar sauce all have their champions.

VARIATION 1: These are delicious hotted up with ½ to 1 teaspoon crushed dried red pepper or about a heaping tablespoon minced fresh hot chili. When the cakes are prepared this way, *salsa cruda*, the simple un-cooked sauce of tomatoes, onions, chilies, and fresh coriander that is the catsup of Mexico, provides the ideal dip. They're good with guacamole, too, especially at cocktail time, and a nice gooey cheese sauce isn't bad either.

VARIATION 2: Like most fairly dry fritter doughs, these will carry up to about ¾ cup of just about any nonwatery addition that strikes your fancy — bits of crisp bacon, tiny cubes of ham or garlic sausage, corn kernels, toasted almonds, thinly sliced green onions, whatever.

FRESHENING SALT COD: Before the fish can be prepared, the salt must be leached out in several changes of cold water and the fish then briefly poached in hot. How long soaking will take depends on how heavily the cod was salted to start with. As a rule, the more pliable the fish, the more readily it will freshen. Instructions below are for the super-market variety; more heavily cured fish will take longer.

Metal utensils tend to discolor the fish, so use stainless steel, earthenware, or glass for both soaking and cooking. Slow soak: Allow at least 12 to 14 hours of refrigerated soaking in cold water. Change the water several times. Fast soak: Cover the fish with cold water and let it soak at room temperature about 4 hours. Drain. Replace water and put the bowl under a gently dripping cold tap for 30 minutes more. Never soak in warm water; doing so leaches flavor as well as salt.

TO PRECOOK: Cover the fish with cold water and bring slowly to a boil. Right *before* boiling is reached, lower the heat and cook at a slow simmer 5 to 15 minutes depending on the thickness of the fish. Drain and proceed with your recipe. Never let salt cod boil, or it will turn stringy.

Unabashedly Anchovy Pizza
(With Walnuts and Rosemary)

For a 12- by 17-inch pizza

Olive oil for pan, about 2 teaspoons
1 batch pizza dough, homemade (recipe follows) or purchased
2 tins (2 ounces each) anchovies packed in olive oil
2 to 3 tablespoons minced garlic, depending on strength
2 to 3 tablespoons fresh rosemary leaves, depending on pungency
6 ounces mozzarella cheese, the higher the quality the better
½ to ⅔ cup coarsely broken walnuts

Quantities are difficult to give exactly here, because so much depends on the quality of the materials, which have very assertive tastes. Anchovy should predominate, being made smoother by the garlic and piqued by the rosemary. If your garlic is very pungent, briefly blanch the cloves in boiling water before mincing. Usually the garlic available in spring has the opposite problem, but you never know.

A pan and a hot oven are the parents of a crisp crust, so preheat the latter to 475°F. and use the olive oil to grease a 12- by 17- by ½-inch baking sheet (or a pair of 10-inch pizza pans, which will require about ⅓ more of each filling material).

Roll the dough out on a lightly floured board until it is almost big enough to fill the pan. Fit it loosely into the pan and let it rest about 5 minutes. At the end of this time it will have relaxed, making it easy for you to push and press until the dough completely covers the bottom, with a generous rim around the edge. Sprinkle most of the oil from the anchovy cans over the surface of the dough, then distribute the minced garlic as evenly as possible. Arrange the anchovies on top of that, then add the rosemary, then make as all-covering a lid as you can from the cheese. Apply the walnuts and a few discrete final drops of anchovy oil. Cheap cheese tends to weep fat, so omit this final oiling if your mozzarella isn't all it could be. Put the pizza into the oven at once and bake about 18 minutes, or until the crust is a nice rich brown. Serve at once and eat it up: The absence of tomato means this is a low-moisture item, and as such it will not reheat well.

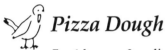 ## Pizza Dough

For 1 large or 2 medium-sized thin-crust pizzas

¼ teaspoon sugar
1 cup lukewarm water
1 tablespoon dry yeast (1 envelope)
2½ to 3 cups unbleached flour or bread flour
Pinch of salt

Combine the sugar with half the water, stir in the yeast until dissolved, and set the mixture aside until foamy. Beat in ¾ cup of the flour, then, when the mixture is smooth, the remaining ½ cup water and the salt. When all is smooth again, start adding flour, switching to a wooden spoon and then to kneading until you have a smooth, elastic, rather hard ball of dough. The more kneading you do, the better, but even a token effort will produce something that works pretty well. (So will a food processor. Just follow the bread-making instructions that came with the machine, using these ingredients.)

Oil a bowl with olive oil and turn the dough therein until it is coated. Cover and set in a warm place to rise double, about 1½ hours. This dough is ready after the first rising but can be punched down and permitted to rise again, or even twice more, before it'll run out of energy.

*I*RISH EATS
For St. Patrick's Sake

"PALEONTOLOGY" . . . "Parnell" . . . "parrotfish" . . . "Pasteur" . . . "Patagonia" . . . "pawnbroking" . . . "Paul, The Apostle" (getting warmer) . . . Here we are — Patrick, Saint. One and a half pages of very tiny type from which I learned a number of things I never knew (I'd always thought he was Irish, for instance) and a number of things I will never remember, such as "the British name of the future apostle was Sucat, to which mod. Welse *hygad,* 'warlike,' corresponds. His Roman name has also survived in a hibernicized form, Cothrige, with the common substitution of Irish *c* for Brythonic *p.*"

What I did not learn was anything about what St. Patrick ate (or didn't eat), and my general knowledge of Middle-Late Celtic cuisine — Patrick was born around A.D. 389 — is too limited to support conjecture. On the other hand, *nothing on God's green earth could make me offer you a recipe for something green,* with lime Jell-O or without it.

Unfortunately, when it comes to recipe writing of the "you are there" school, the sort that enables the willing American cook to concoct a reasonable facsimile of just about any dish, be it ever so exotic, the Irish is a most intractable cuisine; rather, come to think of it, like the cuisine of New England. Everything that's good about it is pretty much a function of fine, very fresh raw materials, prepared as simply as possible.

Out of the cow and into the pitcher, out of the trout stream and into the pan, *that's* what's great about traditional Irish food, a greatness utterly independent of the more complicated kitchen arts and uncompromisingly rural. Spices, prepared foods, and preserved items are used sparingly. Wine, the great mediator, is scarcely used. All this makes it difficult for city dwellers, even those right there on the ould sod, to prepare food that is both ethnographically correct and enjoyable by the non-Irish. Easily translated native dishes, such as bread fried hard in bacon grease, are tough to love if you haven't been brought up to 'em, while treats such as fresh Dublin Bay prawns and thick, unpasteurized country cream, while universally appealing, are nearly unobtainable.

Nevertheless, the situation is far from hopeless for those desiring to take note of the holiday at table. Several fine Irish products do travel pretty well — that bacon, for instance, and the whisky. Other quintessentially Irish foods have equally tasty, very close counterparts here. Salmon comes to mind at once, and let us not forget about the potatoes.

Irish Salmon Stew

Almost a chowder, actually, though innocent of salt pork.

For 4 servings

1 large or 2 small onions, chopped quite fine, about 1½ cups
2 tablespoons butter
¾ pound potatoes, peeled and sliced ⅛ inch thick, about 2 cups prepared
Approximately 1½ cups water or stock from salmon trimmings
3 cups milk, or, for state occasions, 2 cups milk and 1 cup cream
¾ pound boneless, skinless salmon, cut into smallish (about ½-inch) chunks
Salt and white pepper to taste
½ cup finely minced fresh parsley
2 to 3 tablespoons minced fresh chives (optional)

Cook the onion in the butter over medium-high heat, stirring often, until it is golden and starting to brown. Lower heat and arrange the potato slices, in flat layers, on top of the onion. Pour in just enough water or stock to barely cover the potatoes. Cover the pan and simmer 30 to 40 minutes, or until the potatoes are so completely tender they come apart if poked with a knife. Add the milk, stir well, and heat the stew, uncovered. As soon as it is hot again, stir in the salmon.

Continue to cook 5 minutes or so, being careful the liquid doesn't boil. When the fish is cooked through, starting like the potatoes to fall apart, the stew is done. Season with salt and pepper to taste and stir in the herbs right before serving. This tastes even better if you can make it a few hours to a full day in advance. The rest period in the fridge intensifies and blends the flavors. Hold the herbs until serving time, however, so they'll stay fresh and crisp and — happy St. Patrick's Day — green.

Total Potato Tart

For 6 servings

CRUST:
Butter for pan and foil, about 2½ tablespoons
Enough baking-type, starchy potatoes to yield 3 cups prepared, about 1½ pounds

1 egg
3 tablespoons flour
1 teaspoon Dijon mustard
½ teaspoon salt

FILLING:
4 loosely packed cups unseasoned mashed potatoes, approximately 2
  pounds
1 clove garlic, crushed (optional)
¼ cup lightly piled, freshly grated Parmesan cheese, about 1½ ounces
¼ cup minced fresh parsley
2 tablespoons minced green herbs in season (choose from tarragon, dill,
  chervil, and chives in any combination)
1 egg
2 egg yolks
Approximately 3 tablespoons heavy cream or sour cream
Salt to taste
2 egg whites
1½ tablespoons butter, melted

Choose a fairly shallow 10-inch pie plate or quiche pan and butter it *lavishly.* Heavily butter the dull side of a piece of tinfoil large enough to line the pie plate. Move a rack to the upper third of the oven and preheat to 350°F.

Peel the crust potatoes, cut them to potato chip thickness, and cut the slices into match sticks. You should have 3 cups of something that looks like short spaghetti — thin julienne shreds. Some food processors will make these, for which they are to be commended, but it doesn't really take that long to do it by hand. (Grating won't work, as the flat shreds pack and get soggy.)

Mix the potatoes with the other crust ingredients and spread the result in an even layer over the bottom and sides of the prepared pan. Fit the foil on snugly, buttered side down, natch. Either fill the foil with pie weights or dry beans or nestle in another, slightly smaller pan of the same shape. The object is to weight the crust so it cooks without slouching and to spread the heat so the center will cook as well as the outside.

Bake 20 minutes, remove lining materials, and bake 20 to 30 minutes more, or until the crust is dark golden. Take it from the oven and turn the heat up to 375°F.

Meanwhile, make the filling by combining all the ingredients except the egg whites and the melted butter, in the order given. Judge the amount of cream by texture. The potato mixture should be creamy and soft but not so loose as to be liquid. When the crust is ready, beat the egg whites until stiff but still shiny and fold them into the filling.

Pile the filling mixture in the hot shell, swirling the top with the back of the spoon or even putting a final bit through the wide star tip of a pastry tube. Brush all over with melted butter, getting some into every nook and cranny, and return the tart to the oven. Bake 20 minutes, or until the filling is heated and set and the crust well browned and crisp. If you like, set under the broiler about 4 minutes to brown the top.

You can bury a thin layer of almost anything in the middle if you want this to be a one-dish dinner. Consider crabmeat, shrimp, sliced scallops (put these in raw), shredded ham, cubed cooked chicken, shredded cheese — blarney cheese, perhaps. Even leftover curry is good, as long as it's not too liquid.

Soda Bread

This delightful quick bread is right up there with potatoes for coming instantly to mind when you think of Irish food. It comes very quickly to the table as well, taking almost no time to mix and a comparatively short time to bake. Like all breads leavened by the interaction of acid and alkaline ingredients, it should be eaten freshly baked, as it turns stodgy, dries out, and stales much more quickly than yeast bread. Like all unfermented breads that are both lean and (except for salt) unseasoned — in fact, like everything Irish — it is utterly dependent on the flavor of its few raw materials. Fresh stone-ground whole-wheat flour never made more of a difference than it does in soda bread. The bread will be tasty made with ordinary flour, but it won't be in the same league.

Of course, there are limits to all this. The fanatics who insist that the bread be baked the traditional way (in an iron pot at the edge of a glowing peat fire) are not going to get to eat very much in the way of soda bread. Still, once you've bothered to locate good ingredients, it's worth trying to approximate that classic baking method, which produces a light, agreeably moist bread with an excellent crust.

Elizabeth David, in her very fine treatise *English Bread and Yeast Cookery*, recommends baking the bread on a flat sheet, covered with a deep cake tin — a round, straight-sided pan 6 to 8 inches deep. I prefer a deep, heavy, heavy-lidded cast-iron kettle — the old-fashioned Dutch oven (see Note 1). Either way, jury-rigging an oven inside the oven, while not essential, will improve the finished product.

For a good-sized 8- or 9-inch loaf, ample for 4 as a major component of the meal

Butter for the baking pan
1¼ cups unbleached flour
1½ teaspoons salt
1 teaspoon baking soda
2¼ cups fresh stone-ground whole-wheat flour (see Note 2) or 1¾ cups whole-wheat flour and ⅓ cup oat bran
1 to 1½ cups buttermilk

Preheat the oven to 425°F. If you are using a Dutch oven, lightly butter the bottom and preheat it, too. If you are using a baking sheet, butter that, cover it with the cake tin as described above, and preheat both.

In a large bowl, combine the unbleached flour, salt, and baking soda with a wire whisk, stirring thoroughly to be sure the soda is completely distributed. Stir in the whole-wheat flour (then the oat bran). Switch to a wooden spoon, make a well in the middle of the dry ingredients, and slowly pour in the milk, stirring constantly. You want a smooth, quite stiff, not sticky dough, and you want to get there as fast as possible — this riser is even more volatile than baking powder. It's important to add the milk slowly, since you probably won't need it all.

On a floured board, with a few fast motions, form a round, flattish loaf about 1½ to 2 inches tall. Transfer to the baking sheet or bottom of the preheated pan (remember it's hot). Use a very sharp, thin-bladed knife to cut a cross about ½ inch deep in the top of the loaf. Cover and bake about 40 minutes, or until the loaf is well risen and brown and sounds hollow when tapped. Cool on a rack about 10 minutes, then serve while still warm.

VARIATIONS: A friend makes this entirely of unbleached flour, embellished with ¾ cup of raisins and a teaspoon of caraway seeds. All whole-wheat is good too, though flatter and chewier than the version above. Some recipes, the ones in my *Joy of Cooking* and *The Gourmet* cookbooks, for instance, include considerable amounts of butter and sugar. Adding these, you end up with something more like scones, or, in the case of *Joy of Cooking*, coffee cake. Both are tasty, but neither is soda bread as classically understood.

NOTE 1: I have never used an enameled iron kettle of this type and would caution against doing so. The enamel, being empty, might very well crack, and if it is a pale color it will inhibit browning.

NOTE 2: Fresh stone-ground whole-wheat flour can be purchased in health food and specialty stores. It should be refrigerated, and if you're lucky it'll be dated as well. Good home grain mills are quite expensive but possibly worth it if you bake a lot of whole-grain bread and have the storage room. Like pasta machines, grain mills are frequently bought by enthusiasts whose zeal turns out to be temporary, which means they are sometimes obtainable secondhand. Consult the bulletin board at your neighborhood co-op or health food store.

*T*HE JUMP ROPE DIET

THIS BLIZZARD of new reducing diets has gotten out of hand. Every time you turn around there's been another breakthrough, and keeping up with developments has become not just exhausting, but also depressing.

Why not arrange it so all the year's revolutionary, totally amazing, best-ever reducing diets are released at once, in a blockbuster "spring show" the way they do it in the world of High Fashion? There could be a gala party, with proceeds going to a suitable charity — hunger relief, say — and similar fashion show atmospherics: troops of photographers and reporters, an array of dignitaries, perhaps a notable academic or two, to lend tone.

Each candidate for Best-Selling Reducing Diet Designer would parade down a long carpeted aisle, clad in something sufficiently scant to reveal the success of the diet, while celebrity announcers read a few of the grislier instructions from the work under consideration. Well, maybe not that last requirement, since I would be entering myself, with the frequently resorted-to stratagem described in the title.

To follow the jump rope diet, simply keep track of what you eat, then jump rope one time for each calorie consumed. This does not perform miracles; it actually takes about seven jumps to eradicate a calorie. What it does is (a) get you to jump rope for at least twenty minutes a day, long enough to crank up your metabolism so you burn a few more calories just living than you otherwise would, and (b) make you extremely conscious of what you're eating, since you must both write it down and pay for it. This increase in the exercise of both body and superego is remarkably effective.

There are a couple of problems, of course. This diet is pretty athletic. It's hard on the joints unless you have proper shoes and remember to Keep Those Heels Down! Furthermore, though it has enabled me to slim down a whole size, though my posterior is smaller and my cellulite much reduced, the fronts of my thighs are enormous, and my calves look like somebody stuffed baseballs in my socks. "Which does make my ankles look mighty dainty," she reflected, gazing at the bright side.

These difficulties probably would be less severe if I did better at the eating part. Less meat, fat, and sweet; more fish, vegetables, grains, and fruits — this will always be the diet of choice, though it may take a bit of time before it is the diet of desire.

It is getting easier, however, with the palette of fruits and vegetables growing daily more dazzling, and the choices at the fish market expanding apace. Perhaps most important, such low-calorie flavor enhancers as garlic and hot peppers are being welcomed by former meat and potatoes types who would, in pre-Tex-Mex-Szechwan-Cajun days, have recoiled from them in horror.

 ## All-Purpose Low-Calorie Chicken Breast

For 2 servings

1 large chicken breast, ¾ to 1 pound
1 small onion, sliced horizontally into 4 or 5 slices
3 tablespoons dry white wine
1 teaspoon dried herb agreeable to your taste — oregano, rosemary, thyme, or tarragon

Preheat the oven to 350°F. Use a heavy, sharp knife or kitchen shears to trim any protruding piece of bone that might tear the foil. Remove and discard the skin and any loose fat.

Put a large sheet of tinfoil — shiny side down — on a flat pan and center a bed of the onion slices, placed in a single layer, on it. Top them with the chicken breast. Partially fold up the sides of the foil so the wine doesn't run out, then pour the wine over the meat. Sprinkle on the herb (don't add salt; it will draw juice and dry out the chicken).

Finish folding the foil, bringing the long sides in, then the short ones, double-folding the seams so steam doesn't escape. Be sure the seams remain well up so nothing can leak out. Bake approximately 30 minutes, or until the meat is cooked through. The onions should be saved for another purpose, such as soup. The juices in the package are the sauce.

NOTE: This can be multiplied indefinitely, but use a separate package for each chicken breast.

❀ Sort of Szechwan Chicken in Lettuce Leaves

For 20 rolls, sufficient for 6 as part of a Chinese meal or for 3 as the main course of dinner

1 small onion, chopped into small dice, about ½ cup
2 teaspoons peanut oil or other bland vegetable oil
1 whole medium-sized chicken breast, cooked, skinned, and cut or torn into long, very thin shreds, about 2 cups
1 large carrot, grated on the large holes of a grater, about ½ cup shreds
2 tablespoons water
1 teaspoon grated fresh ginger
1 large clove garlic, minced
1 to 1¼ teaspoons crushed dried hot red pepper
2 teaspoons soy sauce
2 teaspoons vinegar
1 teaspoon sugar
3 tablespoons coarsely chopped salted, roasted peanuts (If you use one of the little snack packages, there won't be salted peanuts lying around.)
20 large, tender lettuce leaves from Boston or other delicate lettuce (about 2 heads)

In a medium-sized skillet, fry the onion in the oil until it is wilted and soft, then add the chicken, carrot, and water. Cook, stirring, over medium heat until the ingredients are well amalgamated and the water has boiled away. Stir in the ginger and garlic and cook a minute, then add the red pepper, soy sauce, vinegar, and sugar. Cook and stir 2 or 3 minutes more. Add the peanuts and turn off the heat.

Serve the filling in a pretty bowl, with a suitable spoon for scooping. To eat: Pile about a tablespoon of filling in the middle of a leaf, then fold the leaf around it from the stem end up. The ideal is a two-bite package — bigger than that and they start falling apart.

This is a classic buffet item, but a serving can be arranged on a plate. Accompanied by simply cooked, lightly buttered rice, it makes a painless, low-calorie dinner.

 Oriental Slaw

This pared-down, spiced-up version of the Farm Belt classic is particularly good with that famous coleslaw partner, baked beans.

For 6 servings

6 cups finely shredded firm green cabbage, about 1¼ pounds
1 medium-sized green bell pepper, chopped fine, about ½ cup
1 cup very finely sliced, then shredded, onion, 1 medium-large
2 teaspoons salt
1 very small clove garlic, pressed
1 tablespoon sesame oil
2 tablespoons rice vinegar
2 tablespoons minced fresh hot green pepper
1 cup mixed bean sprouts — lentil, adzuki, mung, etc.
1 can (8 ounces) water chestnuts, rinsed with cold water and cut in thin coins

Combine cabbage, bell pepper, and onion with salt, mixing thoroughly. Allow to sit 1 hour, to wilt, then rinse briefly in cold water and drain well. In a bowl big enough for everything, combine the garlic, oil, and vinegar with the hot pepper, sprouts, and water chestnuts. Stir in the cabbage mixture, allow to marinate at least 15 minutes, and serve. Tightly covered and refrigerated, it will keep several days.

Superlight Strawberries in Sweet Wine Sponge

For 4 to 6 servings

1 tablespoon unflavored gelatin (1 envelope)
¼ cup cold water
⅓ cup sweet wine, preferably Marsala, although sweet sherry will do

2 to 4 tablespoons sugar, depending on the sweetness of the berries
⅓ cup honey
1 pint strawberries, wiped, hulled, and puréed to mush
1¼ cups whole-milk yogurt
2 egg whites
Whole berries and tufts of mint for garnish (Whipped cream is good,
  too, if you're not on too awful a diet.)

Soften the gelatin in the water, then combine it with the wine and sugar in a small saucepan. Heat, stirring, only long enough to dissolve the gelatin and sugar fully. Stir in the honey, remove the pan from the heat, and let the mixture cool to room temperature.

Stir the strawberry purée into the mixture in the pan. In a medium-sized bowl, gently stir the yogurt until it is smooth. Do not beat it or it will liquefy. Add the strawberry mixture, stir well, and chill until thickened but not yet set, about the texture of floppy whipped cream.

Beat the egg whites until they form soft, still shiny peaks. Stir about one-fourth of them into the strawberry mixture to lighten it, then fold in the remainder. Turn the sponge into a pretty serving bowl and chill, tightly covered with plastic wrap, at least 4 hours, as long as a day. Serve with garnish of choice, including thin wafer cookies or amaretti if you want a nice textural contrast.

EASTER
My Hymn To Ham/Dealing with Those Hard-Boiled Eggs

SENSITIVE EATERS can't help having noticed that there is a whole new generation of food taboos in the making. There is an increasing number of foods — formerly okay foods — that a person of delicate social constitution might prefer to consume in the closet, away from prying eyes, ham first and foremost among them.

It's salty, which is bad for the blood pressure. It's smoked, which might give you cancer. It's pork, hence fatty, which is hard on your heart. And generally, it's cured with sugar, condiment of Satan.

Ham. I love it. It's almost always tasty, and quite often it's delicious. It keeps a long time, it's endlessly adaptable, and just a little is enough to flavor a whole dish of healthy, nutritious cheap vegetables and grains.

There are limits, of course. If you go eating nitrate-laden, water-injected, India-rubber supermarket ham, you'll be consuming something indefensible on both nutritional and aesthetic grounds. But getting good ham is no longer difficult, and one is most unlikely to be eating large slabs of it anyway, except perhaps once a year at Easter. And once a year couldn't possibly hurt you, right? Right.

No, the Easter ham is not as much of a problem as it's cracked up to be, and all those delicious leftovers are more than worth the price of admission. It's trying to figure out what to do with all those Easter eggs that's hard.

My edition of the encyclopedic *Larousse Gastronomique* lists 296 recipes (not counting the omelettes) in the egg section, fewer than ten of which are for eggs boiled hard. This is a sensible proportion, in my opinion. But once a year, I wish it were otherwise. Because once a year, thanks to the machinations of a malevolent, mutant rabbit, it is to eggs boiled hard — the very least interesting, to say nothing of the very least digestible, eggs in all creation — that we must, however reluctantly, turn our attention.

A hard-boiled egg is not, contrary to appearances, forever. It will taste best if eaten within a day or two of boiling and will spoil *rapidly* if left out of the refrigerator for long. Before you go making them into something, don't forget that hard eggs are a nice addition to potato salad, marinated vegetable salads, and *salade Niçoise,* as well as the spinach, mushroom, and bacon mixtures currently so popular.

For cooked spinach, broccoli, cauliflower, snap beans, and verdure of other sorts, the eggs can be made into a classic mimosa (named for its resemblance to the flower), an all-purpose garnish if ever there was one, and very pretty, too. Simply chop whites and yolks separately, then toss very lightly to mix. This is to keep things fluffy; any kind of rough treatment turns the chopped egg to paste.

After you've done this, and made stuffed eggs and pickled eggs, that's about it. For the whole eggs, that is. Hard-cooked egg yolks by themselves are considerably more useful, since they provide a way of enriching pastry that does not change the ratio of solid to liquid.

 Sweet-and-Sour Green Cabbage with Ham and Pecans

For 4 servings

SAUCE:
1 tablespoon cornstarch
⅔ cup chicken broth
¼ cup dry sherry or rice wine
¼ cup catsup
3 tablespoons mild vinegar
1 to 2 tablespoons brown sugar, depending on the sweetness of
   the catsup
1 tablespoon soy sauce

PLUS:
½ cup bland vegetable oil
⅔ cup pecan halves

2 large cloves garlic, minced or shredded fine, not pressed
1 tablespoon minced fresh ginger
1½ cups diced strong-flavored, dense-textured country ham, or 2¼ cups
    mild-flavored baked ham, cut into fat match sticks about 1 inch long
6 cups shredded green cabbage (shredded slightly wider than it would
    be for slaw)

This is one of those recipes where the cooking goes very fast, so be sure all ingredients are ready before you start.

Put the cornstarch in a small bowl, slowly stir in the broth, then add the remaining sauce ingredients and stir well. Set aside.

I make this in a large wok. If necessary, use a small saucepan for the pecan frying and a large skillet for everything else. Heat the oil until it shimmers; a frying thermometer should read 360°F. Add the pecans and fry until they are dark gold, about 2 minutes. Remove the pecans with a slotted spoon and put them on absorbent paper to drain.

Pour off all but 2½ tablespoons of the oil and set the pan over medium-high heat. Add the garlic and ginger and fry, stirring, about a minute, just until they are pale gold and smell good. Add the ham and cook about a minute more. Turn the heat to high and add the cabbage, a handful at a time, stirring and turning constantly as you insert the new material. Cook only until the cabbage has turned bright green and begun to wilt.

Stir the sauce mixture to recombine, then stir it into the cabbage and ham. Lower the heat to medium-high and continue to cook, stirring, until the sauce is thickened and clear and the cabbage is tender but still crisp. This will take 2 to 5 minutes more, depending on the size of your pan and the heat of your fire (and the age of your cabbage).

Serve the very instant it's done, topped with the pecans. Chinese flavored though it is, it's great with baked potatoes.

Easter Croquettes

Crusty and brown on the outside, beautifully golden and speckled pink and green within. Pretty as an Easter bonnet and a great deal tastier, these are an excellent way to use up the last crumbs of the holiday ham. Serve as a snack with drinks or as lunch with a big green salad.

For 24 small croquettes, 3 to 4 main dish servings or 6 to 8 appetizers

1 pound parsnips
2 tablespoons not-too-finely minced parsley

2 tablespoons minced onion
¼ cup diced baked ham, about 2½ ounces
1 egg, beaten
1 tablespoon flour
Approximately ¾ cup fine dry bread crumbs
Oil for deep-frying
Coarse salt for garnish

Steam the parsnips until they are very tender, softer than they would be if you planned to serve them plain. Peel and remove cores. You should be able to do this by squeezing, as most of the soft outer flesh will part from the tough core quite readily. Mash the parsnip flesh with a fork or potato masher, or process *very briefly*; the resultant purée should be on the lumpy side, and there should be about 1½ cups of it.

Combine the purée with the next five ingredients. Put the bread crumbs in a shallow bowl and set out a shallow pan or plate to put the croquettes on. The mixture will be too soft to roll into balls, so just drop a walnut-sized spoonful onto the crumbs and gently tease it into a ball shape with your crumb-protected fingertips. Once crumbed, the croquettes can be handled. Finish rolling them gently into balls and place, well separated, on the pan or plate.

Let them sit at room temperature, uncovered, about 30 minutes so the coating can set, then deep-fry for approximately 1 minute in fat heated to 370°F. Drain on absorbent paper and serve at once, with a sprinkling of coarse salt.

Cheesecake Tart

PASTRY:
1½ cups all-purpose flour
1 tablespoon sugar
1 tablespoon finely shredded lemon zest (thin, colored outer rind)
1 teaspoon salt
¾ cup finely grated or powdered almonds (grind with sugar and ¼ cup of the flour if using a processor)
3 hard-cooked egg yolks
⅓ cup butter

FILLING:
¼ cup diced candied lemon or orange peel
¼ cup currants

2 tablespoons brandy
3 hard-cooked egg yolks
8 ounces cream cheese
½ cup sugar
2 egg yolks
1 pound ricotta cheese, well drained
1 teaspoon vanilla
Pinch of ground cloves
3 egg whites
Shaved chocolate and/or additional candied peel for garnish (optional)

Combine the candied peel and currants for the filling with the brandy and set aside in a warm place (such as the back of the stove or on top of the radiator) to plump.

Make the pastry. Combine the flour, sugar, zest, and salt in a wide bowl and stir well with a wire whisk. Stir in the almonds and set aside.

Mash the egg yolks smooth, then work in the butter until the fats are thoroughly combined. Distribute the fat in dabs over the flour mixture and work the two together with your fingertips until the dough coheres. If necessary, add a bit of sweet or sour cream; the dough should hold together when squeezed, but barely.

Set aside about a third of the dough and gently pat the remainder over the bottom and 1 inch up the sides of a 9-inch springform pan. Roll the set-aside portion into a long snake or snakes about ⅓-inch in diameter and use the coil to make a decorative rim at the upper edge of the crust. Pinch the border on firmly, then chill the shell.

To make the filling, mash the hard yolks to a paste, then work in the cream cheese. When the mixture is smooth, add the sugar and beat well.

Beat in the uncooked yolks, one at a time, then the ricotta, vanilla, and cloves. Stir in the brandied fruits and their juices. Preheat the oven to 400°F.

Beat the egg whites until they form stiff but still shiny peaks. Stir a big spoonful into the filling to lighten it, then fold in the remainder. Turn the filling into the chilled shell and smooth the top. Bake 10 minutes, then reduce heat to 350°F. and bake 25 to 35 minutes more, or until the custard is set at the outside edges but still (very slightly) trembly at the center. Turn off the heat, open the oven door halfway, and let the tart cool in situ.

Once the tart is room temperature, cover with plastic wrap and chill thoroughly, still in the pan. At serving time remove the ring, gently slide the tart onto a serving plate, and garnish as desired. Though this is an extremely rich pastry, it does not taste greasy or cloying. In fact, if you didn't know better, you'd think it was *lighter* than regular cheesecake. HA!

THE RADISH RHAPSODY

IT IS WITH a great sigh of relief, a sigh right from the cabbage-laden heart, that New England food lovers greet the arrival of spring. After privation, after expensive lifelike vegetable replicas fashioned in far-off climes, after substitutes that look convincing but taste like plastic when they taste like anything at all, after hard times in the produce department, come wonders without end: fat, crisp asparagus; fine artichokes; innocent new spinach, worlds away from the tired, bagged leaves of winter.

Not surprisingly, The Arrival of the Spring Vegetables calls forth a fair amount of ballyhoo and an avalanche of recipes, very few of which are for radishes. Poor radishes. They tend to get overlooked in the general rush to greenness. I suppose it can't be helped. There really isn't much you can do with them except eat them, and they are, in some fashion, available all year round. But spring radishes are a special, fleeting, truly seasonal treat, and they, too, deserve their day in the sun.

It's a simple enough scenario: A glass or two of fresh white wine, a table set about with friends, and a good dinner in the offing. The radishes are young, spring grown, just picked. Their smooth red skins are as unblemished and fresh looking as their sprightly little tufts of bright green leaves. And their transparent white, slightly peppery flesh is juicy and crisp and sweet. With them you serve plenty of crusty, yeasty, hot French bread and butter that is, as Mark Twain put it, "butter of the most unimpeachable freshness." This classic celebration of the new says "spring" as eloquently as any bundle of fancy asparagus going. With white wine and a baguette for the butter, little red radishes say it in French. To speak German, simply substitute white radishes and dark bread and drink beer instead of wine.

Radishes can also be cooked. But, as more than one skeptic has pointed out, so can grapefruit; that doesn't mean it's a good idea. Sliced red ones provide a nice piquant crunch when added at the last minute to a mixed vegetable stir-fry, and shredded daikon is frequently used to good effect as a garnish for clear soup, but that's about it. Like bean sprouts, radishes are nothing short of horrible if overcooked, so it's probably better not to bother unless you're really desperate for color.

Indeed, color is one of the most appealing things about radishes, which come in everything red from pale blush pink to crimson to lilac, as well as pure white and highly decorative jet black. That last is the black Spanish, a softball-sized winter radish that makes strikingly beautiful slices, the white centers almost glowing in contrast to the dark skin.

Radish Varieties

Black Spanish, like the equally lovely China Rose, is a winter keeper, planted either in very early spring for harvest before the heat comes or in midsummer for fall harvest. Winter keepers take longer to grow and grow larger than the relish types commonly sold. Relish types, which ought to be called spring radishes, might be round or finger shaped, red or pink or white. They are all very quickly grown and good only when quite small. The long, white daikon of the Orient, more and more common here, is less sweet and less peppery, very crisp and refreshing. It is capable of achieving great size, its roots often growing well over a foot long. In spite of these differences, all radishes are closely related, variations of *Raphanus sativus*, the cultivated radish.

Supermarkets generally confine themselves to the relish types, and even at that they seldom carry the tender bunches of spring beauty lauded above. Fortunately, fancy greengrocers, farmers' markets, roadside stands, and Oriental markets make it easy to buy and enjoy a wide variety of appetizing radishes. Well, why not? After all, among their many virtues, they are only 60 calories a pound.

Long or short, red, white, or black, radishes are valued for their roots, and most consumers throw out the leaves without thinking twice about it. Yet these leaves, when they are young and fresh, have a very nice flavor of their own, somewhere between mustard and watercress. Toss them in with a lettuce salad, add some to a batch of panned spinach, or toss a handful into the vegetable soup.

When the radishes aren't springlike enough to be eaten plain with butter, when the greens are insufficiently lovely or absent altogether, consider the radish rose. These days, good old radish roses seem to be getting a lot of bad press. In spite of their continuing popularity, most serious food writers put them in the same sneered-upon class as maraschino cherries on the canned ham: pure ladies' lunch. But there is a reason for radish roses beyond frivolous decor: That cold-water soak not only crisps a cut radish that probably needs it, but also leaches out some of the hot, disagreeably strong flavor storage radishes so often carry. If radish roses are too much to bear, make radish chrysanthemums instead.

HORTICULTURAL NOTE *(for new gardeners and parents):* Radishes are often suggested as ideal for beginning gardeners, especially children. This is presumably because they mature so quickly; a properly grown spring radish will be ready to eat in less than a month from seed. But properly growing a radish is not all that easy, and though you do generally get *something*, the something might not be as fantasized. Radishes need just the right combination of fertility, sunshine, and rain to size up tender and sweet rather than hot and pithy. Once ready, they must be harvested quickly, as their moment of perfection is brief. Furthermore, they are highly attractive to all manner of nibbling pests.

In other words, a pretty bunch of bright-leaved, unblemished, sweet, crisp radishes is no mean horticultural achievement; and while it is perfectly possible, it is not as likely as the Pollyannas make it sound. If you want to start out with something more or less "foolproof," try leaf lettuce, Swiss chard, or perhaps a nice row of early peas.

 ## Radish Chrysanthemums

Cut a thin slice from the base so the radish will stand up. Use a very thin bladed knife to make parallel cuts all across the top, 1/16 inch apart, down to within 1/4 inch of the bottom. Turn the radish 90 degrees and do it again, so the whole thing is deeply crosshatched. Soak in ice water in the fridge 2 to 3 hours, or until the flower opens. These are more fragile than radish roses, but prettier.

 ## Radish and Crabmeat Salad

For 4 appetizer servings

**2 large bunches spring radishes, enough to make 2 generous cups
    prepared
Salt**

DRESSING:
⅓ cup peanut oil
1½ teaspoons dark sesame oil (seasoning)
¼ cup rice vinegar
2 teaspoons sugar
1 teaspoon tamari or other aged soy sauce

PLUS:
4 or 5 ounces crabmeat
3 tablespoons very thinly sliced scallions (green onions)
2 teaspoons finely shredded *beni shōga* (Japanese red pickled ginger
   available at specialty grocers and Oriental markets; optional)

Cut the radishes in very thin slices, layer them in a colander with light sprinklings of salt, and let them drain 20 to 30 minutes, but not more. Rinse them in ice water and lay out on paper towels to dry. They needn't be dried absolutely, but only a small amount of dampness should remain.

Make the dressing by combining the first five ingredients in the order shown and add the prepared radish slices. Let the salad sit 10 minutes or so, then stir in the crabmeat and scallions. Taste. You might want a bit more sugar, or even salt. Distribute the salad among the serving plates and garnish each plate with a pinch of the beni shōga. (I realize this is not the sort of thing most households have lying around, and I certainly wouldn't suggest it is essential. But it *is* nice — both decorative and tasty — and to buy it once is to have it around forever.)

 ## Double-Radish Salad with Sesame Dressing

This has the same cool, crisp appeal as coleslaw or *céleri-rave rémoulade*, the French salad of celery root in spicy mayonnaise. It can be presented on a bed of greens or served on its own, deli-style. It makes a good accompaniment to cold sliced ham, for instance, and it's delicious as the moist part of a sandwich that features roast turkey.

For 4 servings

1 large or 2 small bunches red radishes, about 1½ cups prepared
4- to 5-inch length of daikon radish, roughly 2½ inches diameter,
   enough to make 1½ cups prepared

6 scallions (green onions) sliced thin, including an inch of the green part, about 3 tablespoons

DRESSING:
⅓ cup tahini (sesame paste, available in specialty and health food stores)
2 tablespoons dry sherry
1 tablespoon lemon juice
Pinch each of salt and sugar
Approximately ¼ cup cold water

Prepare the radishes. Slice the red ones ¹⁄₁₆ inch thick. Peel the daikon, slice into sheets about ⅛ inch thick, and cut sheets into match sticks. Cut the match sticks into ½-inch lengths. Combine all radishes with the scallions and set aside.

Make the dressing right in the measuring cup. Glop in the tahini, then slowly stir in the sherry, lemon juice, and seasonings. The paste will stiffen. Thin it back down to creamy dressing consistency with the water, then toss with the prepared radishes.

*T*HE ANNIE REPORT
For My Chocoholic Friend

SOME OF US PINE for the opposite sex,
And some of us long for gold,
But Annie's in love with chocolate,
And her passion is uncontrolled.

From the schlockiest candy bar to the ritziest gâteau, if it's chocolate, Annie wants it. Chocolate *anything*. An entire bag of M&Ms can disappear in minutes, a box of fancy Italian hazelnut-center *baci* even faster, if that's possible. Not even a can of plain old cocoa is safe when this woman is around.

Her often awestricken husband got a hint of what was to come on their very first date, when he discovered she'd eaten two dozen large peanut butter cups before the movie even started. He didn't yet know that she had subsisted, for most of her dollar-free student days, almost exclusively on large chocolate bars — one for morning, one for afternoon — which she hid in her purse and nibbled at surreptitiously, so she wouldn't have to share.

This is a person who once smeared her infant son's mouth with a bit of her chocolate ice cream "just to see how it'll look," and I have even seen her casing my cooking chocolate when she thought I wasn't looking. She calls herself a chocoholic, and she is not joking.

She *is* unrepentant, however, as are the millions who share her addiction. The Aztec emperor Montezuma reportedly drank fifty jars of chocolate a day, and so would Annie if she were king.

Of course, one good thing about having a friend who is famous for this predilection — there's never any difficulty figuring out an appropriate present to bring when visiting. The only problem, given that everyone gives her chocolate, is in deciding just what *sort* of chocolate to bring. The only solution? Selfishness. She gets the chocolate *I* like best — white chocolate, subtlest and most suave of all chocolates going.

Many chocophiles are undoubtedly rising up even now to protest that white chocolate isn't really chocolate at all. The Food and Drug Administration (FDA) agrees. To be labeled "chocolate," a product must contain chocolate liquor, the thing you get when you grind up roasted cocoa beans. Chocolate liquor, represented in retail commerce by unsweetened baking chocolate, is a highly complicated compound of protein, carbohydrates, and fat. Variously treated, sweetened, flavored, and modified, it is the basis of all chocolate confections that include the magic word in their names.

That's why "white chocolate" is such an elusive item. In its finest manifestations, it is based entirely on cocoa butter, the fat component of chocolate liquor, but as it cannot be *called* chocolate, there's no way for the consumer to tell how much if any cocoa butter a given candy contains.

Cocoa butter has a very delicate chocolate flavor and several unique properties very important to candy making. It is highly resistant to rancidity, for instance, and has the ability, because of its low melting point, to give the sensation that it is cooling the mouth. It enhances and binds the flavors of the cocoa bean, while enabling the chocolate liquor to blend more smoothly with sugar. Not surprisingly, it is vital to the production of deluxe chocolates, which are generally characterized by an abundance of added cocoa butter. It also has a number of nonfood uses, primarily in the manufacture of cosmetics.

All this makes cocoa butter much more expensive than most other fats, and as a result, a great deal of what's commonly thought of as "white chocolate" contains very little or none of the one essential ingredient. To complicate the problem further, white chocolate doesn't keep as well as the dark kinds. Like milk chocolate, it contains a large percentage of milk solids in addition to the cocoa butter and sugar. But chocolate liquor contains an element that keeps the milk from turning sour, and that element is missing from cocoa butter by itself.

It is perhaps well to remember at this point that many of the best things in life are hard to find. When it is fresh, when it is well and honestly made, white chocolate has a haunting delicacy that dark chocolate can't match. Exquisite on its own, it is also a perfect foil for soft fruits such as strawberries, peaches, and plums. Tobler Narcisse is the good white chocolate most widely available, but it's not as good as some of the loose types sold in boutique candy stores. Taste around. A good white chocolate will feel cool in the mouth, taste rich and sweet without chemical overtones or the acid of rancidity, and give a decided "chocolate" impression with no unpleasant aftertaste. It might take a bit of research to find one, but the rewards are worth it.

Black-and-White Apricot Mousse Torte

In addition to tasting great and looking dashing, this torte is actually improved by being made a full day in advance. Since several of its parts can also be pre-prepared, it's an ideal dessert for elaborate, time-consuming dinners, multitreat tea parties, and similar occasions.

CRUST:
½ cup finely chopped walnuts
2 cups chocolate wafer crumbs, about 6 ounces
2 tablespoons sugar
5 tablespoons butter, melted
Butter for pan

FILLING AND TOPPING:
8 ounces dried apricots
1½ cups boiling water
2 tablespoons orange liqueur
3 tablespoons white crème de cacao (clear chocolate liqueur)
¾ cup plus 2 tablespoons sugar
1 tablespoon unflavored gelatin (1 envelope)
¼ cup orange juice (one orange's worth)

4 egg yolks
1 cup heavy cream
10 ounces white chocolate, grated or ground fine
4 egg whites
2 tablespoons unsalted butter
3 ounces semisweet chocolate, grated or ground fine

Timetable: On day 1, make the crust, cook the apricots, and set to marinate. Grind the chocolates, keeping them separate. On day 2, finish the torte, leaving at least 12 hours for it to set between finishing and serving.

Preheat oven to 350°F. For the crust, combine all the ingredients thoroughly and press the resultant still-crumbly mixture over the bottom and up the sides of a buttered 9-inch springform pan. Bake 15 minutes and cool on a wire rack.

Put the apricots in a saucepan and cover with the boiling water. Simmer, covered, over medium-low heat 5 minutes. Fish out the ten handsomest apricots and put them in a small bowl with the orange liqueur and 2 tablespoons of the crème de cacao.

Add ½ cup of the sugar to the apricot mixture still in the pan and return it to the heat. Cook, stirring, until the sugar dissolves, then cover the pan and simmer until the apricots are falling apart — about 30 minutes. They will have absorbed most, if not all, of the liquid. Set them aside.

On day 2, prepare the mousse. Drain the liqueur from the marinating apricots into the stewed ones. Lay the drained apricots on a wire rack to dry off. Purée the stewed apricot mixture.

Soak the gelatin in the orange juice. Beat the egg yolks with ¼ cup sugar and ½ cup cream in a small, heavy saucepan (or double boiler) and set it over very low heat (or barely simmering water). Cook, stirring constantly, until the custard thickens enough to coat a spoon — about 10 minutes. Next add the gelatin mixture and cook, stirring, until it is completely dissolved.

Slowly stir in 1¼ cups of the ground white chocolate, dribbling it in a little at a time. As soon as the chocolate is melted, remove the mixture from the heat. Combine it with the puréed apricots, stirring with a wire whisk to be sure everything is well mixed. Chill until just starting to set — the texture of floppy whipped cream.

Beat the egg whites until they form stiff but still shiny peaks and stir one-fourth of them into the apricot mixture. When they are well combined, add the remaining egg whites and fold them in gently but thoroughly. Turn the whole works into the crust, cover with plastic wrap to prevent absorption of odors, and refrigerate at least 12 hours.

At some point during this chilling process, turn your attention to the decor. In a small pan, slowly, *very gently*, melt the remaining white chocolate with the 2 tablespoons of unsalted butter. Melt the dark chocolate in a separate pan and keep both in a warm place. Both chocolates should be melted at the lowest heat possible — on a tepid radiator or in a sunny window is as good as or better than on the stove. (See "Damn Fancy Chocolate Pie" on page 53 for the oven melting method.)

Set out a sheet of waxed paper on a flat pan, to lay the decorations on. Take the now dry marinated apricots from their hiding place. Spread one half of one side of each with a dab of the white chocolate mixture, then coat the other half with the dark chocolate. The apricots are now black and white.

Put the rest of the melted white chocolate in one place on the waxed paper and carefully spread it into a circle about five inches in diameter. Distribute the leftover dark chocolate in artistic dabs around the outside of the circle and use a toothpick or knife point to draw dark lines inward to make a pattern. Alternatively, just put the dark part here and there where it suits you; the idea is to make a flattish chocolate medallion for the middle of the torte.

Set the sheet of decorations aside in a cool place.

At or shortly before serving time, whip the remaining ½ cup cream until it is almost stiff, then slowly beat in the last 2 tablespoons sugar and the remaining tablespoon crème de cacao. Spread it evenly over the torte, right to the edges, completely masking the apricot.

Put the medallion in the center and arrange the black-and-white apricots around the edge so each portion will have one.

All-Purpose Chocolate Sauce

This is, of course, good over ice cream. Also baked pears, pound cake, and *peppermint* ice cream. Use 2 tablespoons sauce to 1½ cups milk and a scoop of chocolate ice cream for milk shakes; 2 tablespoons sauce and 1½ cups milk for hot chocolate.

For about 2 cups sauce

1 cup sugar
3-inch length of vanilla bean, split

½ cup water
2 ounces each baking chocolate and sweet chocolate, chopped small
½ cup semisweet chocolate morsels, chopped small
2 tablespoons butter
Pinch of salt
⅓ cup heavy cream

Combine the sugar with the vanilla bean and water in a small saucepan and cook, stirring, over low heat until sugar is dissolved. Raise heat to medium and let simmer, undisturbed, about 6 minutes, or until a smooth, fairly heavy syrup is formed. Return the heat to very low.

Melt the chocolate as directed in "Damn Fancy Chocolate Pie" (page 53), then slowly add it to the hot syrup, stirring all the while. Add the butter and the salt. As soon as the mixture is smooth, stir in the cream. Continue to cook, stirring, until the sauce is thick and smooth. Leave the bean in for the duration; it will continue to enhance the flavor. The sauce will keep several weeks in the refrigerator, indefinitely in the freezer.

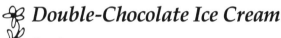 Double-Chocolate Ice Cream

For about 1 quart

1 tablespoon cornstarch
1 cup milk
2 egg yolks, well beaten
1 cup All-Purpose Chocolate Sauce (see recipe on page 51)
Pinch of salt
1½ cups heavy cream
3 ounces first-quality sweet or semisweet chocolate — Lindt, Tobler, or
    similar — chopped to small flakes

Put the cornstarch in a heavy saucepan or double boiler and slowly stir in the milk. Beat in the yolks and cook the custard, stirring constantly, over very low heat until it smoothly coats a spoon. Take the pan from the heat, slowly stir in the chocolate sauce, then the salt, and let the mixture cool. Chill thoroughly.

Whip the cream until it is just thickened and slouchy (don't let it get any stiffer, or the ice cream will taste greasy). Gently stir — fold the cream into the custard and freeze according to the freezer manufacturer's instructions. When the ice cream is slushy — almost but not quite solid — add the chopped chocolate and finish freezing.

Damn Fancy Chocolate Pie

CRUST:

Enough amaretti or other crisp, dry almond macaroons to equal 3 cups
   prepared
⅓ cup cocoa
6 tablespoons butter, melted
1 teaspoon vanilla

FILLING:

8 egg yolks
⅔ cup sugar
1½ cups heavy cream
1 cup semisweet chocolate morsels
4 ounces sweet chocolate
1 ounce baking chocolate
¼ cup unsalted butter
3 tablespoons dark rum
5 egg whites

TOPPING:

1½ cups fresh or unsweetened frozen raspberries
⅓ cup raspberry jam
1 cup heavy cream
¼ cup each superfine Dutch cocoa and superfine sugar, thoroughly
   mixed
½ cup coarsely chopped toasted almonds or (if Annie's coming)
   blanched pistachios

Begin by making the crust. Crush the cookies until they are about the texture of medium oatmeal — don't take them all the way to powder. Mix them with the cocoa, then work in the melted butter and vanilla. The mixture should remain crumbly, holding together when squeezed but not at all pasty.

Using most of the material, make a wreath around the inside edge of a deep 9-inch pie pan. Dump the rest in the middle. Pat and press into an even crust; there won't be much of a rim. Chill the shell.

Make the filling. Beat the yolks with the sugar until pale and thick, then beat in the cream. Turn the mixture into a heavy-bottomed stainless steel or enamel saucepan (or double boiler) and cook over very low heat, stirring constantly, until it is thick enough to hold the impression of a spoon drawn across it — about as thick as soft ice cream. Allow to cool, stirring occasionally to prevent a crust from forming.

Heat the oven to 150°F., then turn it off. While it is heating, chop the chocolates coarsely and put on an approximately 8-inch square of tinfoil. Shortly after turning off the oven, put in the chocolate to melt. The goal is a melting temperature of 100°F. to 120°F. You can skip all this fooling around if your oven has a pilot light; such ovens are hot enough to melt chocolate even when turned off.

Put the butter in a large mixing bowl and beat briefly to soften. Scrape in the chocolate and beat well, then beat in the cooled custard, a little at a time, and add the rum.

Beat the egg whites until they form floppy, shiny peaks. Stir about a quarter of them into the chocolate to lighten it, then fold in the remainder. Turn the filling into the shell and chill the pie, tightly covered, at least 8 hours.

At serving time, push the raspberries through a sieve to make a smooth, seedless purée. Work the purée into the jam, then distribute the topping in dabs over the top of the pie and spread it out to make an even layer. Return the pie to the refrigerator.

Whip the cream until it forms soft peaks, then slowly add, while still whipping, the cocoa and sugar mixture. The resulting cream should be extremely stiff, just this side of butter. Put it in a pastry bag fitted with a large star tip and pipe a heavy, decorated border around the edge of the pie, leaving a 3- or 4-inch bull's eye of jam in the center. Cover the bull's eye with the nuts and serve the pie as soon as possible.

SORREL, THE HERB OF SPRING

"HOW NICE," I remarked, surveying the lavish hedge of sorrel plants at the edge of my friend's small garden. "It really has settled in splendidly."

"Yeah, that's just great," was her response. "Now what the *&#*! do I *do* with the stuff? I tried nibbling just one leaf, and the thing was so sour I couldn't stop salivating for half an hour."

Well, needless to say, what you *don't* do is eat it plain — unless you are the sort of person who enjoys chewing on raw rhubarb. The word "sorrel" comes from the old French for sour, and sour is indeed the name of the game. In addition to that quality, which comes, as does the sourness of rhubarb, from oxalic acid, sorrel is piquant and refreshing, with a pleasant, indefinable "green" taste that makes it an almost universally useful herb.

A few leaves do wonders for salads, for instance, enhancing the palate-cleansing qualities of green leaves in vinaigrette sauce, and cooked sorrel provides a sharp balance for all sorts of heavy-prone protein. In classical French cuisine, it is used as a sauce for rich fish such as salmon and shad, as filling for omelettes, and in a lovely purée soup enriched with egg yolks, called *potage Germiny.* The British have long used it in a sauce for roast goose, and it goes well with bland starches such as potatoes and dried beans.

Buying this wonder herb is getting easier as greengrocery departments expand, but it's still much easier to grow than it is to find in stores. The broad-leaved, comparatively mild-flavored French sorrel, *Rumex scutatus,* is scarcely different in its habits from the assorted weeds, such as *R. acetosella* (wood or sheep sorrel) and *Oxyria digyna* (mountain sorrel), to which it is closely related. It is perennial, inclined to spread, hardy, undemanding, and of no particular interest to bugs. One of the first plants to green up in spring and the last to go by in fall, it will produce all summer if it is constantly cut back. A square foot and a half of ground will support a clump big enough for one family's needs. And if it is less than beautiful, it is at least unobtrusive.

All this should make it an ideal market crop (though it does wilt quickly once cut), and I have no doubt that if the market existed, specialty growers would start producing it. Unfortunately, although it has been popular in western Europe from medieval times, when it was often used in place of the more expensive verjuice (unfermented wine-grape juice) and the extremely expensive lemon, and although it continues to hold a place of honor in Polish and Russian cooking, where sorrel soups and sauces are pretty much taken for granted, the sorrel revolution has yet to hit these shores.

No time like the present. Starting is easy, once you've got the sorrel, because almost all recipes are based on a simple purée made by melting the shredded leaves in butter. "Melted" is the word for it, too. Cooked sorrel doesn't just soften, it disintegrates. It also cooks down, to a degree that puts spinach in the shade. Within about twenty minutes' cooking, six or seven cups of shredded sorrel will reduce to a heaping cup of concentrated olive green sourness. This is very convenient when it comes to preservation — tablespoon-sized lumps of said purée freeze well and thaw fast. Put up a cup or two in season and have the perfect enhancing touch ready for a winter's worth of rich soups and fat meats.

 ## Basic Sorrel Purée

For about 1¼ cups purée (recipe can be reduced)

1 pound fresh sorrel
4 to 6 tablespoons butter
1 small onion, chopped fine, about ¾ cup (optional)

Pick over the sorrel and cut away any tough stems — the older the plants, the more of these there will be. Chop roughly and set aside. Melt the butter over medium heat in a wide skillet. (If you want an onion flavor, sauté the onion in the butter until golden.) Add the sorrel, a handful at a time, stirring as each handful is added and inserting more as soon as there's room. Cook, stirring, until a smoothish purée is achieved. That's it.

SORREL SAUCE I: For each 2 servings, heat ½ cup heavy cream almost to boiling. Rapidly, to avoid curdling, stir it into 2 tablespoons of the purée. Season lightly with salt, white pepper, and nutmeg. Serve with poached fish, roast chicken, open-face grilled fontina and rye bread sandwiches, fresh broad beans, whatever.

SORREL SAUCE II: Make hollandaise sauce. Season with about 2 tablespoons purée for each ½ cup hollandaise. Serve with any of the above, also fried clams, steamed asparagus, artichokes, fiddleheads, broccoli, wild rice, or new potatoes.

SORREL OMELETTE: Allow about a heaping tablespoon of purée for a 3-egg omelette. Spread it down the middle right before folding, when the eggs are almost set. Resist the temptation to add more, or the eggs will be overpowered.

 ## Lamb and Black Beans Swirled with Spring Greens

This is a sort of Frenchified chili, not spicy but rich, lightened and piqued by the freshness of sour greens. It's hearty and filling without being nearly as fattening as it tastes, and it needs only a good supply of crusty bread or warm tortillas for an accompaniment, especially if you have an orgy of fresh fruit on hand for dessert. For the finest flavor and fewest calories, make the meat base a day in advance so it can be completely de-fatted.

For 6 generous servings

STEW BASE:
2 pounds lean stewing lamb from the neck or shoulder, on the bone, cut into large (2- to 3-inch or larger) pieces
1 large onion, stuck with 4 cloves
1 large carrot, chopped small, about ¾ cup
1 generous sprig fresh thyme or 1 teaspoon dried
8 peppercorns
3 cups water

FINISHING:
1 pound (2 cups) dried black beans
Approximately 2 cups water
Salt to taste

GREENS MIXTURE:
12 ounces large fresh sorrel leaves, about 1½ quarts
1 tablespoon olive oil
1 tablespoon butter
1 large clove garlic, minced, not pressed
3 tablespoons snipped fresh chives or thinly sliced scallion tops
1 cup sour cream, as an accompaniment (optional)

Day 1: Cut off any easily removable lumps of fat and set the meat aside. Coarsely chop the fat and slowly render it in a wide, heavy skillet over low heat until there is a generous layer of melted fat in the pan. Scoop out the solids and discard them.

Raise the heat to medium-high and brown the meat on all sides, a few uncrowded pieces at a time. Transfer the meat as it cooks to a heavy, lidded stew pot or kettle. When all the meat has been browned and transferred, add the remaining stew base ingredients to the kettle, using a cup or so of the water to rinse the skillet so you don't lose anything.

Bring the liquid to just under a boil, turn the heat to simmer, cover, and cook until the meat is tender — 45 minutes to an hour. Take the kettle from the stove, remove the meat, and spread it on a plate to cool. As soon as it is cool enough to handle, take the meat from the bones, cover it tightly, and set it in the refrigerator. Return the bones to the kettle, put it back over low heat, and continue to cook, covered, another hour or so. Strain the liquid through something just fine enough to catch the peppercorns, pressing on the vegetables to get all the juice. Let cool, then cover and refrigerate overnight.

Day 2: Pick over the beans and put them in a heatproof bowl. Cover with an inch of boiling water and allow to sit about 10 minutes. Remove and discard the cake of fat from the top of the cooled broth and measure everything else, including the thick stuff at the bottom, into a heavy, lidded kettle. Add enough water to equal 3½ cups liquid altogether, using the water to rinse the broth bowl.

Drain the beans, add them to the kettle, and stir well. Bring just to a simmer, cover, and cook over low heat 1 to 1½ hours, or until the beans are tender and the liquid has evaporated. If necessary, remove the lid and cook rapidly over high heat, stirring often, until there is only a small amount of free liquid left. Chop the reserved meat into small pieces and stir them into the beans, then salt the mixture to taste and let it sit, covered, on the lowest possible heat. Warm a shallow serving dish.

Shred the greens as though for slaw. Put the oil and butter in a heavy skillet over medium heat and add the garlic as soon as the butter melts. Sauté 2 to 3 minutes, or until the garlic starts to turn pale gold. Raise the heat to medium-high, stir in the greenery, and continue to cook until the leaves have softened toward purée. This will take about 3 minutes. As soon as the greens are wilted, stir in the chives.

Transfer the hot bean mixture to the serving dish. Distribute the green purée on top in large dabs, using the back of a spoon to swirl it in so it makes fat streaks. Serve at once, with the sour cream on the side. Like most bean dishes, this one is very tasty with beer.

Lamb Loaf with Sorrel Stuffing

For 6 servings

STUFFING:
¼ cup butter
1 medium onion, chopped fine, about 1 cup
1 tablespoon finely grated lemon zest (thin, colored outer rind)
1 large clove garlic, pressed
½ teaspoon salt
1 teaspoon dried oregano
1¼ cups cooked rice or cracked wheat

½ cup coarse bread crumbs, preferably from unsweetened French bread
2 cups sorrel, chopped if it's the cultivated kind, whole if you use the
    small wild leaves
½ cup diced Emmenthal (Swiss) cheese, about 2 ounces
1 egg, well beaten
Approximately ½ cup milk
½ cup currants (optional)

LAMB LOAF:
1½ pounds lean ground beef (chuck or round)
1 pound ground lamb
1 smallish carrot, chopped fine, about ¼ cup
2 eggs
¼ cup dry red wine
Generous grind of pepper
1 large clove garlic

Make the stuffing. Melt the butter over medium heat in a small skillet, add the onion, and sauté until it is pale gold. Stir in the lemon zest, garlic, salt, and oregano. Turn heat to low and let the seasonings cook together 2 to 3 minutes.

Combine the grain, crumbs, sorrel, and cheese, then stir in the onion mixture. Add the egg and enough milk to make a cohering but not soggy stuffing. Stir in the currants, if you're using them. They add a sweet counterpoint to the sorrel but are by no means essential.

Make the lamb loaf by combining the meats with the carrot, 1 egg, the wine, and the pepper. Stir gently only until blended; overhandling will make the meat tough.

Set a sheet of waxed paper about 20 inches long on the worktable and pat the meat mixture out onto it, making a rectangle a scant ½ inch thick. It should be about 12 by 16 inches, but thickness is more important than exact size.

Cover the meat with the stuffing, leaving an exposed strip about 1½ inches wide along one of the long edges. Press the filling firmly onto the meat. Beat the remaining egg and smear it over the filling, using the palm of your hand for maximum speed and gentle thoroughness. Starting with the filling-free long edge, roll the meat like a jellyroll, tucking and pressing firmly as you go, using the paper to help things along.

Halve the garlic clove, crush slightly, and rub all over the inside of a long loaf pan or two short ones. Insert the lamb loaf (or half the loaf), seam side down. Press gently to flatten the top and even the loaf; it will still rise above the pan a bit. Preheat the oven to 350°F., cover the loaf tightly with foil, and put the pan(s) on a drip-catching baking sheet.

Bake 1¼ to 1½ hours, or until the loaf has shrunk from the sides of the pan, uncovering for the last 30 minutes or so, so the top can brown. Allow the loaf to sit 5 to 10 minutes after removing from the oven so the juices can go back into the meat. No gravy is necessary, but hollandaise, Greek avgelemono sauce, and plain yogurt all make nice accompaniments.

VARIATIONS: The stuffing also is good baked in green peppers or layered in a casserole with slices of grilled eggplant. You can use it to stuff mushrooms, tomatoes, zucchini, cabbage leaves, etc. You also can bake it, covered, in a well-buttered pan and serve it as a starch with a simple roast and plain steamed vegetables — a nice plump chicken, all golden and crisp, and a pile of tender bright green snap beans, for instance.

*T*HE MENU-CHANGING MONTH

NEW ENGLAND April, capable though it may be of springlike days, is still definitely hot lunch time — part of the hearty supper season. Starting to get the garden in, watching the rain fall while greening up goes on with agonizing slowness and the first bulbs grudgingly bloom low to the still-sodden ground — that's pork chop weather yet, when dinner had better be heavy-duty and breakfast ditto.

But May, ah, May, that's menu-changing month, when the sweet air of spring inspires a different sort of hunger. "Just a simple salad for lunch" starts to sound positively attractive, instead of merely dutiful. Balmy evenings invite light dinners, and big, hot breakfasts no longer seem like a smart way to start the day.

The hot cross buns of Easter morning herald the watershed. On the winter side are substantial day-starters like hot oatmeal, pancakes with sausage, and warm baked apples with prunes. On the side that leans toward summer are the airier pleasures of fancy breadstuffs — lemon loaf, English muffins, the kugelhopfs that follow, any or all of them toasted and slathered with cream cheese, accompanied by a small bowl of stewed rhubarb, if it's really May, or perhaps, even better, a handful of fresh strawberries to be picked up by the stems and eaten, unembellished, one by one.

You know it's spring when you start wanting to eat breakfast outdoors in the sunshine. And you know it's spring when the asparagus performs.

Since, as we know, "it takes all kinds," there are presumably people who do not like asparagus. It is difficult, however, to imagine just who these people might be when just about everybody thinks of it as *the* premier vegetable of spring, a position it has held since the beginning of culinary history.

Apparently, everybody has always known know to cook it, too. The phrase "do it as quickly as you would cook asparagus" is widely quoted as attributable to the Roman emperor Augustus (born 63 B.C.), who did not, in all probability, think it up himself.

The other thing that should be done quickly is the bringing of the asparagus from the garden to the table. Those hoary wisdoms about starting the water boiling before picking the corn apply equally to asparagus, though you'd never know it from this vegetable's ubiquity and longevity as a greengrocer's staple. This contradiction is partly a result of the triumph of hope over wisdom, of course, but it's also a result of the fact that asparagus exists in two different states of freshness.

The first is "fresh" as in standing there in the garden and snapping off a stalk of almost unbearably sweet, intensely juicy green-growingness that makes you glad to be alive in spite of everything. The other is "fresh" as in anything between twenty-four hours and about ten days old, because once that exquisite initial bloom has fled, the remaining good qualities of asparagus are actually quite stable. When properly stored, it will remain crisp and relatively tasty, if not transcendental, for a fair amount of time.

Properly stored means well chilled, stem ends kept damp but not sitting in water, the stalks packed tightly enough to remain upright but not jammed so close that rot is encouraged and not bruisingly bound with metal ties, rubber bands, etc. Obviously, it is better to buy from loose displays so that individual stalks can be chosen for their quality — firmness, absence of buds, tightness of head and scales, good color — as well as for the uniformity of size that facilitates even cooking. Some stores that display the stalks bundled or wrapped will let you choose from the crate out back if you ask. It's worth asking, especially early in the season when asparagus is so expensive (and so inclined to be ratty).

It's never cheap, at least partly because it must be harvested by hand. The stalks present themselves over several weeks, the roots shooting up new spears as the previous ones are cut. Still, it is grown on at least a small scale almost everywhere, and as the local product comes into season, prices generally do come down. Almost anywhere it will grow or has grown, it is likely to be growing wild somewhere nearby, free for the picking if you can find it. Birds spread the seed, the plants are hardy, and once a stand is established in a congenial place, it will continue for many years. Just about any forager's guide will give directions for finding it. Euell Gibbons named the granddaddy of them all *Stalking the Wild Asparagus* for good reason.

Asparagus is classically presented steamed. If you want to be *really* classic about it, you peel the lower ends of the stalks, cook them upright in a tall, narrow asparagus steamer, and present them naked (the asparagus, that is) on a white napkin, with the sauce on the side. Diners eat the spears with their fingers, etiquette for once finding such behavior not only permissible but correct. Certainly it is one of the most erotically suggestive ways of consuming a vegetable long reputed to have aphrodisiac qualities (only because of its shape, as far as I know).

Classicism aside, it's difficult to get steamed whole spears right even with the proper pot, because timing really is split-second and the tip-to-base identically sized stalks that would permit this are seldom found. More reliable results are obtained if you cut the tip ends from the thicker stalks and stack those stalks, thickest at the bottom, in a plain old basket steamer. Cook them over boiling water for six minutes or so, depending on amount and individual thickness, then spread the small stalks and tips over the top and cook about four minutes more.

If tradition calls (few meals could be more seductive than a major pile of steamed fresh asparagus with whipped cream–lightened maltaise sauce) and for some reason you don't happen to have an asparagus steamer, use a well-scrubbed, old-fashioned coffee percolator. Remove the center tube. Fashion a lid from a saucepan or generous square of tinfoil if the asparagus is taller than the pot. Leave the woody ends on the stalks so *they* sit in the inch or so of boiling water you need for the operation. Cut them off before serving, and the whole edible length will be in prime condition.

Alternatively, asparagus can be stir-fried. Cut it on the diagonal into one- or two-inch lengths and add to the pan sequentially, thickest pieces first. Use olive oil if you plan marinated asparagus for salad.

Possible sauces are without end. The maltaise mentioned above (a hollandaise flavored with orange, ideally sour orange, instead of lemon) is great, but anything buttery, eggy, or cheesy is bound to be good as long as it doesn't overpower. Salted whipped cream heavily studded with shredded fresh horseradish is terrific when you can find fresh horseradish, a commodity that grows scarce as the asparagus season progresses.

Franco-Chinese Asparagus
(Flavored in the French Manner, Cooked Chinese-Style)

For 6 portions

2 pounds asparagus, trimmed
¼ cup butter
1 teaspoon lightly flavored olive oil
1 small clove garlic, crushed but left whole
Grated zest (thin, colored outer rind) of 1 large lemon
1 tablespoon plus 1 teaspoon lemon juice
Pinch of sugar
6 egg yolks (see Note)
Coarse salt

Cut the asparagus on an exaggerated diagonal into 2-inch lengths. The extreme angle of the cut will expose a large amount of asparagus interior for faster cooking and better flavor absorption. Set the asparagus aside.

Put the butter and oil with the garlic in a heavy, wide skillet or wok and steep over the lowest possible heat for 10 to 15 minutes. Remove and discard the garlic; raise the heat to medium-high. When the fat foams up, add the asparagus by handfuls, stirring as you go. Turn the heat as high as you can get it without burning anything and stir-fry 2 to 3 minutes.

Start tasting (remembering to blow first). As soon as the stuff tastes cooked, while it's still very crunchy, add the lemon zest and keep frying just until it smells toasted. Turn off heat, stir in lemon juice and sugar, and cover the pan. Set it in a warm place about 2 minutes so flavors can blend and asparagus achieves a more French than Chinese texture.

Divide the asparagus into six portions on warmed serving plates. Form each into a nest, making a depression in the middle with the back of the spoon. Put a yolk in each nest and serve at once, lightly sprinkled with coarse salt. The yolk will cook slightly when stirred into the hot asparagus, magically becoming sauce. If you want to present the nests together on a platter, by all means do so. A flat spatula will lift them onto individual plates with no problem.

NOTE: To have the yolks waiting at the critical moment, separate them beforehand and drop them gently into a bowl containing a couple of cups of cold water acidulated with a squeeze of lemon juice. They will stiffen slightly because of the acid but will still be fairly fragile unless they are nicely fresh. Lift them out when you need them, using a slotted spoon or, more gentle, your lightly cupped hand.

 *Basic Kugelhopf*

SPONGE:
1 cup milk
1 tablespoon dry yeast (1 envelope)
1 cup all-purpose flour

CAKE:
Butter for the pan, plus 1 cup
¾ cup shredded or slivered almonds
½ cup sugar
5 eggs
1½ teaspoons vanilla extract
Grated zest (thin, colored outer rind) of 1 large lemon
½ teaspoon salt
3 cups bread flour
1 cup currants or chopped raisins
Confectioners' sugar

Make sure all ingredients are at room temperature when you mix them; it will make a much lighter cake. Begin by making the sponge. Scald the milk, pour it into a medium-sized mixing bowl, and let it cool to lukewarm. Sprinkle the yeast over it and let it dissolve. Stir well, beat in the flour, then cover the mixture with plastic wrap and let it rise in a warm place until it is very light and bubbly — 1 to 3 hours, depending on how warm the warm place is.

Lavishly butter a 2-quart ring or Turk's-head mold, making sure all crevices and convolutions are well greased. Press in the nuts to make as even a coating as possible and set the pan aside.

In a large mixing bowl, cream the 1 cup butter until it is light and fluffy, then thoroughly cream in the sugar. Beat the eggs in one at a time, making sure each is thoroughly incorporated before adding the next. Beat in the vanilla extract, lemon zest, and salt and set the mixture aside.

When the sponge is ready, beat it into the butter mixture. Slowly, a cup at a time, beat in the flour. Beat and beat until the dough is very smooth and elastic. It will be much stiffer than cake batter but much looser than bread. Never in your wildest dreams would you be tempted to start kneading it. Stir in the currants or raisins.

Carefully transfer the batter-dough to the prepared pan. Place it — don't pour it — as you don't want to dislodge the almonds. Cover the pan with plastic wrap and let the kugelhopf rise until it's almost but not quite double in bulk and just about fills the pan, again 1 to 3 hours, depending on the room's temperature.

Preheat the oven to 375°F. Bake the cake 10 minutes, then lower the heat to 350°F. and bake 40 to 60 minutes more, depending on the pan (tubes cook more quickly than the solid Turk's-heads). It's ready when well risen, brown, and shrunken from the edges of the pan.

Turn the kugelhopf out upside-down onto a cooling rack. Dust lavishly with the confectioners' sugar when it's completely cold.

HUNGARIAN VERSION: Substitute ⅔ cup raisins plus ½ cup poppy seeds for the currants and finely chopped walnuts for the almonds.

DELUXE TEATIME *(Not Breakfasttime)* **VERSION:** Increase the sugar to 1 cup. Substitute ½ cup each raisins, poppy seeds, and chopped semisweet chocolate for the currants and use finely chopped pecans or walnuts instead of the almonds.

*M*Y PAEAN TO PEAS

THEY ARE immensely old, peas, one of the very first vegetables to be domesticated. At the same time, they are ever new. For centuries they have been a symbol of summer achieved, of the garden's first full flowering. Eagerly awaited, avidly consumed, and gone before anyone is sated, they are like sweet corn on the ear — a fleeting seasonal pleasure.

For me (as for all gardeners, surely) the beauty of peas on the plate is inextricably mixed with the beauty of peas growing. Green pods among white flowers in the mass of leafy vine, bees everywhere, and in the same garden the blooming sweet peas, fragile, fragrant, most perfect of flowers. The sight of their graceful tendrils reaching from the arching vines is definitely in there with the thrill of that first "mess of peas," with the taste of sweet greenness beyond green, steaming hot, gilded with butter.

Of course, by the time for pea cooking, a good portion of the crop has already been eaten . . . or gobbled, more accurately. After asparagus, peas are the first vegetable a gardener can really *browse* on. Off the plant and into the mouth — no waiting, no washing — instant gratification. Then, far too soon, their moment has passed. Unlike tomatoes, say, or green beans, peas do not continue to produce over a long period. Early peas are followed by late peas and late peas by sugarsnaps, but the whole sequence takes less than two months. They're over and done with by early midsummer, and that is the end of that for another year.

Some people, people who are otherwise, as far as one can tell, sane, profess to enjoy the flavor of canned peas (provided they are the tiny or baby variety). I have long wondered what possessed these people and think it might be that they have caught and been caught by the elusive, slightly richer flavor of true *petits pois*. These are a specific group of varieties whose peas are small even when fully mature. Most of our popular "English" peas, even the tenderest home-garden sorts, are insipid (and rather funny-looking) when immature enough to be that tender and tiny. Petits pois have a strong, distinct flavor, readily identifiable even when they are very young.

The ability to investigate these matters, tasting for yourself the difference between favorites such as, say, Green Arrow, Lincoln, and Waverex, is to some extent a function of where you live. Pea connoisseurs in New England and the Northwest are especially fortunate because the climate that so discourages melons is ideal for the growing of peas. But even in the Deep South, home gardeners and those with access to farmers' markets or stores supplied by small, quality-oriented truck farms are in a very good position to make the most of pea season. They may even get sugarsnaps.

Sugarsnaps resemble Chinese snow peas in that the whole pod is eaten. They are, however, a great leap forward in the deliciousness department. Crisp and flavorful, their fat pods heavy with juice, they are a triumphantly wonderful new vegetable that has not entered mass distribution (yet). And why not, if they're so dandy? Well, for one thing, they're new. New vegetables, no matter how splendid, take a while to catch on outside of trendy restaurants in large cities. Most people are deeply conservative when it comes to the food they eat.

Even more important is the fact that the plant is not well suited to large-scale culture. The sugarsnap pea, a cross between English peas and snow peas, bears later and grows larger than either, and these are major faults in the world of commercial farming. Though seed catalogues optimistically tell you the vines will climb five or six feet, the unfortunate truth is that when they are happy, they are *huge* — eight feet is not all that uncommon. This means they must be supported by more than a few haphazard branches of brush, and picking is no casual matter. Needless to say, plant breeders are hard at it, and I have no doubt that the folks who figured out how to make iron tomatoes will be able to tame the sugar-snap's wayward ways. Already short-vine types are being marketed, though their quality is not as high as the original's. When it becomes so, this novelty will surely turn into an extremely common vegetable in both fresh and frozen forms.

Sugarsnaps are such a revelation that there is a temptation to forswear all other peas, and they do pretty much enable you to stop bothering with snow peas. Still, you have to put in a few English peas, and a few petits pois, too, because the marvelousness of sugarsnaps is not better than — only different from — the marvelousness of green peas.

The nature of marvels, alas, is to be elusive, and whether you grow them or get them from your marvel of a greengrocer, you know that fresh, new green peas of the type over which I've just been swooning are rare on this mortal coil. Once harvested, peas lose their innocent freshness and sweetness with truly appalling speed.

Then, as if this problem weren't enough, there is a tendency on the part of commercial growers to let them peas get *big*, Buddy, before the vines are stripped. A pea grown so fat it has busted its skin has also long since converted to starch every crumb of sugar it ever possessed. Most frozen peas share a similar fault; they may have been *frozen* with model speed, but that doesn't mean they were all that great to start with.

This brings us to the melancholy subject of frozen peas. Might as well get it over with.

1. They are *much* better than the ancient, horsey, so-called "fresh" peas that so often pollute the shelves of even the most fastidious markets, though it must be admitted this is not saying a lot.

2. Freezing tends to toughen the skins. So does salt. Add this to the fact that peas specially bred for freezing tend to be sturdier anyway, and you know why frozen peas are so mean.

3. If you take good fresh peas of a delicate variety (from your garden or from your farmers' market) and freeze them yourself, the results can be pretty tasty. Similarly, there is an enormous difference between brands of frozen peas. Shop around.

4. I can't go on. Not in fresh pea season, when the air is fat with the smell of growing, the sky serene, and bees loud in the thyme.

The recipes that follow are designed to be used with a wide variety of peas. While all are at their best when made with exquisitely fresh young new ones, all except the first (for gazpacho) still come in handy when the bloom is off the rose.

Green Gazpacho with Peas

For 6 generous servings

3 pounds fresh young peas in the pod, enough to make 3 cups shelled
3½ cups light chicken or veal broth (or water)
1¼ teaspoons salt
½ cup coarsely chopped celery
½ cup coarsely chopped green pepper
½ cup peeled, seeded, coarsely chopped cucumber
1 cup coarsely chopped green tomatoes (see Note)
1 small clove garlic, pressed
½ cup whole almonds, ground to a powder
¼ cup very thinly sliced green onions (scallions)
1 or 2 bright-skinned, juicy limes, for garnish

Shell the peas, reserving 3 cups of the nicest-looking pods. Put the peas in a large heatproof bowl. Cut up the pods and combine them with the broth and salt. Put the pan over medium-high heat, bring just to the boil, then lower heat to medium and simmer 30 minutes or so. Strain the simmering broth over the peas in the bowl, stir well, and allow to cool to room temperature.

With a slotted spoon, remove one cup of the peas. Combine them in a processor or blender with the celery, green pepper, cucumber, green tomatoes, garlic, almond powder, and 1 cup of the broth. Grind, turning the machine on and off, only until you have a uniform slush. The chopped vegetables should be about the size of wheat berries or very coarse cornmeal, chunky enough to provide a definite crunch.

Combine the chopped mixture with the peas and broth. Stir in the green onions and chill the soup, covered, at least a few hours, as long as a full day. At serving time, stir well to recombine everything, taste, and adjust the salt. Serve very cold, garnished with wedges of lime.

NOTE: Fully mature tomatoes, still completely green outside and just starting to turn red inside, are ideal for this and fairly easy to find in pea season. Their taste is rather unassuming, but they add just the right touch of piquant acidity to balance the soup.

 # Risi e Bisi
(Rice and Peas)

This jaunty springtime combo is a specialty of Venice, known all over Italy for the quality of its peas. Authentic recipes call for fat bacon or prosciutto in addition to the other seasonings, but I prefer the less complicated flavor of this lighter version.

For 6 large servings or 4 small servings and a batch of **suppli** *(see recipe on page 71)*

4 cups light chicken stock (may not all be used)
1 teaspoon salt, less if stock is salty already
2 tablespoons butter
2 tablespoons olive oil
½ cup minced celery
½ cup minced onion
1 cup arborio rice (Italian risotto rice; see Note)
1½ to 2 cups shelled fresh peas, about 1¾ pounds in the pod
⅓ cup freshly grated Parmesan cheese, about 1½ ounces
4 tablespoons finely minced fresh parsley
Additional Parmesan, to pass at the table

Sometimes Risi e Bisi is listed on menus as a soup, but though it should be very creamy, it also should be firm enough to eat with a fork.

Heat the chicken stock with the salt and keep it warm, just below a simmer. Put the butter and oil in a large, heavy saucepan and place over medium heat. When the fat is fragrant, add the celery and onion and cook, stirring often, until the vegetables are thoroughly cooked and starting to brown a bit around the edges. Stir in the rice and cook 2 to 3 minutes more.

Pour in about 1½ cups of the hot stock and stir well, then adjust the heat so that the liquid bubbles very gently. Keep stirring, adding more liquid as necessary to keep the rice barely surrounded at all times. In 15 minutes or so, you should have rice cooked just al dente — fully tender but firm to the tooth, swimming in a generous amount of extremely thick sauce. There may be a bit of broth left over, depending on the dryness of the rice, your definition of bubbling gently, etc.

While the rice is cooking, evaluate your peas. Fully developed large ones may take as long as 12 to 15 minutes to cook, while young, tender new ones are done enough as soon as they're hot through. Since the idea is to have them just exactly tender at the end of the approximately 25 minutes it takes to cook the rice, subtract projected pea-cooking time from 25 to find out how many minutes should elapse between starting the rice and adding the peas. When their moment arrives, add them, stirring very well to distribute thoroughly.

As soon as the rice hits the al dente stage, stir in the Parmesan, parsley, and (if you have not already done so) the peas. Cover the pan and let the mixture settle 4 to 5 minutes at the back of the stove. Serve at once, as a first course, with additional Parmesan.

NOTE: Arborio rice is sold at specialty shops and Italian groceries. The grain is diamond-shaped, with a white spot at the center and a slightly grayish cast to the overall color. This special rice is essential for proper texture because ordinary white rice will turn to mush if cooked stirred in lots of liquid, and brown rice, though it will hold up better, will not make the creamy wavelike sauce for which Risi e Bisi is famous.

SUPPLI: If you plan to make these lovely croquettes (see the following recipe) be sure to spread the leftover Risi e Bisi in a shallow dish at once and refrigerate promptly. Since the mixture will be reheated later, you want it to cool as fast as possible so the held heat doesn't overcook it.

Suppli al Telefono

These toothsome croquettes are a study in textural contrasts — crisp crust, smooth filling, and unctuous, slightly chewy melted cheese at the heart. They get their name from the long strings — telephone wires — for which melted mozzarella is famous. Serve plain, garnished with lemon wedges, as a substantial finger food or as a first course, 2 or 3 to a plate, capped with a light tomato sauce.

For 1 dozen golf ball–sized croquettes

1¾ to 2 cups leftover Risi e Bisi (see recipe on page 69)
3 ounces prosciutto or other flavorful dry-cured ham, cut in ¼-inch
    cubes, about ½ cup
3 tablespoons grated Parmesan cheese
2 tablespoons finely minced fresh parsley
1 egg, beaten to mix
12 ½-inch cubes mozzarella cheese (see Note), about 3 ounces
Flour
Oil for deep-frying

COATING:
Reserved egg from croquettes
3 tablespoons milk
½ cup fine dry bread crumbs
½ cup blanched almonds, ground to powder
1 tablespoon finely shredded lemon zest (thin, colored outer rind)
½ teaspoon salt

Combine Risi e Bisi, prosciutto, Parmesan, parsley, and 1 tablespoon of the egg (reserve the remainder). Spread in a shallow pan, such as a brownie pan, and chill thoroughly, lightly covered, so it can firm up a bit.

To make the coating, combine the reserved egg with the milk and set aside. Mix bread crumbs, almonds, lemon zest, and salt in a shallow bowl.

Set out a shallow bowl of flour. Line a flat pan with waxed paper to put the suppli on. Working quickly, divide the rice mixture into 12 parts. Form each into a ball with a cube of mozzarella at the center, not worrying if the cheese isn't completely enclosed but trying to get it surrounded as best you can. The mixture will be gooey and stick to your fingers. Persevere. The stickier the stuff is now, the creamier it'll be once it's cooked. If necessary, lightly flour your fingertips to keep the rice from sticking. As each ball is formed, drop it in the flour, roll to dust it as lightly as possible, and transfer to the sheet.

When all the suppli are formed, go back and dip each first in the egg mixture, then in the coating. Arrange well apart on the sheet and allow the coating to set. This will take about 30 minutes at room temperature. Suppli can be refrigerated at this point, loosely covered, for several hours or overnight. Be sure to allow them to return to room temperature, uncovered, before you proceed.

In a heavy, wide pan, slowly heat a 3-inch layer of oil to 365°F. Fry the croquettes, uncrowded, about 4 minutes, turning once. Regulate the heat so temperature stays steady — much over 365°F. and the crust will burn before the cheese is melted, much under and they'll absorb oil and get greasy. Drain finished suppli on absorbent paper on a flat sheet and put them in a 250°F. oven with the door cracked open to keep them warm.

NOTE: There's mozzarella and there's mozzarella. Fresh imported *mozzarella di bufalo* is so soft you can barely cube it, and it melts very quickly; the *fresh* domestic product can be almost as good. Rubbery, firm, commercial mozzarella is pretty heat resistant. If you have the latter type, shred it instead of cubing and put a pinch of the more easily melted shreds in the center of the suppli.

 ## *The Goodwife's Peas*
(*Petits Pois à la Bonne Femme or à la Française*)

This most classic of classic recipes is a rather aggressive treatment. Clearly the goodwife of the title used it toward the end of the season, when the peas were somewhat larger and coarser than the sweet new peas of spring.

For 4 to 6 servings

3½ ounces lean salt pork, diced, about ½ cup
3 tablespoons butter
12 tiny white boiling onions, peeled, about a heaping half cup
Firm inner leaves of 1 small head of tender lettuce (see Note), shredded
    as though for slaw, enough to make 4 cups, lightly piled
3 cups shelled peas, about 3 pounds in the pod
Bouquet of 3 sprigs each parsley and thyme (and chervil, if you can get
    it)
Pinch of sugar
⅓ cup water

Drop the cubed salt pork in a generous amount of boiling water. Turn off the heat and let it sit 2 minutes, then drain thoroughly.

In a heavy skillet, melt 1 tablespoon of the butter over medium heat. Add the pork and fry, stirring almost constantly, until the cubes are golden brown. Remove them with a slotted spoon, drain on absorbent paper, and reserve.

Add the onions to the pan and fry them, stirring frequently, until they are translucent and starting to brown, almost but not quite cooked — about 10 minutes. Remove the onions with a slotted spoon and reserve. Drain and discard all fat and return the pan, unwashed, to the heat.

Put the onions back in with the lettuce shreds, peas, bouquet, and sugar. Add the water and bring the liquid to a boil. Lower the heat to medium-low, half-cover the pan, and simmer 8 to 15 minutes, or until the peas are very tender and well imbued with the onion flavor. The lettuce will have more or less vanished.

Remove the bouquet and add the remaining 2 tablespoons butter, cut into 3 or 4 pieces. Gently tilt the pan this way and that until the butter melts and thickens the sauce. Turn into a warmed vegetable dish and serve at once, sprinkled with the reserved cubes of crisp pork.

NOTE: You want a soft-leaved, tender lettuce that will break down rapidly without shedding too much water. Bibb (Boston), buttercrunch, Deertongue, and Black-Seeded Simpson (early salad bowl) all work well. For gardeners, this is a good place to put those lettuces that are just about to bolt and turn bitter. Their sharper flavor is a wonderful accent for the peas.

CONCERNING CRABMEAT
Northern Crabmeat Especially

THE FISH MARKET was lined with white tile, gleaming, reassuringly clean. Nestled in the ice-filled display case were trays of vaguely familiar, not quite identifiable fish. "What's that?" I asked, pointing to a tray of absolutely even, perfectly rectangular slabs of something white, which bore the label "Flownder, $2.98." "We sell lots of that," the clerk replied. "Glad to hear it," said I. "What is it?" "Two ninety-eight a pound," she replied. "Yes, so I see, but what is it?" "We have a service where we can bread it for you right here, if you like." "But *what is it?*" I screamed, which woke me up.

This nightmare was, I have no doubt, inspired by the fear that surimi is about to take over the world. Surimi is an all-purpose fish paste currently used to make ersatz shellfish — crabmeat, lobster, etc. Like its land-based counterpart, textured vegetable protein (TVP on the thousands of labels it adorns), surimi is a protean substance that can be made to assume the appearance, texture, and flavor of many different foods. Invented, perfected, and still largely manufactured (where else?) in Japan, it is by all accounts America's fastest growing seafood. Six million pounds were sold in 1981; by 1987 the figure was one hundred forty million. A billion is projected by 1990.

The surimi base is usually made from Alaskan pollock, a comparatively bland, off-white, extremely abundant fish that was called, before surimi, an "underutilized species." It is mangled and minced and put through several washings, mixed with a sweet stabilizer, and now ready to be turned into any of a number of "shellfish analogues," frozen for future use.

So far, the most popular surimi product seems to be fake crabmeat, sold under names such as Sea Legs, Krab Fingers, and King Krab. These offerings vary quite a bit among themselves — some contain a substantial proportion (as much as a third) of actual crabmeat, others are flavored with a crab extract made from the shells, and still others depend completely on artificial flavoring. Similar differences exist in choices of binders, additives such as monosodium glutamate (MSG), additional sweeteners, and the red colorings used to add that final touch of verisimilitude.

Though most fish markets sell imitation crabmeat by the pound, from display trays that do not display a description of the formula, the box in which the stuff was originally packed should carry a list of the contents of its contents.

The technology is pretty good; all these products do taste crablike — some of them quite convincingly, others quite horribly. All of them are crablike in the same way, however, with a sort of generic "crab" flavor utterly lacking in character.

After all, real crabmeat is, among its other virtues, a many-hued pleasure. Alaskan king crab, Dungeness crab from the West Coast, Florida stone crab, Jonah crab from Maine, the "beautiful swimmers" (*Callinectes sapidus*) of Chesapeake Bay — each has its distinctive savor, unmistakably the taste of crab, yet also delicately, subtly, the taste of its own special place and species.

The crabs of Maine are small and scarce compared to the types from the South and Northwest, but they are every bit as delicious, maybe even a little more so. If they are less famous, it may simply be because the people who love them have not gone around bragging about it.

Up north in Hancock County, Maine, crabmeat is a growing industry, but as far as the rest of the state is concerned — and the rest of New England as well — demand far exceeds supply. Except at the height of the season (which runs from April to September), fresh crabmeat is not reliably available in any quantity at all, a scarcity that's hardly surprising, since the meat is waste-free, almost all protein, easily digestible, nonfattening, and among the most delicious foods in all creation.

The price of picked-out meat is high, but you're paying for a lot of labor. Professional pickers, who usually are paid by the pound, might turn out as much as four pounds an hour. That's almost sixty-five crabs, since the official yield is calculated at about one ounce per crab. Cooked crabmeat costs $8 or $9 a pound, whereas live crabs sell for $2 or $3 a dozen. But I can't say I really care about the cost. Even if I have to buy it, I get to eat it, which means I'm very lucky indeed.

Crab Buyer's Guide

Maine crab is sold mostly in Maine, though some is shipped as far south as Boston and New York. Almost all Maine crab is rock crab (*Cancer irroratus*) caught off a muddy (not rocky) bottom fairly close to shore. A small proportion is Jonah crab (*Cancer borealis*) caught in deeper water. The primary difference is that the Jonah claws are bigger. Some people claim Jonah meat is coarse tasting, but this is debatable.

Live crabs are rare, both in and out of season, though you might find them if you have access to the coast or, better yet, a lobsterman. Fish markets near sources of supply do sell whole cooked crabs, but these are invariably overcooked, old, and not worth even their comparatively low price.

Picked crab is widely available, even quite far from the coast. It is usually sold in six- or eight-ounce containers. The meat should look opaque, plump, and moist, and it should smell sweet with no trace of ammonia. Don't be shy — give your crabmeat the sniff test before you leave the market. Crabmeat sold by pickers with "Fresh Crabmeat" signs on the lawn usually is freshest.

Cooking and Picking Crabs from Scratch

Make sure you have lively crabs, complete with all their legs. Put them in a big tub of warm water and scrub the shells with a stiff brush. Hold them carefully, right behind the claws, so they can't reach around and pinch you. The warm-water bath will tranquilize as well as clean, and the crabs will therefore be less likely to drop their claws when you dump them in a large pot of boiling water.

I prefer boiling over steaming because that way I can cook more at a time, more quickly, and more evenly. The "crab boil spices" popular for use with southern crabs overwhelm the more delicate flavor of the northern ones and should be avoided. But a bay leaf, a lemon wedge, and a clove or two of garlic will do no harm, and neither will a dollop of wine. Keep the water at a solid but not violent boil. The crabs will be cooked in about 10 minutes unless they are very large. Overcooked crab will be tough and shreddy and much harder to pick out, so it's better to err on the undercooked side. You can always finish them in a bit of butter, cream, or fish stock if need be.

Most crab lovers who cook their own have favorite homemade tools for picking. One woman I know uses a small curved knife her lobsterman husband fashioned from an already short-bladed parer. I rely mostly on hairpins and the long, thin, pointed bamboo skewers made for hibachi cooking. Hard-shelled claws call for a hammer. A hammer is better than a pair of conventional crackers, which are likely to crush shell fragments into the tender claw meat. Whatever you plan to use, find it and set it out.

Equipment assembled, set yourself up a work surface covered with paper or plastic. Get out two bowls, one for white meat and one for brown. Station yourself at the sink to start with — crabs hold a lot of juice.

Take the biggest crab you've got (to give yourself encouragement) and turn it on its back, head facing away from you. Grasp each leg at the joint closest to the body and twist up and backward. The legs should come off flush with the jagged, triangular apron. Set the legs aside. You can see and feel the place at the tail where the body will, if encouraged, come away. Force the body from the shell and set it aside, too. You are now holding the shell, which is holding the inedible stomach and a lot of tasty liver, fat, and other soft (brown) meat. Remove the stomach by pressing down on the mouth section, underneath the eyes, and gently lift out both the mouth and the attached stomach. Throw them out. Hold the shell over the brown meat bowl and empty the contents into it. Run a fingertip around the inside of the shell to be sure you get everything. This rich meat is delicious in chowders, crab cakes, and casseroles, but it's too soft for sandwiches and salads.

Retire to the worktable. Twist the legs apart and pile them in like-sized piles. Use the hammer where necessary to crack the claws. Set them on edge and whack *lightly*; you want them to come apart at what would be the seam.

There is meat in each of the eight body sections that correspond to the tops of the legs. Poke your curved tool into the holes to extract big lumps of it.

Freshly cooked and picked crabmeat will stay wholesome for two or three days if kept cold, but it will be deteriorating at every moment. Eat it quickly to enjoy it most. You can freeze crabmeat, but neither taste nor texture will be the same.

 Crab Spread with Almonds

For about 1½ cups

¼ **cup butter**
½ **cup chopped, unblanched almonds**
1 **small onion, chopped**
3 **ounces cream cheese, preferably the gum-free, natural kind**
6 **or 7 ounces crabmeat**
1 **tablespoon brandy**
¼ **teaspoon ground mace**
Salt to taste

Melt the butter over medium heat in a small skillet. When it foams, add the almonds. Turn the heat to low and sauté the almonds, stirring often, until they are golden brown. Remove them with a slotted spoon and reserve.

Cook the onion in the same butter, stirring often, until it is wilted and just starting to turn gold. Remove from pan. Reserve the butter.

Use a processor, blender, or mortar and pestle to crush the almonds and onions to a smooth paste. In a small bowl, work the cream cheese until it is soft, then work in the almond and onion purée. Stir in the crabmeat, brandy, and seasonings, adding the reserved butter last.

Let the pâté mellow 15 minutes or so, then taste it and adjust the salt. Serve with crusty French bread or simple crackers so the delicate flavor comes through.

This pâté will stay good for 3 or 4 days in the refrigerator. Let it come almost to room temperature before serving.

Seashell Pasta with Crab and Mushrooms
(For Parties)

Although crabmeat, cream, and prosciutto are pretty pricey ingredients, the magic of pasta means this is actually an inexpensive dish. The sauce can be assembled in the time it takes to cook the shells, making it a real timesaver in addition to its other virtues.

For 8 to 10 servings

2 teaspoons salt
1 teaspoon olive oil
1¾ cups whipping cream (30% butterfat, not ultrapasteurized)
1 pound cooked crabmeat, picked over to remove any bits of shell
¼ teaspoon freshly grated nutmeg
4 tablespoons butter
2 cups very fresh mushrooms, wiped but not washed, and coarsely chopped
2 pounds small seashell pasta
1½ cups fresh peas, about 1½ pounds in the shell
1¼ cups lightly piled freshly grated Parmesan cheese, about 4 ounces
¼ pound super-thinly sliced prosciutto or Westphalian ham, cut into thin slivers
Kosher salt

Combine the salt and oil with at least a gallon of water in a large kettle, cover, and put on to boil for the pasta. Put the cream, crabmeat, and nutmeg in a small, heavy saucepan and put it somewhere warm to heat and infuse without actually cooking — the back of the stove, if you have that kind of stove. Warm the serving plates.

In a small skillet, melt the butter over medium-high heat and add the mushrooms when it foams. Sauté them, stirring often, until they are well browned, then set them aside in the same place as the crabmeat cream to keep warm.

When the water boils, uncover the pan and slowly stir in the pasta, dribbling it a bit at a time so the water never stops boiling. Cook about 8 minutes, or until a test shell is almost, but not quite, done. Add the peas and cook 2 minutes more, then drain thoroughly and return to the pot.

Pour in the crabmeat cream and toss madly, then add everything else except the kosher salt, stirring and tossing as you add so the tidbits are well distributed. Portion the pasta onto the warm plates and pass the kosher salt for the diners to sprinkle at will.

BOSTON CREAM PIE
The Mystery Explored

NEVER WAS there a more enigmatic piece of pastry. As almost everyone knows, it isn't pie, it's cake — plain old American butter cake — and a rather flabby one at that, without so much as a trace of crust in sight.

In his wide-ranging *Dictionary of American Food and Drink*, John F. Mariani credits Boston's Parker House with having invented the assemblage of cake layers, custard filling, and chocolate icing we call Boston cream pie, tracing the first mention of the term to 1855. Since the Parker House hotel didn't open until 1856, this implies the pastry was already a specialty in Mr. Parker's restaurant, which came first.

If the thing is indeed that old, it's a safe bet the original cake wasn't much like the fluffy, buttery layers we associate with the pastry today, since the baking powders that leaven those layers did not become widespread until the 1870s and 1880s and the highly emulsified shortenings that characterize the commercial pastry were not invented until the 1930s.

More mysterious than the composition of the cake, of course, is the matter of nomenclature. Why pie? The *Oxford English Dictionary* has a great deal to say on the subject of pie, an English word that doesn't seem to have come from anywhere else. But consistently, from the earliest citations (twelfth century), pie means something cooked in its enclosing crusts, the filling being an integral part of the original creation. It can be savory or sweet. It can even be assembled from separate parts. But a pie always holds its contents in a tight embrace, which that Boston cream thing does not.

My theory, utterly unsubstantiated, is based entirely on my research into the construction of the tastiest. It is, simply, that (perhaps) the term came from baking the cake layers in pie tins. If you do that, you get a somewhat funny-looking cake, one that does not much resemble those in magazine illustrations. But you also get the largest possible surface to put the cream on, as well as a thinnish confection whose total loft more nearly resembles that of pie than conventional cake.

Regardless of the pan shape and general composition, the pastry itself seems always to have been a special-occasion treat, something you got when you were out — a restaurant-fancy dessert that came from a commercial rather than a home kitchen.

A friend of mine, born and raised on the Maine coast, though widely traveled since, put the situation neatly when I asked for his recollections. "*Regular* pie — apple, blueberry, stuff like that — we had that every day. But Boston cream pie . . . . " His eyes took on a faraway look, as did the eyes of most of the men consulted in my informal survey. Women, on the other hand, mostly said they could live happily without it.

Thus we are left with one more mystery: Why is this particular pastry a gender-specific pleasure? Answer that one and you win the cream pie.

Boston Cream Pie
(Iconoclast's Version)

Not being male, I've always found the classic Boston cream pie to be a singularly boring pastry. I mean, why eat Boston cream pie when you could be eating trifle? After all, it is the nature of even the moistest cake to be on the dry side, needful of filling and icing and fruit and liqueurs to soften it into attractiveness. This being the case, only Puritans (maybe that's where the Boston part comes in) would content themselves with the small amount of custard prescribed in conventional Boston cream pie recipes.

The cream pie that follows is, therefore, what is these days popularly called an interpretation. It looks and tastes enough like the classic to be clearly recognizable, but I have made a number of alterations.

There is a lot more custard, you will not be surprised to hear. And the chocolate icing (which there is no avoiding if it's going to be Boston cream pie at all) is a very firm, candylike layer. This is so it can be neatly peeled off by those who feel, as I do, that the flavor of chocolate overwhelms the subtle vanilla perfume of the cake and its silken filling.

In conformation with my theory about the origin of the name, the cake is baked in pie tins. In contradistinction to said theory, it doesn't look very pielike, since the giant layer of custard in the middle lends considerable height.

For a 9-inch pie, about 8 servings (It's quite rich.)

CAKE*:
Butter for the pans plus 6 tablespoons
1¾ cups sifted cake flour (sift before measuring)
2 teaspoons baking powder
¼ teaspoon salt
2 tablespoons solid vegetable shortening such as Crisco
¾ cup minus 1 tablespoon sugar
3 egg yolks
2 teaspoons vanilla extract
¾ cup milk

ICING:
4 ounces high-quality bittersweet chocolate, such as Lindt or Tobler, chopped, about ½ cup (Do not use chocolate chips.)
2 tablespoons butter
3 tablespoons sweet, clear liqueur — Triple Sec, amaretto, crème de cacao, etc.

FILLING:
1 vanilla bean
1½ cups milk
5 egg yolks
⅓ cup sugar

---

*All ingredients should be at room temperature.

¼ cup flour
1 tablespoon unflavored gelatin (1 envelope)
2 tablespoons cold water
½ cup heavy cream

Begin with the cake layers. Preheat the oven to 375°F. Butter two shallow 9-inch pie pans, line the bottoms with baking parchment (or waxed paper), and butter the paper.

Sift flour, baking powder, and salt and set aside. Cream the 6 table-spoons butter and shortening until fluffy, then slowly beat in the sugar. Keep beating until the mixture is smooth and light; thorough beating ensures a fine-textured, moist cake.

Beat in the egg yolks one at a time, mixing each in thoroughly before adding the next. Beat in the vanilla extract.

Still beating, alternately add a third of the flour mixture, half the milk, another third of the flour, the rest of the milk, and the rest of the flour. Each addition should be well mixed in before the next is attempted, but overbeating at this stage is to be avoided.

As soon as the batter is smooth, divide it between the pans, smooth the tops, and put the pans in the oven. Bake 10 minutes, lower heat to 350°F., and bake 10 to 15 minutes more, or until the cakes shrink from the pans, the tops are lightly browned, and a toothpick emerges clean. Reverse onto wire racks, peel off the paper, and let them cool.

Make the icing. Put the chocolate and butter in a small, heavy pan and melt over the lowest possible heat. A sunny windowsill, the back of the stove, and similar approximately 100°F. locations are ideal. When all is melted, stir in the liqueur, a little at a time. The amount of icing will seem scant. Fear not.

Line a pair of flat plates, pan bottoms, or the like with plastic wrap and transfer the cake layers onto them, wide faces down. Choose the smoother, prettier layer to be the cake top and spread a very thin layer of still-warm icing over the small face and sides. Ice only the sides of the layer that will be the bottom one. The icing will sink in and look mingy, but that's okay; this first layer sets and seals the cake so the next one will be professionally smooth.

Let the icing cool to room temperature, then give the cake another coat. Allow the icing to set. The layers may be prepared up to this point a day ahead. Keep them cool but do not refrigerate.

Make the filling. Split the vanilla bean the long way a few times, combine it with the milk in a saucepan, and heat slowly until bubbles form around the edge. In a heavy saucepan, beat the egg yolks with the sugar until well combined, then beat in the flour.

Stirring constantly, add the milk in a thin stream. Add the vanilla bean, too. Put the pan over low heat or over simmering water and cook, stirring, until the custard is so thick the spoon leaves a trail when drawn across the pan. Do not let it boil.

Sprinkle the gelatin on the water to soften, then add it to the hot custard and stir until it is completely melted in. Strain the mixture into a wide, shallow bowl and chill in the refrigerator or over ice. Stir occasionally as it chills so you don't get lumps (the custard that's next to the sides of the bowl sets faster than the middle).

When the custard is almost but not quite set, beat the cream until very stiff and fold it in. Reverse the bottom cake layer onto a serving platter so the wide side now faces up. Spread on the filling, making an even layer, and chill until it is completely set.

Hold the top layer on your palm and peel away the plastic, then place it carefully, wide side down, natch, on the filling-topped bottom layer. Decoration is definitely against the rules, though that flat, smooth, dark surface does invite whipped cream rosettes, real flowers, or loving messages spelled out in melted chocolate. For easiest service, cut with a serrated knife.

 ## Boston Cream Torte

On my first go at the preceding recipe, for reasons too embarrassing to detail, the cake did not come out well. Heavy? Uranium is as eiderdown in comparison. But I wanted, having just *baked* a cake, not to have to bake another damn cake immediately (I wanted to go plant the peas). So since I had already prepared the custard and icing (another long story), I made them into a torte.

For a 9-inch torte

Ingredients for cake, filling, and icing as described in recipe on page 80
Butter for the baking sheets
1 package (10 ounces) frozen raspberries in syrup or 1 pint fresh raspberries combined with ⅓ cup sugar and allowed to sit 1 hour to release juices
¼ cup Triple Sec or other orange liqueur
1 tablespoon rum
¾ cup whipping cream

Bake the cake as described in the previous recipe. When it is cool, split each layer with a long serrated knife. The four layers you now have will be very thin and probably a bit uneven. No problem.

Lightly butter a pair of baking sheets, set the cake layers on them, not touching, and dry out in a 250°F. oven until they resemble Melba toast — about 20 minutes, but keep your eye on them. Let them cool.

Choose the better-looking of the 2 larger layers and ice it as described in the previous recipe. (There will be some icing left over but not enough for a whole cake. Might as well drop it by half teaspoons onto waxed paper and eat the hardened wafers as candy.)

Make the filling and get ready to assemble the torte. Drain the berries, saving the juice. Mix the juice with the liqueur and rum. Find a pretty serving plate.

Put the not-iced large cake layer on the plate, sprinkle a bit more than a third of the berries on it, and carefully pour on about a third of the juice, encouraging the cake to suck it up. When the custard is almost set, apply a third of that. Top with one of the smaller layers and repeat the berries, juice, and custard. Put on the remaining smaller layer and the remaining enhancements. Top with the iced layer and press it on firmly.

Refrigerate the torte to mellow for at least an hour, not more than half a day. At serving time, tidy up any extra juice that may have leaked out of the cake. Whip the cream until it's stiff but still glossy and use it to ice the sides of the torte, hiding all imperfections and presenting a face of perfect intent to the world.

EARLY VERSION DEPARTMENT: According to *The Taste of America* by John and Karen Hess, the original 1837 version of *Miss Leslie's New Cookery Book* had an "exceptionally fine recipe for Boston Cream Cakes. It calls for . . . [i]ndividual cakes (very rich ones) filled with a custard made with 12 egg yolks, flavored with 'a vanilla bean and a stick of the best Ceylon cinnamon' and a glass of rose water." You will notice there is no mention of chocolate.

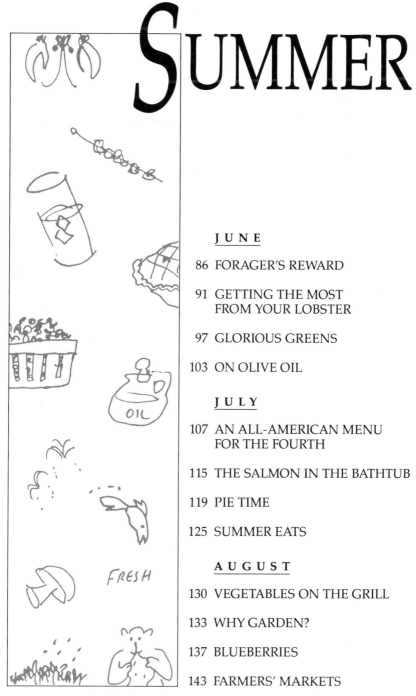

SUMMER

FORAGER'S REWARD

JULY AND AUGUST in Maine are summer run amok, producing a mindless riot of visitors, seasonal businesses, and, above all else, *food*. The gardens are well along in the swelling progression from lettuce to tomatoes. Every berry — straw, black, and blue, rasp and elder — fruits in its time with mad abandon among the shrubbery, while rain-hatched mushrooms spring underfoot in ever more confusing profusion. Mackerel jump from the water, while the rocky places rest thick with mussels, and the flats are fat with clams.

The world around us is swelling like a half-grown tornado, spinning faster and faster toward the big payoff — autumn in New England. And just around the corner, too, Ducky, almost before it's fairly summer yet, as anyone who's lived here for longer than a single summer knows. Carpe diem, in other words, is my advice to you.

Conveniently, just as nature has provided the forager with an abundance of free food, commerce has provided a large number of handbooks, articles, and field guides full of advice on what to get and how to get it. Unhappily, many of these are so exuberant and encyclopedic they probably scare away more people than they attract.

An hour of dedicated shelling produces a handful of beach peas. A parboiling and discard of boiling water removes most of the bitterness (and flavor and vitamins) from milkweed. It's easy to get the idea that wild foods are more trouble than they're worth unless you're starving or writing a book. In the case of things such as beach peas, this is probably correct, but no one needs to be convinced of the worth of blueberries or of the luscious wild blackberries that reward anyone who takes the trouble to armor up against their formidable thorns. Rose hips, mussels, and dandelions are also cases in point.

Rose hips are the fruit of the rose. They contain a great deal of vitamin C and a very pleasant, rather sharp flavor. You can't really eat them out of hand; they are sour and thin fleshed, and the seeds are an irritant. But they are easily dried (in which condition they will brew into an invigorating tea), and they make a tasty preserve that's especially good as a sauce for bread pudding, a condiment with fat meats, or anywhere you want to balance something very rich or starchy.

Though all roses will make hips, those of *rugosa* roses (a very hardy species that grows well without protection even in northern New England) are particularly good — large, fleshy, and of good flavor.

Mussels are no longer exactly on the "scorned except by the knowledgeable" list. In fact, they are New England's fastest growing native seafood export, and professional harvesters have put quite the dent in formerly dense beds. But they are still among the most easily gathered and most gratifying of Maine's wild free foods.

To get the best ones, free or nearly free of the tooth-breaking little pearls to which wild mussels are so prone, gather those that are still under the surface of the water when the tide is lowest, those attached to rock or wood far from the sandy bottom. The tastiest are the tiniest, but unless you have a lot of time, the ones to go for are those with shells about 2½ inches long. There are larger ones, in fact there are (or were) immense ones, but the bigger they are, the likelier they are to be tough. Ignore any that are not attached to anything and any whose shells can be moved apart. They're dead. Very heavy mussels are probably full of mud, not meat. Finally, be sure to check with the fisheries department about the location of red tide.

Dandelions need no introduction, being one of the more successful weeds ever to invade these shores. To be at their best, they should be gathered in early spring, before the buds have begun to rise from their hiding place within the crown. But fall often provides a second generation, and there are occasional anomalous summer plants that are, for some reason, not bitter.

Be sure to wash them thoroughly, as grit tends to linger even though the leaves aren't all that curly. Soaking them in cold water for an hour or two will reduce the bitterness of those that are almost all right but not quite. I do not recommend the parboil-throw-out-the-water routine — too much flavor is lost with the bitterness. If you're determined to have dandelions out of dandelion season, cover the plants with overturned baskets and blanch them into submission.

About wild mushrooms, which grow abundantly all over New England, in wildly flavorful and not infrequently lethal variety, I have so much to say I have nothing to say, echoing the popular old song "If they asked me, I could write a book." Several people already have, of course. I use the *Audubon Society Field Guide to North American Mushrooms* (Gary H. Lincoff, Knopf, 1981) and *The Complete Book of Mushrooms* (Augusto Rinaldi and Vassili Tyndalo, Crown, 1974) most often for identification. Jane Grigson's excellent *The Mushroom Feast* is a good source of recipes, recipe ideas, and plain old culinary entertainment when it's time to eat what you have gathered.

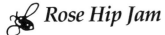 Rose Hip Jam

For about a pint

2 cups rose hips, carefully picked over, spiky blossom ends removed
2-inch cinnamon stick
1 cup water
Approximately 1 cup sugar

Put the hips and cinnamon stick in a small saucepan with the water and simmer, covered, over medium-low heat until the fruits are very soft. Remove the cinnamon and purée the fruit pulp through a mouli or coarse sieve.

Measure the purée, return it to the pan, and stir in an equal amount of sugar. Cook, stirring constantly, over low heat until the sugar is dissolved and the preserve is thick.

VARIATION: Herbed rose hip jam is great with things such as roast pork or lamb, functioning rather like mint sauce to sharpen and flavor. Replace the cinnamon with a garlic clove and don't bother to remove it. Add 1½ teaspoons finely minced fresh thyme with the sugar.

Mussels Marinière

This is a recipe that knows no teaspoons or tablespoons. It is the Ur-recipe, the basic recipe, as variable as the tastes and raw materials of its millions of makers. It is a good method to use when you want cooked mussels to add to salads, to stuff and bake, after the manner of clams, or to add to seafood combinations. To give a sense of general proportions, I have suggested quantities, but feel free to improvise.

For 4 servings

About 3 tablespoons butter

Small handful minced shallots or large handful minced onions (shallots are better)

1 or 2 cloves garlic, minced, not pressed (optional)

Several sprigs parsley plus a good handful chopped parsley

2 or 3 turns of the coarse pepper grinder

1 cup dry white wine

50 to 75 mussels, about 3 quarts, depending on size, scrubbed and de-bearded (Yank off beards while scrubbing.)

½ small bay leaf

2 to 3 more tablespoons butter or about 1 cup heavy cream, boiled down by half

Lots of crusty French bread for juice-sopping (This is a crucial ingredient. Neither whole-wheat nor balloon bread will do, so don't even think about it.)

Melt a generous film of butter in a big, wide-bottomed kettle with a tight-fitting lid. Add the shallots and cook, stirring, over medium heat until golden and translucent but not brown. Stir in the garlic, then the parsley, pepper, and white wine. Bring the liquid to a boil, stir in the mussels, then bury the bay leaf in the middle.

Cover the pan, raise the heat to high, and boil until the mussels open, usually about 6 to 10 minutes, though this will depend on how hot your stove is and the shape of the pan. As soon as they're open, they're ready. Transfer them to serving bowls, discarding any that failed to open, and keep them warm.

There will be some salty liquid in the pan. The saltiness will vary each time you prepare the recipe, so taste it before proceeding. If it's quite mild, use 2½ cups of it. If it's salty, use ½ cup of it, diluted with 2 cups of fish stock or clam broth. Strain the liquid through cheesecloth, to remove all sand, into a small saucepan. Bring it to a simmer, add the butter or cream, and tilt the pan (don't stir) to mix.

Pour the sauce over the mussels, sprinkle lavishly with parsley, and serve at once.

A NOTE *about Purchased Mussels:* Most of the mussels available for sale are harvested from the wild, sorted, and washed by the packers. They must be carefully picked over for broken or otherwise dead individuals — a single dead one will taint the whole batch if it gets into the pot by accident — but they are usually of good quality. Plan to buy about one-fourth more than you need, just to be on the safe side.

Mussels must be stored loose or in perforated bags. If they can't drain, they'll drown in their own liquid. As they drain, however, they change texture, flavor, and, of course, moisture. Do not expect nearly as much juice as you get with freshly foraged mussels. The fish consumers' newletter *Seafood Soundings* (available from Raquel Boehmer, Monhegan Island, Maine 05852) suggests soaking the mussels as you would clams, in a pail of water with a handful of salt, to rehydrate them before cooking. Don't leave them in longer than 2 hours.

A NOTE *about Rope-cultured Mussels:* These will be labeled as such and will cost more than the wild ones. Because they are very quickly raised on supports suspended in the water, rather than on the bottom, they are free of the little pearls sometimes found in the wild kind, and the care put into their cultivation means they are top quality: uniform, plump, and flavorful.

⋅☼⋅ Wilted Dandelion Salad, Pennsylvania-German Style

For 2 main dish or 6 side dish servings

⅓ to ½ **pound bacon**
3 **quarts tender dandelion greens**
⅓ **cup water**
⅓ **cup cider vinegar**
¼ **cup brown sugar**
1½ **teaspoons coarsely ground black pepper**
1 **small clove garlic, minced fine (optional, not authentic but good)**
2 **hard-boiled eggs, cut in thin slices**

Slowly try out the bacon until it is thoroughly crisp, then drain it, reserving ⅓ cup of the fat. Do not wash the skillet. Crumble the bacon and set it aside.

While the bacon is frying, tear the greens into bite-sized pieces, put them in a big bowl, and put the bowl somewhere warm, such as the back of the stove, so the leaves can start to wilt a bit.

Put the bacon fat back in the skillet with the water, vinegar, and sugar. Stir until the sugar is mostly dissolved, then put the pan over medium-high heat, add the pepper (and garlic), and bring the liquid to a full rolling boil.

Let it roil around for about 40 seconds, then pour the boiling dressing over the greens. Toss with vigor and dedication until everything is well coated. Add the bacon, toss again, and serve garnished with the hard-boiled eggs.

GETTING THE MOST FROM YOUR LOBSTER

ACCORDING TO food historian Waverley Root, the seventeenth-century New England colonists had more lobsters than almost anything else. "When there was a storm at Plymouth, lobsters piled up in windrows two feet high on the beach; they were so plentiful and so easily gathered that they were considered fit only for the poor . . . ." There was, in fact, a brief lobster strike at Maine's Popham colony in the early part of the century, when settlers got fed up with an enforced regimen of lobsters and lobsters only for breakfast, lunch, and dinner.

Though often told, these and other stories of abundance are no longer good for much except inspiring lamentations. Landings have remained steady or decreased slightly over the years (depending on which authority you consult), while public demand has increased. Unless we can figure out a way to "farm" lobsters successfully, their meat, which is certainly a luxury the way good steak is a luxury, will become instead a rare delicacy, like caviar.

Fortunately, at least so far, stories where lobsters cost their weight in gold are only stories. These richest of shellfish, though admittedly not cheap, are still a comparative bargain, especially if you follow the sensible French example and use the whole thing. There is quite a bit of flavorful meat in the too often discarded body of a lobster, and there is a wonderful cache of flavor in the almost always discarded shell. These neglected parts can be used to make two very handy items: a flavorful stock for use as a base in stews, soups, and sauces and an exquisite coral-pink butter that gives a fine, lobster-flavored flourish to any seafood preparation.

Making these things is not difficult, time-consuming, or unpleasant, particularly if you do it in the aftermath of a classic lobster feed, when you're already good and messy. That's what I do. Then I'm ready at a moment's notice to make impressive dishes such as Pasta Primavera with Lobster Sauce or the very luxurious but very easy Lobster Pâté with Pistachio Nuts. The recipes are simple, once you have the basics ready. You can even make them with purchased cooked lobster meat (if you trust your fishmonger). And they are surprisingly inexpensive, since with the aid of your special flavor enhancers, you can wring up to four respectably meaty portions from only one large lobster.

An Important Distinction

All lobsters are not created equal. Hard-shelled winter lobsters are much meatier than the so-called soft-shells of summer, and their meat is firmer and less sweet. Even though the shells themselves are heavier, winter lobsters give you more meat per pound. It's not only because the body meat is firm enough to pick but also because there is considerable "soft meat" (mostly fat) lining the shells.

Connoisseurs are divided on the subject of which is better. The tender-meated soft-shells are unquestionably the sweetest, but the firm flesh of the winter lobster has its own robust charms, and there is, after all, *more* of it — a definite virtue. Speaking personally, I never met a properly cooked lobster I didn't like; it's just a matter of knowing what raw material you're dealing with so you can use it to its best advantage. To get 1½ cups of lobster meat you will need one 1½-pound winter lobster or two 1-pound soft-shells. Soft-shells, by the way, should be flexible but not so soft you can poke a finger through them when raw. That's too soft — the sign of a lobster that changed its shell so recently that the flesh will be unpleasantly flabby and watery.

Getting the Raw Material

Generally, you get lobster bodies and lobster shells by having a big lobster feed. Most people do not bother to pick anything but claws and tails, especially if there are enough of both to produce satiation. There is, however, another excellent source of lobster bodies — lobster bodies with the tomalley still in them — though it is, alas, a source to which comparatively few have access. The source is those fish markets that sell lobster meat that has been picked out on the premises. Because the labor it would take to pick the bodies is prohibitively expensive and there is not (as yet) any market for the tomalley, the bodies are sold simply as is, usually for not more than $3 a dozen.

Being fortunate enough to live near a town that bills itself as "The Lobster Capital of the World," I use the bodies frequently, sometimes to make the following recipes, but even more often as a sort of "diet dinner deluxe." It is almost impossible to pick out enough lobster body meat to get fat on before you die of boredom, and in the meantime, you've taken plenty of time to eat and enjoy one of the world's tastiest dinners.

WARNING NOTE: The lobsters chosen to be cooked and picked are likely to be those lobsters that were not long for this world, lobsters on their last legs, as it were. Since lobster is highly perishable even under the best of conditions, and the body part, where the stomach and liver are, is the most perishable of all, be sure if you buy lobster bodies that they were picked out that day and that you eat them that day.

✦ Lobster Stock

Plan to use the water from the initial lobster cooking as your base. Omit the rockweed, which makes overstrong broth, and whether you steam or boil, save the water. Set the liquid to cool as soon as the lobsters have cooked and refrigerate it, covered, until needed. Live lobsters usually are pretty clean just as sold, but if they look like they could use it, give them a *very quick* rinse before cooking. Pick them up right behind the head so they can't reach back and pinch you.

For a little more than 2 quarts

Picked-out bodies, heads, and 2 smallest legs of four 1½-pound winter lobsters or the bodies, heads, and 4 smaller legs of five 1¼-pound soft-shells
1 large carrot, peeled and cut in chunks
1 large onion, sliced
2 large stalks of celery plus a few celery leaves
1 very small piece of bay leaf — about ⅓ inch square
5 or 6 whole peppercorns
10 cups liquid left from the original lobster cooking (Make up the difference with water if you don't have enough.)

Combine everything, bring to just under a boil, then lower the heat and simmer, uncovered, 40 to 45 minutes. Strain, pressing hard on the solids to get out all the flavor, and refrigerate as soon as possible. Like all fish stocks, this one should be used within a day of its manufacture. Freeze it if you don't need it right away; it will keep at 0°F. about 6 months. Use it as a foundation for bisques, chowders — even bouillabaisse — or any sauce to be served with fish or shellfish.

 Lobster Butter

For about 12 ounces (That's a lot — it's very rich.)

**Brightly colored leg, claw, and body shells of 4 cooked winter lobsters
or 5 cooked soft-shells
1 pound unsalted butter, as fresh as possible**

WINTER LOBSTERS: Distribute the shells on a cookie sheet or other flat pan and dry them in a 175°F. oven about 40 minutes, stirring frequently so all surfaces are exposed. The idea is to desiccate the shells, making them brittle and easy to crush. Do not overheat; if they actually cook, both flavor and color will be diminished.

Let the dried shells cool, then dump them into a heavy brown paper bag and pound with the flat of a hammer or other wide blunt instrument until they are thoroughly crushed — the finer the better. This crushing ideally should be done with a big marble mortar and pestle. Classic French cookbooks want the stuff as fine as powder, but "well busted up" — all pieces ½ inch or smaller — will do just fine.

SUMMER LOBSTERS: Grind the assorted shell through the fine plate of a meat grinder or pulverize it in small batches in a blender. Do not use a processor; the plastic workbowl can't take it.

WINTER OR SUMMER, SECOND STEP: Combine the mangled shells with the butter in a deep, heavy saucepan. Put it over *very* low heat — a heat spreader on the smallest flame, the side of the woodstove, or atop a tepid radiator are all suitable locations. Let the mixture steep, stirring occasionally, 1 to 1½ hours. Once again, actually *cooking* the mixture would be injurious; the idea is to extract color and flavor in as gentle a manner as possible. At the end of the steeping period, put the mixture through a cheesecloth-lined strainer, stirring, then squeezing, to get as much butter out as possible. Set the lobster butter aside to cool, then refrigerate, tightly covered.

Some of the precious substance will still be clinging to the shells. Combine them with 1½ quarts boiling water and stir well; the butter will wash off and rise to the surface. Pour the liquid into a tall, narrow, heatproof container, carefully leaving the shells in the bottom of the pan, and chill until the butter forms a solid, easily removable cake. This second pressing will have a grainier texture than the pristine product. Use it to enhance soups, sauces, and other fairly liquid preparations, adding it at the very last minute so it just barely melts before serving. Both butters should be frozen promptly if they are not to be used within a day or two. (The butter will keep longer under refrigeration than the stock, but not by a whole lot.)

This stuff is universal: Use it as a garnish for chowder, in a hollandaise sauce for poached salmon, or as the cooking butter for any delicate fillet.

☼ *Pasta Primavera with Lobster Sauce*

This colorful, creamy lobster and tomato sauce is so richly flavored you can get 4 servings from a single large lobster, which is not to say a bit more shellfish is necessarily a bad idea. If you want a truly luxurious dish and more lobster is beyond your budget, consider adding some cooked crabmeat, a few scallops, or a handful of cooked mussels.

For 4 generous servings

1½ to 2½ cups cooked lobster meat, chopped coarsely
1 cup light cream
1 cup chopped onion, about 1 medium
2 tablespoons Lobster Butter (recipe on page 94)
½ cup white wine, preferably the wine you intend to drink with the pasta
1 tablespoon tomato paste
4 tablespoons finely minced fresh parsley leaves
2 medium-sized genuinely ripe tomatoes, peeled, seeded, drained, and cut into ¼-inch cubes, about ¾ cup (When it isn't tomato time, canned, peeled, first-quality Italian plum tomatoes should be used in preference to those styrofoam monstrosities duplicitously labeled with the name of this most seasonal of fruits.)
2 quarts lobster stock (or water)
1 teaspoon salt
1 teaspoon olive oil
¾ pound small seashell pasta
1 cup barely cooked seasonal green vegetable, cut into small pieces about the same size as the lobster (Use asparagus tips, broccoli florets, green peas, snap beans, very young zucchini, etc., alone or in combination.)

Combine the lobster and cream in a small saucepan and set in a warm place to steep. In a heavy saucepan over medium-low heat, slowly simmer the onion in the lobster butter until it is limp, transparent, and completely cooked. Add the wine, raise the heat slightly, and allow to bubble until the liquid is reduced to ¼ cup or slightly less. Add the tomato paste, 2 tablespoons of the parsley, and the tomato cubes. Set the mixture aside in a warm place.

Combine the lobster stock or water with the salt and olive oil in a large pot. Bring to a boil, covered, then uncover and add the pasta, dribbling it in slowly so the boiling never stops. Cook according to time suggested on the package, usually about 8 to 10 minutes.

While the pasta is cooking, finish the sauce by adding the creamed lobster, all at once, to the tomato mixture. Do not pour it in slowly, or it might curdle. Stir to combine the sauce thoroughly and let it simmer over very low heat until the pasta is finished. When the pasta is done, drain away the stock, quickly toss in the vegetable, and mound the mixture on a heated platter. Thoroughly blanket it with sauce, garnish with the remaining 2 tablespoons of parsley, and pass any extra sauce separately.

Lobster Pâté with Pistachio Nuts

For a little more than 2 cups

½ cup shelled, unsalted, raw pistachio nuts (available at health food
   stores and Middle Eastern and Indian markets)
¼ pound flounder or other tender, sweet white fish fillets
4 tablespoons Lobster Butter (recipe on page 94)
1½ cups cooked lobster meat, including some body meat and fat,
   if possible, and any coral
2 teaspoons cognac or brandy
½ teaspoon salt
Scraping of nutmeg

Spread the nuts in a shallow pan and toast them in a very low oven, 200°F., for 10 minutes, or until the skins get papery. Then gently rub them together in a tea towel to remove as much of the skin as possible. Chop into coarse crumbs and set aside.

Cut the fish into 1-inch dice and, over low heat, slowly cook in the lobster butter until it just turns opaque, about 3 minutes. Transfer the mixture to the container of a processor, a meat grinder, or a large marble mortar, and add 1 cup of the lobster meat, including the fat and other soft parts, and coral.

Process, grind, or push that pestle until the mixture is completely puréed and smooth, then stir in the cognac or brandy, salt, nutmeg, and pistachios. Chop the remaining ½ cup lobster meat into small but still recognizable chunks and stir them in, too. Taste and adjust the salt, then mound the pâté in a decorative crock, cover tightly, and refrigerate to mellow for at least 2 hours. Let the mixture return to room temperature before you serve it, preferably with crusty French bread, Melba toast made from unsweetened brioche, or another egg bread. Whatever the vehicle, make sure its flavor is delicate and unobtrusive. Even something as seemingly bland as a saltine can overpower the delicate, sweet shellfish flavor of this regal spread.

LORIOUS GREENS

FOR MANY YEARS some vegetable-loving friends, people whose thumbs are in most respects quite verdant, were doomed to a garden of bitten-off stems, rank herbs, and hard-skinned gourds because they are (or were) landlords to a largish colony of woodchucks. Voracious woodchucks. Woodchucks that defied wire fencing, dried blood, mothballs, fantastic cat's cradles of creosoted string, and, on one highly memorable occasion, a good solid whack on the head. Finally, after years of frustration, deliverance! Raccoons, evidently, are woodchuck repellent.

Now that only corn is on the forbidden list, my liberated friends are stuffing themselves with all manner of homegrown produce, especially greens, glorious greens. Not only are there beet and turnip tops, tender lettuces, and flag-sized chard, there is kale and there are collards and there are spinach and roquette and that delicious volunteer, that so-called weed, that favorite of the unlamented woodchucks, lamb's-quarters.

Not only is all this leafage delicious, but it's good for you, too — and that not only for the digestion-enhancing factor known in former days as roughage, but also because it is a source of that ever-desirable item, dietary calcium.

Getting enough dietary calcium is, after all, a problem. The most widely recommended, cheapest, most accessible sources are dairy products. Yet most dairy products, especially the more palatable ones such as whole milk, hard cheese, and ice cream, are freighted with many calories and carry rather a lot of cholesterol, too much of which is hard on your heart. It is therefore a great relief to learn that greens — low-calorie, cholesterol-free greens — carry quite a bit of this valuable mineral.

Or it is a great relief until you turn to your cookbook, where you quickly learn that most traditional recipes for greens also call for smoked pork in the form of ham, sausage, bacon, or possibly all three. From the nutritional point of view, this is roughly equivalent to being told you should cook them with Twinkies.

Though fatty smoked meat and classic greens, especially the cabbage-family ones, have an aesthetic affinity that cannot be denied (and should surely be indulged in occasionally by all but the most grievously heart attack–prone), there are plenty of other options, including those on the following pages: an assortment of green soups that are all based on one master recipe, a simple Mediterranean favorite accented with raisins and pine nuts, and a Chinese sweet-and-sour treatment.

⚙ *Cream of Green*

For about 2 quarts

¼ cup plus 3 tablespoons butter
2½ cups thinly sliced leeks (2 cups thinly sliced onions may be
   substituted, but they won't be as good)
Approximately 12 cups (a loosely filled brown grocery bag full)
   greens,* cleaned, picked over, and shredded as though for slaw
1½ quarts light chicken or veal stock or water
1 cup soft white wine such as Moselle
2 sprigs fresh thyme or ½ teaspoon dried
1 large clove garlic, peeled but left whole
3 tablespoons flour

---

*Any and every green can be used, in just about any combination. Avoid using as more than about one-fourth of the total strong-flavored items such as the cole family — kale, collards, etc. — and the mustards — radishes, turnip tops, mustard itself. Don't forget dandelions (when young and tender), cresses, and lettuces that have started to bolt but are not yet beyond the pale.

2 cups finely shredded greens**
2 cups light cream or 1 cup each heavy cream and half and half
Salt to taste

Melt ¼ cup of the butter in a large soup pot over medium heat, stir in the leeks, and cook, stirring occasionally, until they are just golden and wilted, not really browned.

Stir in the 12 cups of greens a few handfuls at a time until they are all in there, wilted and well mixed with the leeks. Add the stock, wine, thyme, and garlic. Stir well and raise the heat to bring the liquid to a boil.

Lower the heat, partially cover the pot, and simmer about 45 minutes, or until the greens are falling apart. Put the soup through the mouli or purée it in a blender or processor.

Wipe but don't bother to wash the soup pot. Put in the 3 tablespoons of butter and melt it over low heat. Stir in the flour and cook, stirring, about 5 minutes, or until the flour is light gold. Using a wire whisk, stir in the soup, a cup at a time at first so there aren't any lumps. Cook until soup thickens slightly.

Add the 2 cups of shredded greens, raise the heat to medium-high, and bring the soup to just below the boiling point, by which time the new greenery should be barely cooked, still a fresh, bright color. Add the cream, adjust the salt, and serve as soon as the cream is hot. Do not let it boil after adding the cream, and do not cook it further if you intend to freeze the soup for future use rather than serve it at once.

Pints are the ideal-sized freezer containers, and they are called for in the variations on the following pages. Each variation will, when completed, make lunch for 2 or rather spare first-course portions for 4. (When packing, don't forget to leave room for the freezing soup to expand.)

🌹 Mushroom Green

3 tablespoons butter
1 cup coarsely chopped mushrooms
2 tablespoons flour
1½ cups milk
¼ to ½ cup dry sherry
1 pint Cream of Green (recipe on page 98)

**All those listed in the preceding note, plus up to a cup of not too strongly flavored herbs such as parsley, chervil, dill tips, nasturtium leaves, and purslane.

Salt to taste
Small scraping of nutmeg
⅓ cup sliced almonds, toasted gold, for garnish (optional)

Melt the butter in a heavy saucepan over medium heat. Add the mushrooms and cook, stirring often, until they are well browned and much reduced in volume. Sprinkle on the flour and cook, stirring constantly, until the flour is golden — about 5 minutes.

Using a whisk, slowly stir in the milk. When it has heated through, add the sherry, a little at a time to help prevent curdling. When the soup is smooth and hot, stir in the Cream of Green. As soon as all is hot through, the soup is done. Adjust the salt, scrape in the nutmeg, and garnish, if desired, with the almonds.

Corn Is Green

2 cups corn kernels, with scraped-out milk from cobs, about 2 large ears
1½ cups milk
½ teaspoon sugar (optional, add only if corn is old and flat)
½ teaspoon ground cumin
1 tablespoon minced fresh oregano or ½ teaspoon dried
1 pint Cream of Green (recipe on page 98)
Salt to taste

In a heavy saucepan, combine the corn with the milk, sugar (if used), and seasonings. Heat very slowly, stirring often. Do not let it boil. When the mixture is hot, add the Cream of Green and heat it, again permitting no boiling. The soup is ready as soon as it's hot. Adjust the salt and serve at once so the corn doesn't get tough.

It's somewhat shaming to admit, but the truth is that crumbled crisp bacon or a few cubes of tried-out salt pork are probably the best garnish.

Green Chowder

2 tablespoons butter
1 cup peeled, thinly sliced boiling potatoes
2 cups milk
1 cup shucked clams or oysters, with their liquor
1 pint Cream of Green (recipe on page 98)

> ¼ cup minced fresh chervil, 2 tablespoons minced fresh tarragon, or 2
> teaspoons dried tarragon
> Salt to taste

Melt the butter in a large saucepan over low heat, then cook the potatoes in it, stirring occasionally, until they are transparent but not colored. Add the milk and cook very slowly until the potatoes are falling apart — about 40 minutes.

Stir in the liquor from the bivalves, the Cream of Green, and the chervil and heat through. Add the bivalves themselves and continue cooking only until they are heated through — curly around the edges and plump. Salt to taste and serve at once.

✿ *Mediterranean Mustard Greens*

Actually, they don't eat mustard greens much in that part of the world. This treatment is in fact used there on Swiss chard and spinach. It works very nicely on mustard greens, though, bringing out their latent sweetness. Try it as a side dish with fried or grilled fish and corn bread.

For 4 servings

> 2 medium-large bunches mustard greens, 1½ to 1¾ pounds total
> 2 tablespoons butter
> 2 ounces pine nuts (pignoli), about ⅓ cup
> 2 tablespoons raisins
> 1 small clove garlic, pressed
> 1 tablespoon plus 1 teaspoon lemon juice
> ½ cup finely sliced scallions (green onions), including some of the
> green part

Rinse the greens and pick them over, discarding anything wilted or discolored. Cut off and discard the tough stem bottoms, then slice across the leaves so you have strips about 4 inches wide.

Put a shallow layer — about ¼ inch — of water in a deep kettle, bring to a boil, and add the greens. Lower the heat to medium and partially cover the pan. Like spinach, the greenery will shrink something considerable. Stir it from time to time as it does so. Continue to simmer about 20 minutes, or until the greens are tender but not falling to shreds; they should be neither so crisp as something Chinese nor so soft as something deep southern.

At this point, the water should be all cooked away except for a couple of tablespoons. If it isn't, remove the mustard so it won't overcook and keep it warm while you rapidly boil away excess liquid. (It's too full of vitamins and flavor to be simply drained away.) Return the greens to the pot when the liquid level is right.

While the greens are cooking, make the sauce. Melt the butter in a small skillet, add the pine nuts, and simmer over low heat until both nuts and butter are lightly browned. Stir in the raisins and garlic and set the mixture where it will keep warm without actually cooking.

When the greens are cooked, stir in the lemon juice. After it is thoroughly mixed in, add the sauce and the scallions and stir very well again. Serve at once. The salt in the butter usually is enough.

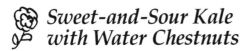 ## Sweet-and-Sour Kale with Water Chestnuts

For 4 servings

1 pound kale
1 small onion, sliced in thin shreds, about ⅔ cup
2 tablespoons bland vegetable oil
½ cup chicken broth or other light stock
2 tablespoons cider vinegar
2 tablespoons sherry, Madeira, or other sweet, fortified wine
2 tablespoons brown sugar
1 tablespoon soy sauce
1 large clove garlic, shredded on the fine holes of a grater
½ teaspoon finely shredded fresh ginger root
1 tablespoon cornstarch
¼ cup orange juice
1 can (6½ to 8 ounces) water chestnuts

Wash, shake, and shred the kale. In a large, deep saucepan, sauté the onion in the oil over medium-high heat, stirring often, until most of the shreds are well browned. They won't color evenly, but that's okay. While the onion is cooking, combine ¼ cup of the broth with the vinegar, wine, sugar, soy sauce, garlic, and ginger. Dissolve the cornstarch in the orange juice and set it aside. Drain the water chestnuts, rinse with cold water, and cut them in half if they're large.

When the onion is done, add the kale, stirring well as the kale starts collapsing to be sure the vegetables are thoroughly mixed. Pour in the remaining ¼ cup of broth and lower the heat slightly. Cook, stirring often, about 10 minutes, until the kale is wilted and nearly tender and the liquid about cooked away. Add the sauce mixture, give it a few minutes to flavor the greens, and finish cooking. Stir in the water chestnuts, then recombine the cornstarch and orange juice mixture and stir it in. In about 2 minutes, the sauce will have thickened and become clear, at which point it is done. Serve at once, as cornstarch-thickened sauces break down if they're overcooked. This is nice with buckwheat noodles, by the way.

IMPORTANT WARNING: As a rule, the darker the green, the more vitamin filled it is. All greens are very nutritious. Don't forget turnip tops, dandelions, and watercress. But be careful of spinach, chard, beet greens, parsley, sorrel, and purslane. They all contain oxalic acid, which blocks calcium absorption.

N OLIVE OIL

FOR ONCE THERE is good news on the health front. A former pleasure has been restored to respectability. Just when things seemed really hopeless in the flavorful fat department, just when it looked like there was no way around "polyunsaturate or die," it turns out olive oil is actually good for you. And not only that, there's even a possibility that olive oil is *better* for you than the health-consciousness classics, safflower, corn, soy, and all their bland ilk.

For years we've been told that polyunsaturates help remove the dangerous (artery-clogging) blood cholesterol we've piled on by eating too many saturated fats like butter and coconut oil. The tasty villains were duly proscribed. Monounsaturated fats like olive and peanut oils, both supposedly neutral in their effects on cholesterol, were to be used only sparingly so we'd have more room for the polyunsaturated kinds. All this was supported by studies showing that the Finns, who eat a lot of butter and fat meat, have lots of early heart attacks, while the Japanese, who eat mostly polyunsaturates, are comparatively free of cardiac problems. Italians and Greeks, both champion consumers of olive oil, also had noticeably healthy hearts, but that connection went unexplored for a good many years.

Now, at last, there have been studies, one of which was published in the *Journal of Lipid Research* and brought to public attention by *New York Times* columnist Jane Brody, that seems to prove that (a) monounsaturates *do* lower blood cholesterol levels, and (b) unlike polyunsaturates, which lower everything indiscriminately, monounsaturates lower only the damaging kinds of cholesterol (low-density lipoproteins), leaving the beneficial ones (high-density lipoproteins) "relatively unscathed."

I think we should declare a national holiday. After all, if olive oil can be redeemed, can butter be far behind?

Choosing Olive Oils

It may seem rather sour-spirited to equate acidity with sexual experience, but there it is. According to Italian law, virgin olive oil cannot be more than 4 percent oleic acid. Fine virgin is 3 percent, superfine virgin 1.5, and extra virgin 1 percent or less. In France that sequence is the same. The United States Department of Agriculture is equally strict about "extra virgin," allows 3.3 percent oleic acid in "virgin" oils, and skips the other fine distinctions. Regardless of the oil's origins, if the magic word does not appear, the oil is likely to have been refined and may (though this is unlikely) have come from a second (or third) solvent or hot water assisted pressing.

The ritziest estate-bottled vintage varietal olive oils will, of course, cost large sums, but good extra-virgin oils are relatively inexpensive, so there's no reason to settle for less than the best. The flavor is determined by the same factors that influence wine: the quality and type of olives or blend thereof, the place it is made, and the fruit's ripeness when pressed — generally speaking, the greener the olive, the greener the oil, with fully ripe olives yielding oil of a more golden color. Unlike wine, olive oil does not improve with age and should be consumed promptly. Store in dark glass, away from light, and decant large quantities into smaller bottles so the oil isn't exposed to air.

⦂Ö⦂ *Leeks in Olive Oil with Berry Vinegar*

This odd-sounding trio works beautifully, producing an addictive salad born for summer buffets. Fresh berries are an ideal garnish if used sparingly. Five or 6 is plenty.

For 4 to 6 small servings

1½ pounds leeks, white and pale chartreuse parts only
¼ cup olive oil
½ teaspoon salt
2 or 3 tablespoons blackberry or raspberry vinegar (available in
    specialty stores)
5 or 6 fresh blackberries or raspberries as garnish (optional)

Trim and clean the leeks and cut into 1-inch lengths. Put the olive oil in a heavy, lidded skillet big enough to hold the pieces in one layer and arrange the leeks in the pan. Sprinkle them with the salt, cover, and place over very low heat. Steam-braise, shaking the pan so the leeks cook evenly, 20 to 25 minutes, or until they are very tender when tested with a knife point. Try not to let them brown.

Transfer the cooked leeks and their juices to a shallow serving dish, mix in 2 tablespoons of the vinegar, and allow to cool. Let marinate at room temperature for an hour or so, then taste and adjust the vinegar if necessary. These keep well, refrigerated, though the berry dye they absorb from the vinegar eventually makes them a rather strange color. Garnish with berries if desired.

🐝 *Herbed Feta Cheese in Olive Oil*

If you are not a feta fan, this can be made with cubes of a milder cheese, something like Monterey Jack. The taste and texture will, of course, be substantially different, but the result will still be tasty.

For 8 to 10 appetizer portions

1 pound feta cheese
1½ cups olive oil, the greener the better
1 large clove garlic, minced fine
2 tablespoons minced fresh chives
½ cup minced fresh parsley
3 tablespoons minced fresh oregano or 1 tablespoon dried
1 tablespoon fresh thyme leaves or 1 teaspoon dried
½ teaspoon cracked black pepper
1 teaspoon shredded lemon zest (thin, colored outer rind)

Cut the cheese into small cubes, about ½ inch each. Save the crumbs. (Even very firm feta will crumble a little when cut. If yours doesn't, you have been sold a cake of library paste. Taste before proceeding to be sure the project is worth it.)

Combine the oil and seasonings in a shallow bowl. Add the feta and its crumbs and stir to coat everything well. If the cubes are completely submerged, so much the better, but submersion isn't essential. Cover tightly and marinate, stirring occasionally, 3 to 4 hours at room temperature or overnight in the refrigerator. (Allow to return to room temperature before serving.) It will continue to improve for 2 to 3 days, after which the herbs will get tired and flat tasting.

To serve, set out the cheese, still in its oil, and provide toothpicks for spearing (and crusty bread for drip-catching). After all the feta is gone, there will be this delicious, highly flavored oil filled with cheese crumbs. Add a little lemon juice and pour it over your salad.

The oil also is terrific as a moistener for hero sandwiches. One of my favorites calls for crusty French bread well moistened with the oil. Sprinkle one slice (or one side of the roll) with some of the marinated cheese, then top with grilled fresh eggplant and sliced tomatoes. Apply the other piece of bread. The longer it sits, the better it gets (within reason, of course). This is a good sandwich for making in the morning and inserting in a brown bag.

AN ALL-AMERICAN MENU FOR THE FOURTH

HEAVEN KNOWS it's easy to get fed up with discussing the currently fashionable question "What is American food?" — particularly when the answer turns out to be something like blue-corn pancakes garnished with three kinds of native caviar. But it's a fascinating subject all the same, and it isn't unimportant.

After all, you don't need a Ph.D. to know that food is a primary vehicle for cultural bonding, that the sharing of daily sustenance is a big chunk of the glue that ties the child to the parent and the parent to the child. It is over meals, with friends, with schoolmates, with coworkers, with neighbors, that people are gradually bound to the communities in which they live.

Food habits have much to tell us about who we are, what we cherish, who is important, the history of our soil and climate, our ceremonies and rites of passage. All this being the case, an interest in "What is American food?" isn't frivolous — it's inevitable. Ours is a young country in the recorded history department, and one chock-a-block with immigrants. It may well be a little soon to go calling ourselves a culture, but that doesn't keep the whole thing from being fun to think about.

AN ALL-AMERICAN MENU
Raw Clams and/or Oysters on the Half Shell
Corn Pasta with Succotash Sauce*
Sliced Tomatoes/Coleslaw*
Ice Cream, Fresh Fruit, and Intoxicating Chocolate Drops*

*Recipes given.

This little feast was designed to feature a few of the undeniable, universally acknowledged strains in our food culture. It is "American" in being easy to prepare, quite sweet, abundant, and largely based on New World foodstuffs. It includes native food presentation that is ancient (the shellfish and succotash), Colonial (the slaw), and modern (the chocolate drops, based on ground-up store cookies). While the latter are not a recent invention, they are as emblematic of mid-twentieth-century American food as anything fit to eat (if you want to make a Jell-O salad with marshmallows in it, that's your own business).

Dress the tomatoes with a sprinkle of sugar, midwestern-style, make the ice cream strawberry, and you'll probably start hearing the Sousa band even before the fireworks begin.

Of course, there are some people who cannot imagine anything so outlandish as pasta on a day like the glorious Fourth, when everybody in New England knows the sacred, the *only*, menu was, is now, and ever shall be salmon with egg sauce, new potatoes, and peas. On the theory that even died-in-the-egg-sauce traditionalists might like at least a little bit of a change, I'm also including an alternate first course that rings a major change on the pea component of the classic trinity.

Concerning Coleslaw

Culinary logic and an appreciation for the appropriate suggest coleslaw should be a fall and winter specialty, those being the seasons when cabbage is at its best. But as soon as swift shipping and cold storage made it a summer possibility, custom made it a summer staple, and though slaw is actually a salad that knows no season, it's a safe bet far more of it will be forked down on the Fourth of July than was ever consumed at Christmas.

The incongruity of the cabbage aside, this makes a lot of sense. For one thing, the stuff is durable, not only okay when prepared in advance but generally improved by a bit of marination. Furthermore, it's compact. Ten portions of coleslaw take up a lot less space than ten portions of green salad, an important consideration when the fridge is full of beer and watermelon. Finally, it's tidy, easy to eat at picnics, barbecues, and other informal occasions — no flapping leaves, no drippy dressing, no elusive, unspearable cherry tomatoes to careen off the plate into Aunt Maude's decolletage. When you add to these advantages the fact that it's almost impossible to make bad coleslaw *and* almost impossible to spend much time making it, well, no wonder it's just about the national salad.

Coleslaw's history in America is a long one, dating from the late eighteenth century if not earlier. Most authorities describe it as a Dutch import, the name coming from the New World Dutch *kool sla* (or *slaa*), which translates to "cabbage salad." Food historians John and Karen Hess point out (in *The Taste of America*) that "cole" is old English for cabbage (whence we get "cole crops" to describe the whole family from broccoli to kale) and that cabbage is *kohl* in German. They state flatly that "slaw is a simple corruption of salad" and do not say a word about the Dutch.

They do, however, agree that the original dressing was not mayonnaise but what is classically called "boiled dressing," a cooked mixture of vinegar, seasonings, and eggs that often includes milk, cream, or sour cream as well. Though capable of considerable tastiness, boiled dressing often is remembered as something far better forgotten. In the hands of unskilled cooks it can be floury, sour, and lumpy, and it seems to have seldom been seasoned with the herbs, garlic, onion, etc., we have come to associate with salad. The eminent food writer M.F.K. Fisher called it "dreadful stuff — enough to harm one's soul." The boiled dressing Fisher's talking about, a dressing remembered from childhood that has haunted her for sixty or seventy years, was made, she's pretty sure, of nothing but vinegar and flour. So no wonder.

Sometime around the mid-1800s, coleslaw began being called cold slaw, a change that can only be attributed to mishearing, since the salad often was served immediately after having been mixed with the hot dressing. It wasn't until somewhat later that unthickened dressings began to appear.

Commercial mayonnaise manufacture began in 1912, and mayonnaise-based dressing rapidly replaced boiled dressing except in old-fashioned households, particularly those in the Midwest. Vinaigrette-style has never really taken hold, though slaws so dressed do enjoy great popularity in some places, especially parts of the South and the Southwest. Pineapple, raisins, nuts, and marshmallows are not, by the way, an inspiration of the 1950s. They were already showing up in salads of all sorts, including coleslaw, when the twenties began to roar.

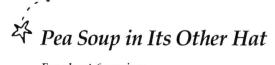

✿ *Pea Soup in Its Other Hat*

For about 6 servings

Enough fresh peas to equal 3 cups shelled, about 3 pounds
4 tablespoons butter
1 large onion, chopped small, about 1½ cups

Coarsely grated zest (thin, colored outer rind) of 1 lemon
3 large sprigs fresh thyme or 1 heaping teaspoon dried
1 teaspoon salt
½ bay leaf
2 quarts light chicken stock
½ cup rice
1 small head Boston lettuce, shredded as though for slaw
3 egg yolks
⅓ cup cream
1½ cups snow peas or sugarsnaps
Salt to taste
Pinch of sugar (may not be needed)
6 small florets of fresh mint

Shell the peas, saving 1½ cups of the freshest looking pods. Melt the butter over medium heat in a soup kettle and sauté the onion and lemon zest in it until the onion is limp and the zest is fragrant but neither is at all brown. Add the reserved pea pods, thyme, salt, bay leaf, and stock. Bring to a boil, then lower heat to simmer and cook, uncovered, 45 minutes to an hour. Strain, discarding the solids.

Put the liquid back in the kettle with the rice and lettuce and cook over medium heat about 10 minutes. Add the shelled peas and cook 15 to 20 minutes more, or until the peas are thoroughly cooked — very soft but not yet disintegrating. Put the whole works through a food mill or purée in a blender. Strain again if necessary. The soup should, at this point, be very smooth.

Beat the egg yolks with the cream and beat in a bit of the hot soup, enough to thin and warm the egg mixture. Being sure the soup proper is well below boiling, beat in the egg-cream mixture and cook, stirring constantly, over low heat until the soup is slightly thickened and smooth. Chill well.

Bring a large pan of water to the boil and drop in the snow peas or sugarsnaps. As soon as the color brightens, drain them and either plunge into ice water or spread over ice cubes to stop the cooking. Shred the pods into thin slivers and reserve, chilled, until serving time.

Taste the chilled soup and correct the salt. If the pea flavor is fainter than it should be, try adding a pinch of sugar as well. Garnish with the prepared snow peas and mint sprigs and serve at once.

☆ Corn Pasta with Succotash Sauce

For 6 to 8 servings

½ to ¾ pound mild cured baked ham, enough to make 2 cups of
  ½-inch cubes
1 tablespoon butter (may not be needed)
1 large onion, diced fine, about 1½ cups
2 cups shelled fresh lima beans, about 2 pounds in the shell, or 1
  package (10 ounces) frozen beans
1½ cups light cream or 1 cup heavy cream and ½ cup half-and-half
2 cups fresh corn kernels, 3 to 5 ears, depending on size, or 1 package
  (10 ounces) frozen kernels
1 medium-sized sweet red bell pepper, cut into ½-inch cubes,
  about 1 cup
3 tablespoons finely minced fresh parsley
¼ cup snipped fresh chives
1 pound corn pasta ribbons

Put the pasta water on to boil. (See "Concerning Corn Pasta" following.) Trim the fat from the ham and cut the lean into ½-inch cubes. Chop the fat and cook it in a wide skillet over medium-low heat until enough has melted to grease the pan generously. If necessary, add the butter. Remove and discard solids.

Turn the heat to medium-high, add the ham, and cook, stirring frequently, until the meat has firmed up and taken a bit of color. Remove it with a slotted spoon and set it aside. Add the onion and cook, stirring often, until it is well browned and reduced in volume. Stop here until the pasta water is about ready. It will take approximately 10 minutes to finish the sauce, 8 minutes to cook the pasta. If anybody has to wait, it ought to be the sauce, so time things accordingly.

To finish the sauce, add the lima beans and cream to the onions in the pan, turn the heat to high, and boil about 6 minutes, or until the beans are almost but not quite cooked. By now the pasta is cooking. Add the corn to the beans and keep boiling. In 3 to 4 minutes, you should have a thick sauce of reduced cream with vegetable lumps. Stir in the red pepper, parsley, chives, and reserved ham cubes. Immediately turn the heat to low and keep the mixture just warm.

Drain the pasta and return it to the kettle. Pour on the sauce and toss gently, just enough to mix well. Serve at once.

VARIATION: In classic American fashion, this can be served as a casserole. Prepare as described above, as much as a full day in advance.

Spread the noodle mixture in a shallow buttered baking dish about 12 by 14 by 2 inches and cover the top, either with a tight-fitting lid of tinfoil or a loose blanket of lightly buttered corn bread crumbs (about 1½ cups crumbs and 2 tablespoons melted butter). Bake in a preheated oven — 350°F. for the tinfoil, 375°F. for the crumbs — until the noodle mixture is thoroughly heated, about 25 minutes. Do not overcook; if the crumbs aren't brown enough, put the casserole briefly under the broiler.

VEGETARIAN VERSION: This is still delicious without the ham, and it's probably even more nourishing, all things considered. Just omit the meat and sauté the onion in 2 tablespoons butter. Luxurious protein in the form of cooked crabmeat, shrimp, or lobster can be added to tasty effect, but it will shift the flavor emphasis away from the corn in a way that ham does not.

CONCERNING CORN PASTA: It's sold primarily in health food stores, having found its original market among those who cannot eat wheat products. Increasingly, however, people are discovering how delicious it is. The corn flavor, though gentle, is unmistakable, and the texture is a great deal more delicate than that of conventional noodles. This is because the basic dough is only about one-third as dense as wheat dough.

Because it contains no gluten to hold it together, corn pasta will disintegrate if overcooked. You have only about 1½ minutes between underdone and that unhappy state, so keep your eye on the pot and keep tasting.

To cook corn pasta, allow 1 quart of water for each 1½ cups of noodles and salt it generously. Allow 6 to 8 minutes for spaghetti or ribbons and 8 to 10 minutes for elbows, shells, and other thicker shapes. If the pasta is ready before its sauce, drain, rinse gently with hot water, and keep warm in a partially covered pot.

A Slaw for Our Time

A brief salt bath tempers the strength of cold-storage cabbage while moderating the heat of chili peppers. The dressing is influenced (mildly) by Oriental sauces often used for cold noodles. Don't be alarmed by the peanut butter; most people won't be able to tell *what* makes the dressing seem so smooth and rich and yet is scarcely there. Though peanut butter is a high-calorie item, there isn't much of it in here and the finished slaw is less fattening than most.

For 6 to 8 servings

1 medium-sized head of firm green cabbage, about 2 pounds
2 medium-sized bell peppers, 1 red and 1 green, each about 4 ounces
1 medium-sized onion, about 4 ounces
1 or 2 long hot fresh green peppers, cayenne type, enough to make 2 to
    3 tablespoons prepared
2 teaspoons salt
3½ tablespoons unsalted chunky peanut butter (pure, all-peanut type)
½-inch cube of peeled fresh ginger root (measured after peeling)
2 medium-sized cloves garlic
2 teaspoons sugar
1 tablespoon lime juice, about 1 small lime
1 teaspoon soy sauce

Remove the coarse outer leaves and core from the cabbage, then chop into small pieces — not too fine, about ⅓ inch square. A processor works fine as long as you don't let it get carried away. Chop the bell peppers and onion to the same size. Remove all but about ¼ teaspoon of the hot peppers' seeds, then chop them a bit smaller than the other vegetables. The object is a gentle heat, not a roaring fire.

Combine the prepared vegetables in a large bowl with the salt, stir thoroughly, and allow to sit an hour or so at room temperature, stirring occasionally. Turn the mixture into a colander or large strainer and drain, pressing, stirring, and pressing again so as much juice as possible is removed.

Make the dressing. Put the peanut butter in a small bowl, position a grater over it, and grate in the ginger and garlic, using the small (⅛-inch) round holes. You should get thin shreds, not crumbs. Add sugar and stir well. Stir in the lime juice and soy sauce, then enough water to make a dressing the texture of mayonnaise — about 2 tablespoons. The amount will seem scant, but it will be enough.

Combine the dressing with the salad, let it marinate 20 minutes or so, then taste. Depending on the thoroughness of the draining, it may need salt. Depending on what the slaw will be served with, you may also want a bit more sourness; but be careful not to upset the subtle balance that distinguishes this version of the old favorite. It's particularly nice with grilled fish.

✮ Intoxicating Chocolate Drops

For about 100 small confections

2 cups pecans, about 8 ounces
1½ cups sifted confectioners' sugar
2 packages (8½ ounces each) plain chocolate wafer cookies, crushed to
    powder, 4 cups
3 tablespoons cocoa
Pinch of salt
2 tablespoons maple syrup
¾ cup bourbon (may not all be needed)

Spread half the pecans on a flat pan and toast them in a 350°F. oven 10 to 12 minutes, or until they are light gold. Let them cool. Combine them with the untoasted nutmeats and grate the mixture to fine crumbs. If you use a processor, add about half the sugar to the pecans before grinding to make sure they grind to bits instead of to butter.

Transfer the mixture to a large bowl and stir in the sugar, cookie crumbs, cocoa, and salt. Mix the maple syrup with ½ cup of the bourbon and pour it into the dry mixture, stirring as you do. Use a wooden spoon to mash and stir, working toward a soft, fairly sticky paste, adding more bourbon as necessary. At first it will seem as though there isn't enough moisture, but the paste will gradually come together, so be miserly with the hooch. You want a dough with the texture of soft mashed potatoes. (If by some chance it *does* get too gooey, slowly add confectioners' sugar until malleability is restored.) Cover and allow to rest for 20 minutes of so, then knead briefly.

Pinch off small pieces and roll into balls the size of large marbles, a bit less than an inch in diameter. Store airtight overnight to mellow, then keep airtight until they're all gone, which should be within a few days.

PAINTING THE LILY: These come out really black and smooth, with a faint shine — slightly sinister looking. If you have the time, you can use confectioners' sugar icing to transform them into art deco delights.

Beat an egg white just enough to mix and thin it, then stir in enough confectioners' sugar to make a thick icing that will flow without spreading. Put it in a pastry bag fitted with a fine plain tip or in a small plastic sandwich bag with a tiny corner snipped off. Decorate the chocolate drops with tick-tack-toe boards, polka dots, stars, initials, etc., and let dry until the icing sets. Serve promptly; they don't store well once decorated.

HE SALMON IN THE BATHTUB

I WILL SPARE you the details of the misunderstanding. Suffice it to say that the project began in the laundry room of a comfortable, old-fashioned Maine mansion. In the classic deep double sink, embedded like a pair of ·champagne bottles in outsized buckets of ice, were two large fish. Two *very* large fish. One of them measured three feet eight inches. The other was longer. Both were commensurately plump.

The monsters were destined to become cold salmon with green mayonnaise for seventy wedding guests. It was my job to cook them. It was not required that I cook them whole. It wasn't even suggested. One can only suppose the devil made me do it.

After all, it stands to reason that anyone *not* actually possessed would have poached the salmon in pieces, then reassembled the parts. A bit of decor in appropriate places and nobody the wiser.

But there's something about the challenge of cooking creatures that size that excites the latent vanity of even the most modest chef. When the chef is *not* any too modest, and when her employer is also a skilled cook and contemplator of challenges, the result is bound to be something like Poached Salmon à la Bathtub.

The fish were served proudly seamless, glistening with aspic and wreathed with nasturtium flowers — a tour de force of no mean proportions for which we garnered much congratulation.

The inspiration came from dimly remembered stories about how the Indians lived. According to the leader of my old Brownie troop, the Indians had cooked large objects in hollowed logs filled with water. They heated the water by dropping hot stones into it. We did exactly the same thing, lowering rather than dropping the stones, in deference to the bathtub, and adding wine, lemons, etc., which the Indians did not.

If *you* acquire a large fish and wish to follow our example, you will need:

1. A bathtub. It has to be porcelain, uncracked and unchipped in the business section, so you can scrub it clean enough and so it won't melt when you put the stones in. It should be small, so as to require the smallest amount of water and seasonings. And it should

be close to the kitchen, for obvious reasons. (Allow me, on the basis of experience, to suggest that a bathtub on the second floor at the top of a narrow flight of rickety stairs is not a good idea.)

2. Rocks. These should be cobbles, granite, brick, or another explosionproof material. They shouldn't weigh much more than five or six pounds, since you must handle them when they're hot.

3. A support for the fish. This could be a section of bookshelf wrapped well in tinfoil, a large grill from a barbecue unit, or any big sheet of something rigid that isn't poison or peculiarly flavored and doesn't weigh much. You need it to support the fish while it cooks and while it cools. It needn't be exactly fish length, especially if you wind the fish tight enough with . . .

4. Cheesecloth, lots of cheesecloth.

You will need the seasonings that are commonly used with poached fish — lemons, peppercorns, mustard and/or coriander seeds, celery, carrots, onions, parsley, and, of course, white wine. You can make a proper court-bouillon if you are feeling ambitious, but a big fish means a lot of liquid, and it's not really necessary. You will, however, need at least enough of the seasonings to stuff the fish partially.

Be sure there are plenty of tea towels, pot holders, and similar articles on hand. Start thinking about a presentation platter. We were able to use the marble top of a Victorian hall table, but only because someone strong enough to lift it happened to be handy.

Having someone strong and long-armed to help is a good idea in general. Otherwise, just lowering the salmon into its waiting bathtub takes a bit of engineering.

Begin by putting the rocks (enough to pave the tub by about one-third) into a cold oven. Turn the heat to 200°F. and bake 20 minutes. Raise the heat to 375°F. and bake at least 1½ hours more.

Heat several large pots of water while you are heating the rocks. Put seasonings in if you're inclined toward court-bouillon. Bathtubs and giant fish vary so much that it's hard to suggest quantities, but a 4-foot fish in a 5-foot tub will require about 10 to 15 gallons of liquid, 3 pounds each of carrots and celery, 5 or 6 big onions, 8 lemons, 2 bunches of parsley, 5 or 6 bay leaves, and ¼ cup peppercorns.

Of course, you won't need nearly so much if you just use the seasonings to stuff the fish. This "stuffing" is partly to provide flavor and partly to keep the top and bottom of the fish slightly ajar so the heat can get all the way to the backbone from both directions.

Lay out four long pieces of cheesecloth in a crisscross to make a square and lay the fish thereon. Insert the vegetables, cut in rough chunks. Completely wrap the fish in cheesecloth, pulling it tight. Tie it in a few places with kitchen twine. This binding up will help the fish keep its shape during the cooking process. Put the fish on its support and let it come to room temperature.

Clean the bathtub. First scrub mightily with cleanser, then rinse with the greatest possible thoroughness. After you've given the final rise, go back and wipe out the whole tub with a vinegar-soaked cloth. Rinse again. Fill the tub with hot tap water and let it heat thoroughly.

Okay — everybody ready? Drain the tub. Lower in the fish on its support. Pour the heated (seasoned) water over and around the fish. Position a heated rock on a tea towel and lower it into the water. Roll the rock off the towel, as close to the fish as it will go without touching. Position the rest in the same way.

Now inspect the water level. If it doesn't come halfway up the fish, add hot tap water until it does. Arm yourself with a small saucepan and start ladling the hot water over the fish. Keep it up, concentrating on the thicker sections and not worrying overmuch about the head. A fish four inches thick will take about an hour.

When you think the fish is cooked, use a razor blade to cut right through the cheesecloth into the fish at the thick part near the backbone. As soon as the flesh there is almost opaque, the cooking is complete. A thin layer of still-translucent meat next to the bone is okay. Held heat will continue the cooking for some time after the tub is drained.

Let the fish cool in situ, if you can. There are few things more awkward to handle than a big, hot, wet fish.

The thing should, however, still be slightly tepid when you transfer it to the serving platter, because a warm fish is so much easier to peel. Film the platter and the support with cold water so the fish will slide around easily. Move the fish gently off the support onto the platter, proceeding cautiously so it doesn't break. Cut away the cheesecloth.

Remove and discard the stuffing. Carefully peel away most of the fish skin, leaving a decorative bit near the tail and, of course, the head. Have a flat knife handy in case you need to help free the creamy pink meat.

Now either glaze the salmon with aspic (see your all-purpose cook-book) or cover the exposed portion with plastic wrap so it doesn't dry out.

To chill the fish and keep it cold, put the platter on a strong support back into the faithful bathtub. Surround it with ice. Be sure the support is tall enough to keep the platter out of the melted ice.

At serving time surround the fish with leaves and flowers and pass a nice green sauce separately.

🐝 *Green Mayonnaise*

This classic sauce is always flavored with a purée of herbs. Spinach and watercress are the foundation and coloring agent. The traditional flavorings are tarragon and parsley, but dill, chervil, or even a few green coriander leaves can be used to good effect.

For about 2 cups

¼ pound fresh spinach leaves, all coarse stems removed
1 bunch watercress, leaves only
4 tablespoons minced fresh parsley
3 tablespoons fresh tarragon
3 egg yolks
2 to 3 tablespoons lemon juice
1 teaspoon dry mustard
Tiny pinch of sugar
½ cup olive oil
1 cup peanut oil

Purée the spinach, watercress, parsley, and tarragon. A processor works well. Wrap the mass in the corner of an expendable dish towel or double layer of cheesecloth and squeeze it to extract all possible juice. Drink the juice if you need vitamins and set the purée aside.

Use the remaining ingredients to make mayonnaise according to the instructions in your all-purpose cookbook. Stir the wrung-out greenery into the mayonnaise. Let it sit at room temperature 5 minutes, then taste it and add salt and lemon juice as necessary.

Please notice I have not suggested you can substitute ordinary store mayonnaise. You can't. Its sweet flavor is all wrong for this sophisticated sauce.

Green Mayonnaise will keep in the refrigerator 4 to 5 days and is great not only on poached salmon but also on hard-boiled eggs, potato salad, fresh tomatoes, and clam fritters, to say nothing of cold roast beef, turkey sandwiches, and, in all probability, your grandfather's old boot. Only 80,000 calories a tablespoon.

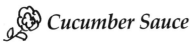
Cucumber Sauce

1 large or 2 medium-sized cucumbers
1 tablespoon prepared mustard of the smooth, slightly sweet
    Scandinavian type
1 teaspoon sugar
2 tablespoons peanut oil
Pinch of ginger
⅓ cup white wine vinegar or rice vinegar
2 cups whole-milk yogurt or sour cream
½ cup snipped fresh dill
Salt to taste

Peel the cucumber(s). Quarter them the long way and cut out the seeds. Grate the meat on the large holes of a grater and spread the shreds on absorbent paper to dry. Let them sit about 5 minutes.

Beat the mustard, sugar, oil, and ginger until the mixture is well combined, then slowly beat in the vinegar. Stir in the shredded cucumber and marinate, refrigerated, 1 to 3 hours, but not longer.

At serving time, drain the cucumbers, reserving the marinade. Stir the yogurt or sour cream until it's smooth, then slowly stir in the marinade to make a sauce just a little thicker than heavy cream. Fold in the cucumber, dill, and salt to taste. Serve at once.

The texture of the sauce does not hold well, but it does continue to taste good even after it looks terrible. When I end up with leftover sauce, I stir it into potato salad.

PIE TIME

JULY 13: "Oh, what nice cherries. Are you going to make a pie?"

JULY 22: "My goodness, those are lovely looking plums! Making a pie?"

JULY 26: "What's the column going to be about this week? I'll bet you're going to do one on *pie*, huh? Aren't you?"

Hope springs eternal in the breasts of those who have reason to think they can pry a pie out of a friend who cooks. There is, at this point, no treasure more rare than good old-fashioned American-style fruit pie, flaky in the crust, full of fresh fruit, served bubbling hot at the moment of just-baked perfection.

At first glance, it seems as though there ought to be more good pie around than ever, as record numbers of enthusiasts buy books, take classes, and otherwise school themselves in culinary artistry. Alas for art, the classic fruit pie is known territory, its roots firmly set and its rules established, while most of today's creative cooks spend their time in the kitchen striking out for new frontiers.

This has had the interesting effect of making pie — the one dessert that used to be dependably good no matter where it was made — the one dessert that is dependably bad from coast to coast. All the good cooks are hard at work making French cakes, Viennese pastries, and baklava, leaving the task of pie making to the greedy ovens of commerce.

But fruit pie is a national treasure, an edible American anthem. So be patriotic; seize the sweet fruits of summer and bake a pie today. Posterity will thank you, and the long-starved pie lovers in your dining room will rise up and call you blessed.

About Easy as Pie

To a great many cooks, this has always been a singularly aggravating expression, since for them plain old pie crust seems to be about as elusive as puff paste. Forbearing the usual homilies about chilling everything well, handling it minimally, etc., I will take this opportunity to say the best way to make a pie crust that is adequate for most usual pie crust purposes is to use the recipe for pâté brisée that came with your processor, and to further suggest that if you do not *have* a processor and are a person who cannot make pie crust, then the pie crust is an excellent reason to go out and get one. Though it does not have the lovely flakiness that distinguishes classic pie crust and is a bit on the rich side, the processor crust is rife with virtue, crumbly and short, resistant to sog, and easy to work with as long as (as usual) it is kept cool. It is also very tender unless overhandled, which brings me to my final word in the handy hint department: *waxed paper.*

Rolling out the dough between sheets of waxed paper obviates the need for sprinkling the board with flour. It enables you to turn the dough over without stretching it and to rechill a partially rolled sheet if the dough seems to be softening in an untoward way. It wrinkles up far less than plastic wrap, but it does wrinkle up, so you have to stop every now and then, peel away the sheets, and resmooth them. Small price to pay, if you ask me.

Several rolled sheets of pastry can be stored stacked in the original waxed paper if you don't plan to store them for long, but as waxed paper does absorb moisture (and does not protect from odors), rolled dough should be wrapped in plastic if you plan to store it for longer than a couple of hours. Come to think of it, why would you want to do that? Your business. Just don't do it in waxed paper.

 ## Deep-Dish Plum and Black Cherry Pie

For an approximately 9- by 12-inch pie

CRUST:
2¼ cups all-purpose flour
½ teaspoon salt
½ cup leaf lard (see Note) or vegetable shortening such as Crisco
¼ cup butter
¼ cup ice water
1 tablespoon lemon juice
1 tablespoon milk
1 tablespoon sugar

FILLING:
3½ cups pitted sweet cherries
3½ cups sliced red or purple round plums
⅓ cup sugar (approximately)
½ teaspoon mace
Pinch of salt
3 tablespoons butter

Combine the flour with the salt. With your fingertips, rub ¼ cup of the lard into it until the mixture resembles very fine meal; the lard will pretty much disappear.

Distribute the butter and the remaining lard in tablespoon-sized dabs over the surface, then use a pastry blender, 2 knives, or your fingertips to cut the fat into the flour until it forms lumps no smaller than peas.

Combine the ice water with the lemon juice and dribble it into the flour mixture as you stir with a fork. Work *just* until the dough holds together — it's better to add a few more drops of ice water than to torture the pastry into toughness trying to get a smooth mass.

Gather the dough into a flattened circle (or square, depending on the pan it's to fit). Wrap tightly in plastic wrap and chill several hours or overnight. Remove from the refrigerator and allow to come almost to room temperature before you roll it out.

Preheat the oven to 400°F. Choose a large, deep pie pan or a square baking dish about 2 inches deep. Envision servings with a comfortable proportion of fruit to crust, and choose your pan accordingly.

To make the filling, taste a plum slice and a cherry together, considering the sugar situation. If both fruits are at the peak of ripeness, ¼ cup of sugar may be enough. If the mixture tastes decidedly tart, as much as ½ cup may be needed. Remember that hot fruit tastes sweeter than cold fruit, other things being equal, and that commercial ice cream is sugar city. Keep the fruit mixture tart if you plan to serve your pie à la mode.

Combine the sugar, mace, and salt. Put half the plums in the pan, top with the cherries, and apply the remaining plums, sprinkling a bit of the sugar mixture and dabbing some of the butter on each layer of fruit. Roll the pastry out ⅛ inch thick and fit it over the pan, crimping up a generous rim and pressing it firmly around the edges. Cut a few vent slashes so steam can escape and brush the surface with the milk. Sprinkle the tablespoon of sugar on top, then bake 35 minutes, or until the crust is richly browned. The pie is best served hot, but not *right* out of the oven. Cool 5 or 10 minutes so juices thicken slightly and go back into the fruit.

 Deep-Dish Peach-Amaretto Pie

CRUST:
Ingredients for recipe on page 121, plus ½ cup ground almonds and ¼ cup sliced almonds

FILLING:
7 cups peeled, sliced peaches
2 teaspoons lemon juice
½ cup brown sugar, slightly less if peaches are very sweet
¼ teaspoon almond extract
1 tablespoon cornstarch
⅓ cup amaretto
¼ cup butter

Make the crust as described on pages 121-122. After chilling, roll out a rectangle ¼ inch thick and sprinkle evenly with the ground almonds. Fold the dough in thirds lengthwise, as though folding a letter, then fold that (approximate) rectangle in thirds across, to make a not necessarily very neat looking square. Fold in the points of the square to make something vaguely circular. Wrap tightly in plastic wrap and rechill.

Combine the peaches, lemon juice, brown sugar, and almond extract. Dissolve the cornstarch in the amaretto and stir the mixture into the peaches. Allow the filling to sit 15 minutes, then stir well again.

Remove the peach slices with a slotted spoon and layer them, dotted with butter, in your deep pie pan or baking dish; I use a rectangular pan 9 by 12 by 2 inches. Pour the juices over them.

Roll the dough out not quite ⅛ inch thick. Arrange the sliced almonds over the dough and roll them into it with the last few strokes of the pin. Attach the dough to the pan, glaze, and bake as described on page 122. Especially nice with extra-rich French vanilla ice cream.

A NOTE *about Shortening in Pie Crust:* Lard — real leaf lard from the fat that cushions pork kidneys — carefully rendered and unadulterated by stabilizers, emulsifiers, and preservatives, is the fat that made American pie crust famous for its flaky tenderness. Consider this still-accurate passage from *The New England Cookbook*, published in 1905: "Except in puff-paste, lard and butter in about equal proportions make the best crust; if made of butter alone, it is almost sure to be tough. That of lard alone, though tender, is usually white and insipid." I prefer a bit more butter than that book suggests and have found solid shortening better than ordinary commercial lard. The real stuff is now considerably more difficult to obtain than fresh caviar, but some specialty butchers do sell it and it's not hard to make your own.

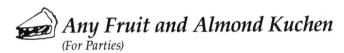 *Any Fruit and Almond Kuchen*
(For Parties)

This large, flat tart is delicious with sweet or sour cherries, peaches, plums, apricots, and blueberries. Apples and pears are good but must be poached beforehand unless they are very soft. Strawberries, alas, and raspberries, are too soft, period.

For 24 servings

CRUST:
Butter for pan, plus 1 cup
2¾ cups all-purpose flour
½ cup sugar
½ teaspoon baking powder
2 eggs

FILLING:

4 heaping cups fruit (see above), pitted and sliced (where necessary) into bite-sized pieces

12 ounces cream cheese

1 cup confectioners' sugar

½ cup granulated sugar

½ teaspoon almond extract

Grated zest (thin, colored outer rind) of 1 lemon, about 1 heaping tablespoon

4 eggs

½ cup milk

¾ cup flour

½ teaspoon salt

2 teaspoons baking powder

1 cup almonds, ground fine

TOPPING:

2 cups whipping cream

¼ cup sugar

¼ teaspoon almond extract

¼ cup amaretto

Butter an approximately 13- by 17-inch jellyroll pan. Preheat the oven to 400°F. Combine the flour, sugar, and baking powder for the crust in a large bowl, stirring with a wire whisk to mix thoroughly. Using your fingertips or a pastry blender, work in the 1 cup butter until the mixture resembles cornmeal, then quickly blend in the eggs. Dough will be soft.

Distribute the dough in dabs on the prepared pan, then refrigerate or freeze briefly to chill the whole works. Spread the dough as evenly as possible over the bottom and up the sides, using lightly floured fingertips. Spread the prepared fruit over the crust and bake 15 minutes, or until the fruit is soft and the crust is set and starting to brown.

While the fruit is baking, make the rest of the filling. Beat the cream cheese with the sugars, almond extract, and zest until light and fluffy, then beat in the eggs, one at a time. Beat in the milk.

Sift the flour with the salt and baking powder, then stir it into the cheese mixture, as gently as possible. As soon as the flour is thoroughly dampened, add the almonds. Stir only until the filling is completely mixed.

When the fruit is done, spread the filling over the fruit, lower the heat to 350°F., and bake the kuchen 25 to 35 minutes longer, or until a toothpick emerges clean. The top will be only a pale gold. Run the kuchen briefly under the broiler if you want it to look browned. This last is a purely cosmetic step, however. Cool on a wire rack.

Prepare the topping at serving time. Beat the cream until it forms soft peaks, then beat in the sugar and almond extract. Fold in the amaretto and serve alongside the kuchen, which should be precut with a very sharp knife into 24 squares.

SUMMER EATS

I ADMIT it isn't common, but even on the coast of Maine it occasionally gets hot — unpleasantly hot. Searing hot in the garden, where even the cayenne peppers are wilting in the sunlight. Blistering hot in the open fields, where even the indomitable, bloodsucking bugs are lying doggo, done in by high temperatures. Swelteringly hot, even down by the river, where the putatively cooling breezes seem to be composed largely of lukewarm dishwater and second-hand salt.

No one is keen to cook on such days, when the overwhelming desire must be a hunger for coolth. Oh, to be an ice cube in Antarctica, cool as Jack Kerouac or maybe James Dean, to be as cool (how could it be otherwise?) as a cucumber.

Actually, once you come to think on it, it's clear that "cool as a cucumber" is rather an odd simile. The cucumber is not, after all, cool in and of itself, any more than apple pie is easy. What's cool, presumably, is you as you eat the cucumber, just as what's easy about the pie is forking it down.

As a matter of fact, cucumbers only grow well when it's good and hot, being as they are closely related to melons in their growing habits as well as their (supposedly) cooling juiciness. Thus high summer is the height of cucumber season, when fat, warty picklers, long green Armenians, and roadside-stand miscellaneous slicers finally bump those waxy-skinned monstrosities from their usual monopoly and cooling comestibles made with cucumbers are at their most appealing.

Sometimes, of course, the liquidity of cucumbers is insufficient, and the summer-beleaguered do not pass Go or collect $200 but go directly to beer, with which they will, perversely, want something salty or peppery, just to set it off. Alternatively, truly thirsty types might prefer iced tea, made, I need scarcely add, from tea, not from some sort of foul crystals, or lemonade (one of the great thirst quenchers of all time), made from lemons, dammit, not from a can. And should these old favorites fail to thrill, there's Agua de Flor de Jamaica, a bright pink, slightly sweet-sour infusion made from the dried flowers of a tropical hibiscus.

✵ *Cucumber Soup*

In one form or another, this is a staple all over the Middle East, where they know from hot.

For 4 to 6 servings

2 large cucumbers, preferably unwaxed so they needn't be peeled
1 or 2 large cloves garlic
1 teaspoon salt
2 cups whole-milk yogurt
⅓ to ½ cup finely minced green herbs (Chives, dill, parsley, and mint
  are good in almost any combination, except not too much mint if
  you're inviting me.)
1 quart good water or light broth
⅓ to ½ cup plumped raisins, roughly chopped (optional)

Peel the cucumbers if they have been waxed. Grate all but about half of one on the large holes of a grater and reserve the remainder. Let the grated material sit 15 or 20 minutes to shed water, then drain, pressing well.

Put the garlic and salt in the bottom of a large bowl and crush them with a pestle until they form a paste. Beat in the yogurt, then, when the yogurt is lumpless and smooth, the herbs and grated cucumber. Now beat in the broth, a little at a time to prevent lumps.

Either chop the remaining cucumber or cut it into tiny dice — depending on your energy for such projects, given the heat — and add that. Stir in the raisins if you want 'em. Nothing in the world will keep them from plummeting to the bottom of the bowl, where the cucumber pieces already are. Such is life; this is no time for thick soup.

Ideally, you should chill the soup for several hours to blend and bind the flavors and intensify the cucumber quality, but if you like you can serve it at once, with a couple of ice cubes floating around to make it look (and taste) chilly. Oddly enough, they don't make it taste weak.

☼ Cucumber and Shrimp Salad with Beets

This was inspired by *chlodnik*, a famous Polish cold soup employing cucumbers; beets; either shrimp, crayfish, or veal; and plenty of sour cream. It makes a nice first course, followed by something like roast chicken, and is an ideal luncheon dish accompanied by black bread. It's very pretty, the pale pink–spotted green salad wreathed by the red beets, and it spreads a small amount of shrimp for quite a distance.

For 4 to 5 appetizers or 2 to 3 main dish servings

DRESSING:
2½ tablespoons tarragon vinegar
¼ cup corn oil or other light vegetable oil
1 tablespoon minced fresh tarragon or 1 teaspoon dried
2 heaping tablespoons minced fresh dill
½ teaspoon sugar
¼ teaspoon each salt and pepper

SALAD:
4 smallish beets, about 1 pound
1 long cucumber (Oriental, burpless, or Armenian), about 1 pound
1 teaspoon salt
½ cup sweet red onion cut in thin shreds, about half a medium-sized one
1 tablespoon capers, chopped if they are large
8 ounces cooked shrimp, cut in ½-inch pieces (crayfish tails may be substituted if you wish to accent the Polish)
½ cup sour cream
Dill sprigs for garnish

Make the dressing by whisking together all the ingredients. Set aside 2 tablespoons and put the remainder in a shallow bowl.

Wash the beets, being careful not to break the skin, and put them in a deep saucepan. Cover with boiling water. Cover the pan and cook over medium heat until they are just tender, about 45 minutes. Remove from the water.

As soon as they are cool enough to handle, peel and cut in slices a bit less than ¼ inch thick. Put the hot slices in the shallow bowl and turn until all are well coated with dressing. Marinate, stirring from time to time, at least an hour, as long as half a day. Chill thoroughly.

Cut the cucumber in half across, then halve each piece lengthwise. Cut each quarter into three the long way so you have a dozen long, thin sticks. Cut off the seed-bearing edges, then bundle the sticks and slice across at ½-inch intervals so you have a bunch of small, fairly uniform cubes. Combine the cubes with the salt and let them sit 30 minutes or so.

Drain the cucumber, stirring and pressing to remove all possible liquid, and further dry it by wrapping in a tea towel. Combine the cucumber with the onion, capers, and shrimp, then stir in the reserved 2 tablespoons dressing. Let the salad marinate at least 30 minutes, up to 3 hours. Longer won't be a catastrophe, but this part doesn't keep as long as the beets.

At serving time, drain the beets and arrange in overlapping petals around the edges of the serving plates. Drain the cucumber salad, mix in the sour cream, taste, and adjust salt and sugar. Pile the mixture in the middle of the beet ring, garnish with the dill sprigs, and serve at once.

Mexican Beer Nuts

These crisply roasted peanuts, hot and sour with lime juice and chili, are addictive; to eat 2 or 3 is immediately to desire at least a carload. Not surprisingly, more and more manufactured versions of this classic treat are appearing, vacuum-packed, in cans and bottles and jars. As is usual with manufactured versions, these products are expensive. As if expensive weren't painful enough, they contain unwholesome preservatives to aggravate even further the eater's guilt and apprehension. Homemade, they are a great deal cheaper, far more delicious, and (marginally) better for you. Though classically served plain as an accompaniment for drinks, they are great sprinkled over salads or folded at the last minute into simply steamed rice.

For about 2 cups

1 pound skinless *lightly* dry-roasted peanuts (cheapest if bought in
   bulk from a health food store)
2 tablespoons plus 1 teaspoon bland vegetable oil
5 teaspoons powdered pasilla chile or chili powder
2 tablespoons lime juice, or a bit more
1 teaspoon coarse salt, or a bit more
Cayenne pepper (may not be needed)

Preheat oven to 350°F. Mix the nuts with the oil in a shallow pan and roast 15 minutes, stirring occasionally. They should turn dark gold, not darker.

Sprinkle on the chili, stirring well to be sure each nut is coated. Turn the heat down to 300°F. and roast about 5 minutes longer.

Turn the nuts out onto absorbent paper and let cool. A bit of chili will rub off but not much. When they are cool, toss in a big bowl with the lime juice and salt. Taste. They should be hot (if they ain't peppery, they ain't right), and they should be good and sour. Add lime juice, salt, and cayenne until you like the flavor.

This makes enough for quite a crowd. They do not keep well once lime-juiced, but the chili-roasted nuts will store indefinitely, tightly covered, in a dry, cool place. I usually make a double batch and add the lime juice and salt to taste each time I want to serve some.

Agua de Flor de Jamaica

Herb tea aficionados probably have enjoyed the bright red color and fresh flavor of hibiscus flowers in the mixture called Red Zinger (put out by Celestial Seasonings), but that seems to be about the extent of its use outside the enclaves of Hispanic cuisine. A pity, given that Jamaica water is the ideal summer drink: easy to make, comparatively low in calories, without unpleasant side effects, and very, very pretty. A libation for our time.

The packaged dried flowers, sometimes labeled "red sorrel," are widely available in stores that cater to Hispanics. If none of these stores is in your area, try ordering through your local co-op or health food or gourmet emporium. They're cheap, and they keep forever.

For about 1½ quarts

1 cup dried hibiscus flowers (*Hibiscus sabdariffa*)
2½ cups water
⅓ cup sugar, or to taste
1 quart additional water

Because the infusion is quite acid, be sure to use noncorrodible vessels for cooking and storing.

Put the flowers and the 2½ cups water in a saucepan. Bring to a boil, then turn down the heat and simmer 3 to 4 minutes. Add the sugar and cook, stirring, until it is dissolved. Let the mixture cool, then combine in a big pot with the rest of the water. Marinate, refrigerated, 4 hours to a full day. Strain off the liquid, put in a jug or jar, and serve well chilled. It will keep in a tightly closed jar in the refrigerator up to a week.

VEGETABLES ON THE GRILL

AS OF THIS writing, the forecast looks mixed for that fine old American cooking technique, charcoal grilling. Where until rather recently "charcoal-broiled" came in only two basic flavors, Suburban Backyard and Burger Joint — with, admittedly, a small subset of Meat Palace, which involved expert chefs grilling thick steaks and double lamb chops to mouth-watering, if expensive, perfection — we now have chic restaurants otherwise awash in goat cheese and kiwi fruit that pride themselves more than all else on the splendor of their mesquite grills. Inevitably, we also have dire warnings from an increasing number of killjoy nutritionists who say, "Other things being equal, food cooked in the smoke of wood fires is likely to (you guessed it) cause cancer."

In the vast lexicon of environmental evils, this one is still pretty low on the list, in my opinion, and if you set the sillier extremes aside, it's easy to welcome the revival of interest in what was, after all, the *original* method of cooking things, the method that preceded all others — put it on a stick and hold it over the fire.

Unlike most modern methods, this one is chancy — no matter how many fire-tending skills you develop, a bed of coals in the open air is capable of surprises no electrical appliance could dream of. This forces the cook to pay close attention to the proceedings (never a bad idea), and as a bonus it keeps away the mosquitoes.

Sweet Potatoes on the Grill

All you need are potatoes, bamboo skewers, and butter; fancier seasoning is completely unnecessary.

Use the big orange sweet potatoes commonly known as yams. Remove spots but otherwise don't bother to peel. Cut them into 1½-inch cubes, allowing about ⅔ cup cubes for each serving. Steam the cubes over boiling water for about 12 minutes, or until they are just barely tender — be sure not to let them cook completely. Let them cool.

Soak the skewers in warm water for an hour or so, so they won't get charred, then string the potato cubes on them, close but not touching. Paint liberally with melted butter then grill over medium-hot coals about 3 minutes a side. Keep buttering and turning until the outsides are well browned and caramelized and crisp and wonderful, about 15 minutes if the coals are right. Sprinkle with coarse salt and serve at once. Try not to burn your mouth.

(✻) *Ratatouille on a Stick,* *with Tomato-Basil Cream*

Late summer's eggplant, peppers, summer squash, and onions have a great affinity for the grill, which brings out their latent sweetness to a remarkable degree. No oil or other fat is required, and the truth is that while the sauce is delicious, *it* isn't required either. Like truly fresh corn on the cob, vegetables prepared in this manner require absolutely nothing else, not even salt, to taste great.

For 4 portions

1 medium-sized firm eggplant, 2½ cups prepared
2 medium (6- to 8-inch) zucchini, 2 cups prepared
1 medium-large onion, about 1 cup prepared
1 large red, yellow, or green bell pepper, about 1 cup prepared
12 bamboo barbecue skewers

SAUCE:
4 medium-sized firm ripe tomatoes, 2 cups prepared
2 tablespoons olive oil
2 large cloves garlic, minced
1 cup firmly but not tightly packed fresh basil
½ cup firmly but not tightly packed fresh flat-leaf parsley
1 cup heavy cream

Prepare the vegetables any time up to 3 hours in advance. Cut the eggplant into 1-inch cubes, leaving the skin on. Cut the squash into coins about ⅓ inch thick. Quarter the onion from root to tip, halve the quarters crosswise, and separate the leaves. Cut the pepper into slabs about 1 inch square.

Alternate the vegetables on the skewers, running the point through the rim of the squash pieces so they present their wide face to the fire. Cram them close together; they'll shrink as they cook. Set the vegetables aside, covered and refrigerated if they must wait more than an hour or so.

The sauce also can be prepared in advance, then reheated when wanted, though it is never as good as when consumed within the hour of its confection. Peel the tomatoes, cut them into wedges, and remove all seeds and free liquid. Chop the wedges into small dice. They will be pretty loose, of course, but they shouldn't be purée.

Put the oil in a wide, fairly shallow skillet over low heat. Add the garlic and cook, stirring occasionally, until the garlic is pale gold. While it's cooking, mince the herbs to fine shreds — a processor works well — and set them aside.

When the garlic is ready, add the tomatoes to the skillet, turn the heat to high, and cook, stirring continuously, about 6 minutes, or until the tomatoes have reduced and formed a very thick, chunky sauce. The liquid will spatter, so be prepared. As soon as the tomatoes are ready, stir in the minced herbs. As soon as they are added, stir in the cream. Pour it in as quickly as you can get it amalgamated so the tomatoes don't have a chance to curdle the proceedings.

Continue to stir and boil 2 to 3 minutes, or until the sauce is reduced to the texture you want — I like it on the thin side. Once the desired texture is achieved, turn the heat as low as it'll go. Put the pot on the side of the stove or transfer the sauce to the top of a double boiler, where it can keep warm without cooking further.

The vegetables take only 3 to 4 minutes a side over medium-hot to hot coals. They might pick up a few black bars while appearing otherwise raw, but they taste cooked before they look cooked because all you really need to do is soften and heat them, a transformation that comes quickly indeed. Any unsauced leftovers are a delicious addition to vinaigrette-dressed salad; I often prepare extras just to have them for this purpose.

Lemon-Sesame Sauce for Grilled Vegetables

For about 1½ cups

> 2 large or 3 small cloves garlic
> 1 teaspoon salt

¾ cup tahini (roasted sesame paste)
⅓ cup lemon juice
⅓ cup minced fresh green herbs such as parsley, chives, chervil, or dill
¼ cup sesame seeds
Salt to taste

In a mortar or small bowl, crush the garlic to paste with the salt. Stir in the tahini, then the sesame oil and lemon juice. At this point the sauce will be almost solid and very difficult to stir.

Add cold water, 2 tablespoons or so at a time, until the sauce has the texture of sauce. This will take about half a cup of water altogether, but much depends on factors such as the weather and the brand of tahini. Stir in the herbs and set aside.

Spread the sesame seeds on a flat sheet and toast them in a 350°F. oven until they are a rich gold — about 8 minutes. Set them aside to cool.

Taste the sauce, adjust the salt, and stir in the sesame seeds. That's it. The sauce keeps well in the refrigerator, but the garlic flavor will intensify as it sits, so if you are deliberately making it in advance, cut back on the garlic a bit. Thinned with yogurt or sour cream, this makes a nice dip.

WHY GARDEN?

IF YOUR PURSE no longer bulges and you've lost your golden treasure
If at times you think you're lonely and have hungry grown for pleasure
Don't sit by your hearth and grumble, don't let mind and spirit harden
If it's thrills of joy you wish for, get to work and plant a garden.

Edgar Guest

Though the thrills of joy part may be moot, there's no question that more and more people are discovering (or rediscovering) that gardening is an occupation rife with blame-free benefits; self-sufficiency, for instance (or, more accurately in most cases, a better understanding thereof) and excellent outdoor exercise, to name two; plus three of the basic needs of life — nourishment, aesthetic pleasure, and sensual gratification. All this and tax-exempt, too.

My garden is way too big for me and getting bigger, in spite of my best intentions, every year. But you don't need to get grandiose to get the goodies. And you don't have to be especially skillful, either, because just in the nature of things, the seed would rather grow. This is equally true of hundreds of pounds of hybrid corn in the rich black fields of an Iowa farm and four basil seeds in a can of potting soil on a fire escape twenty stories above New York.

If you have a yard, plow some of it up. If you don't have a yard, find or found a community garden. If you're living on a boat or in a balloon, go anchor near something tillable. One way or another, do whatever you must so you can get out there and plant those peas! Gardening is what distinguishes humans from the apes.

Vegetables and fruits consumed in or near the gardens that produced them restore to "fresh" a meaning that far transcends "neither canned nor frozen." The taste of earth and light and rain is in them; they are sweet with life. In many cases, furthermore, this extra-special savor is fullest when the vegetables are raw, and gardeners often discover their summer meals are mostly a matter of taking a stroll through the truck patch, browsing as they go.

To stand in sunlight among tangled tomato plants, eating the perfectly ripe red fruits while the air around you is suffused with the unmistakable tomato sap fragrance that heat raises from the leaves, is to enter a natural role reversal — consumed by the tomato instead of the other way around.

Naturally, the gardenless who wish to harvest similar pleasures must cultivate gardening friends or seek out genuine farmers' markets; the freshness lauded in these lines is fleeting in the extreme. One way or another, though, it *is* possible to get the best, and the pleasure of eating same raw in the garden is closely followed by eating it raw at the table.

When that time comes, at least a bit of embellishment usually is in order, although it should be something that will enhance without, as Alice B. Toklas put it, "interfering with the poor vegetable's leading a life of its own." Dips, in all their dazzling — nay, discouraging — variety usually are the embellishments of choice. They enable the cook to make pretty still lifes of the orange carrots, the red and green peppers, the white cauliflower, the black Spanish radishes, etc., well in advance; they give the diner an opportunity to season at will; and they are, one and all, easy to make.

Vegetables to be served with dips are generally prepared in advance and kept crisp by being kept damp and cool. They will taste best if allowed to warm up to cool room temperature and will provide a more adhesive surface for the dip if they are thoroughly dry.

☆ Spiced Yogurt
For about 2½ cups

2 tablespoons peanut oil
1-inch cube peeled fresh ginger root, grated fine
1 large red onion, minced fine, about 1½ cups
1 teaspoon each ground cumin, coriander seed, and turmeric
1 large clove garlic, crushed or pressed
2 cups whole-milk yogurt
Salt to taste

Heat the oil in a small skillet over low heat. Add the ginger and half the onion and cook, stirring, until they are translucent and pale gold.

Stir in the spices. Cook, stirring, over very low heat about 2 minutes. Be sure not to let them scorch. Then add the garlic. Turn off the heat, cover the pan, and let contents "sweat" in a warm place 5 minutes more.

Allow the spiced onion mixture to cool, then gently stir in the yogurt. Transfer the mixture to a bowl, stir in the remaining onion, then cover tightly and chill at least an hour to allow the flavors to blend. Taste before serving and add salt if you wish.

WARNING: Just in case you were thinking of employing a blender or processor, don't. Subjecting yogurt to those whirring blades thins it to liquidity.

⚬ Cashew Chutney
(A Party Dip to Be Reckoned With)

This subtly hot, rich-flavored pale green sauce looks a lot like guacamole and has the same "enhances everything" appeal. The flavor is an ideal blend of fresh ginger, hot green chilies, cashew nuts, and parsley. Serve it as a dip for raw vegetables, a sauce for fish, or a topping for baked squash or sweet potatoes. Thin it with yogurt or plain water and use it as a dressing almost anywhere you'd use mayonnaise — potato salad, for instance, or tuna fish, which by the simple addition of this product, is unutterably transformed. This recipe is from *The Yogi Cookbook* by Yogi Vithaldas and Susan Roberts (Pyramid Books, 1968), now, unfortunately, out of print.

For about 1½ cups

1 cup raw cashew nuts
2 green chili peppers such as jalapeños, enough to make about 2
    tablespoons
¼ cup chopped, peeled, fresh ginger root
¼ cup fresh parsley leaves
1 teaspoon salt
Juice of 1 lemon

Use a blender or processor to grind the nuts to paste, then add the chili, ginger root, and parsley and grind again. If necessary, add just enough water to make blending possible. A smooth, creamy paste the consistency of thick mayonnaise should be the result. Add the salt and lemon juice and stir well. The chutney will keep, covered and refrigerated, several days.

NOTE: These are the yogi's proportions. I have used both more and less of every one of the character ingredients, almost always with success.

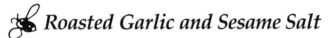 Roasted Garlic and Sesame Salt

For about ⅓ cup

3 large cloves garlic, unpeeled
2 tablespoons hulled sesame seeds
¼ cup coarse salt, either kosher or sea salt
½ teaspoon whole peppercorns

Heat a heavy skillet, preferably cast-iron, over low heat until a drop of water dances. Turn the heat down, lay on the garlic, and toast, turning once or twice, until it is soft and roasted-smelling. Skins might be scorched in a couple of places. Reserve the garlic.

Toast the sesame seeds in the same pan, shaking it to prevent scorching. They'll start turning gold and popping almost at once. As soon as they do, remove them and set aside. Add the salt and peppercorns to the pan and keep toasting and shaking 3 to 4 minutes more. When it's fragrant, it's done. Let everything cool completely.

Peel the garlic, combine it with the sesame salt, and crush the whole works with a mortar and pestle or in a blender. (If using a blender grind salt and pepper first then add other ingredients.) You'll have a mixture about like wet sand. Spread it in a shallow pan and dry it out in a very low (150°F.) oven, stirring occasionally, until it is shakable. Let it cool, then store airtight in a cool, dry place. The amount is small but very pungent, so a little goes the proverbial long way.

Crab Dip with Capers and Watermelon Rind

For 2 generous cups

1 cup freshly cooked crabmeat, picked over to free of shells
²⁄₃ to 1 cup homemade mayonnaise made with lemon juice and half olive, half peanut oils
2 tablespoons each finely minced fresh parsley, watercress, and dill
1 tablespoon coarsely chopped capers
1 tablespoon finely chopped sweet-pickled watermelon rind
Salt and lemon juice to taste

Mix 'em up, making sure the crab gets thoroughly shredded for even distribution. The two cups are enough for 6 people's worth of fresh vegetables, assuming the people are not especially greedy.

*B*LUEBERRIES

EVERY YEAR, from the balmy end of July to the frosts of mid-September, wild blueberries blanket the coastal strip of Maine, which provides about 95 percent of the country's commercial supply. The sweet-sharp little fruits are everywhere: underfoot if you're on a seaside cliff, exploring the meadows and bogs, or walking the woodland clearings; ten feet away if you're strolling down a dusty country road; as close as the peddlers' pickups dotting the verge if you're in your car on the highway.

Go to a restaurant, and there's blueberry pie on the menu. Go to a gift shop, and it's Blueberry City; their image garnishes everything imaginable, from T-shirts, tote bags, and tea towels to wall plaques and the pottery to put the pie on. There is blueberry conserve and chutney and jam. There's even, I'm sorry to say, blueberry wine, for those whose enthusiasm knows no bounds. Next to lobsters, wild blueberries are unquestionably Maine's major contribution to America's gastronomic wealth, and if they are not exactly a secret, they are still, perhaps, less famous than they ought to be.

Most consumers know them only in processed form, frozen or canned, baked into muffins and pies. This is hardly surprising given that almost the entire crop goes to the big processors as soon as it leaves the fields. But it certainly is a shame, given the incomparable deliciousness of the fresh fruit.

The finest of the finest, of course, is the fresh fruit you pick yourself. Kneel once in the tangle of sweet fern, wild strawberries, and delicate grasses that so often share blueberry ground; roll the perfect dark blue spheres into your palm and eat them one by one. That wild-tinged taste is now tied forever to the blue-sky perfection of a late summer day in Maine . . . or, in truth, New Hampshire, New York, or Michigan. Wild blueberries grow all over the northern tier; it's just that they are most abundant along the northern New England coast.

Though some pioneers are starting to ship the fresh fruits outside New England, the unhappy truth is that, for most people, all fresh blueberries are the cultivated highbush kind, which is to say almost worthless. Wild lowbush blueberries, *Vaccinium augustifolium* and related species, are tiny, seldom more than a quarter inch across, tender inside a tight skin, with a tartness that helps to set off the winey sweetness of the flavor. Cultivated berries are much larger; nursery catalogues proudly trumpet fruit the size of quarters. This about ends the catalogue of their virtues, cultivated blueberries being nearly the last word in insipidity — mushy, flavorless, and flat.

That distinction made, I trust, perfectly clear, it must be added that wild blueberries are one of the world's more intractable fruits. No matter what you do with them, they taste like blueberries; no matter what you make with them, it tastes like some comestible or other with blueberries in it. In the case of pie, fine; in the case of muffins, fine, especially if you don't make them too sweet; in the case of lobster salad, emphatically not fine, no matter how innovative and clever.

Keeping Blueberries

As long as they were dry when they were picked (and have not been suffocated and made to sweat by a lid of plastic film), blueberries should store well for several days in the refrigerator. If they're damp when you buy them, spread them out and let them dry before you store them. Of course, they will keep best if you pick them over to remove the bad ones before storage. A rotten blueberry won't spoil the whole basket, but it will spoil its immediate neighbors.

Like cranberries, to which they are closely related, blueberries freeze very well, requiring neither advance preparation nor the addition of sugar. Just pick 'em over, spread 'em out on a cookie sheet, and freeze, as quickly as possible. Once frozen, store in tightly closed plastic bags. Though like all frozen fruit they will soften and weep upon thawing, they can be used straight from the freezer, lightly dusted with flour, for any recipe in which they will be cooked completely. It's nice to save at least a few to combine with blackberries for an unusual and delicious jam. (The sweetness of the blueberries balances the sharpness of the blackberries, and the color is wonderful.)

Blueberries also can be dried, assuming three days without fog. Though this is a dangerous assumption in coastal Maine, in most places the process is easy. Colonial housewives used them in place of currants, which is still a very nice idea.

🦋 Maple-Blueberry Corncake

Other than blueberry, there are few flavors with the peculiar quality of being simultaneously retiring and indefatigable, but maple syrup is one. For whatever reason, these two unlikely partners suit each other very well. Each is further enhanced by the corn, a decidedly sweet grain. This "cake" is somewhere between a muffin and a coffee cake: definitely sweet, but more like breakfast than dessert; definitely rich, but not so rich you would absolutely never want to put butter on it.

For a 10-inch cake

10½-inch iron skillet or other heavy, shallow pan
1½ cups stone-ground cornmeal
1 cup all-purpose flour
1 tablespoon baking powder
¼ teaspoon salt
¼ cup butter, melted, plus butter for the pan

2 eggs, well beaten
½ cup milk
½ cup maple syrup
1½ cups picked-over blueberries

Preheat the oven to 425°F., then put the pan in it to heat up. Thoroughly combine the dry ingredients. In a separate bowl, beat the melted butter, eggs, milk, and syrup until the mixture is foamy. Remove the hot pan from the oven and butter it thoroughly — a pastry brush works well. Dump the liquid into the dry ingredients and give the mixture about 6 stirs, at which point it should look a mess, by no means combined. Add the blueberries and stir a few more times. You should have a barely mixed batter with well-distributed berries. (If you wait till the batter is mixed before you add the fruit, it'll end up overworked.)

At once turn the prepared batter into the pan. Smooth the top, return the pan to the oven, and bake until a toothpick comes out clean and the cake is well browned on the bottom, about 25 minutes. Allow to cool slightly and serve while still warm. If you plan to bake the cake in advance, take it out of the oven a little before it's done — the held heat in the heavy pan will continue the cooking.

Uptown Blueberry Dessert
(Hazelnut Dacquoise with Lemon-Blueberry Mousse Filling)

An ineffably light, crunchy crust around an airy, not-too-sweet filling. If it weren't covered with whipped cream it just might float away. All but the finishing can be done well in advance, so it's nice for parties. Though similar in texture, this is less fussy to make than meringues, but you do need a dry day. Should damp weather persist during blueberry season, don't let it deprive you of the mousse part — just put it in a regular baked pie shell. Use a very thin, crisp, flaky one if possible, or a crumb crust based on zwieback and toasted almonds if absolutely necessary. And, of course, the mousse is tasty all by itself. Pile in wine glasses before chilling and top with a pouf of whipped cream.

FILLING:
1 tablespoon unflavored gelatin (1 envelope)
¼ cup cold water
4 egg yolks
½ cup sugar

⅓ cup heavy cream (not ultrapasteurized)
Finely grated zest (thin, colored outer rind) of 1 large lemon, about 1
    tablespoon
⅓ cup lemon juice, about 1 very large lemon
3 tablespoons Triple Sec or other orange liqueur
2 egg whites
⅓ cup sugar
½ cup heavy cream (not ultrapasteurized)
3 cups picked-over fresh blueberries

CRUST:
Butter and flour for tinfoil
4 egg whites
7 tablespoons sugar
¾ cup ground blanched hazelnuts

TOPPING:
½ cup heavy cream (not ultrapasteurized)
2 tablespoons Triple Sec or other orange liqueur

Begin with the filling. Rinse out a deep, 9-inch cake pan with cold water and line it with plastic wrap, keeping the lining as wrinkle-free as possible. Set aside. Sprinkle the gelatin over the water and set aside.

In a heavy, noncorrodible saucepan, beat the yolks with the ½ cup sugar, ⅓ cup cream, lemon zest, and lemon juice, added in that order. Cook, stirring, over simmering water or very low heat until the custard thickly coats a spoon. Stir in the gelatin, then, as soon as that's dissolved, remove the pan from the heat. Cool to tepid, stirring occasionally. Add the 3 tablespoons of Triple Sec. Chill briefly, just until it starts to gel. It should be very thick but not too thick to stir.

Shortly before you think the custard is about to gel, beat the egg whites with the ⅓ cup sugar, sprinkling the sugar in slowly as you go, until you have a stiff-peaked meringue. In a separate bowl, beat ½ cup cream until it forms firm peaks.

Working quickly, scrape the custard mixture onto the meringue and start folding. When the two are almost amalgamated, add the whipped cream, then the blueberries. Turn the mixture into the prepared cake pan and cover with plastic wrap. Chill at least 6 hours, as long as a day.

Make the crust. Lightly butter and flour a large sheet of tinfoil, then outline a pair of 9-inch circles on it. Place circle-side up on a baking sheet and set aside. Preheat oven to 225°F.

Slowly beat the egg whites until they form stiff but still shiny peaks, sprinkling in the sugar as you go. When the meringue is stiff and glossy, fold in the ground nuts. Divide the batter between the two circles and spread it to fill them — you should have a pair of layers about ½ inch thick. Bake 1¼ hours, or until the layers are golden brown and completely dried out. They might be slightly soft when hot but should crisp as they cool. Let them cool, then carefully peel off the tinfoil. Store airtight, away from moisture, if you don't plan to use them right away.

To assemble the dessert, beat the ½ cup cream for the topping until it forms firm peaks, then fold in the liqueur. Peel the plastic from the top of the filling and put one baked meringue layer on the filling. Reverse the whole works onto a serving platter. Don't worry if the crust cracks — no one will ever see. Peel the remaining plastic from the filling and top with the other meringue layer, prettier side out. Use the whipped cream to mask the sides completely, then decorate with the remainder, put through a pastry tube or not, depending on your strength for such things at this point.

Black and Blueberry Jam

For about 2½ pints

5 cups barely ripe blackberries
6 cups sugar
1 large lemon
4 cloves
4 cups wild blueberries

In a wide, shallow kettle about 4 to 5 inches deep, combine the blackberries and sugar, crushing as you stir to help start the release of juice. Put the pan over low heat and cook, stirring frequently, crushing the berries as you do, until the sugar is dissolved and you have what amounts to seeds floating in liquid. Strain the mixture to remove the seeds, pressing to get all possible pulp. Discard the seeds and return the rest to the unwashed pan.

Peel a 6-inch strip of rind from the lemon, stud it with the cloves, and add it to the blackberries. Stir in the blueberries, return the pan to low heat, and cook, stirring, until the blueberries have softened and yielded their juice. Raise the heat to medium-high and cook, stirring with greater and greater dedication, until the mixture has thickened to jam consistency. This will take anywhere from 15 to 30 minutes, depending on the heat, the pan, and the ripeness of the blackberries; ripe ones have less pectin, so the riper they are, the longer it'll take.

Test according to your favorite jelling test. I drop a bit on a chilled plate and figure it's done when it stays put. When the jam is ready, stir in the juice of the lemon and pack at once into sterilized jars.

*F*ARMERS' MARKETS

IT USED TO BE, in the bad old days, that the produce department of one's local super did not make the heart leap up. It often seemed the only thing worse than the selection was the quality of what was offered — limp lettuces, badly bruised squash, beans floppy with fatigue. These days the supermarket produce section is a thing of (approximate) beauty, largely thanks to farmers' markets.

That old-fashioned marketing system is flourishing lately, summoned and supported by an ever-waxing American love affair with fresh vegetables and fruits. All over the country supermarkets are at last being forced to compete, not only with farmers' markets but with specialty greengrocers, too. Ironically, the supers are often responding so well, massively improving the quality and variety of the produce they offer, that it's easy to get lazy and neglect the farmers' markets that were partly responsible for driving them to it in the first place.

What a mistake that would be! Only direct contact with the grower gives ordinary food shoppers a chance to get next to the finest produce at affordable prices: corn that is genuinely "fresh picked"; properly small squash, their skins unblemished, an occasional blossom still attached; tomatoes and peaches grown for their taste and harvested — it *can* be done — when they are fully ripe.

There is also, let us not forget to mention, the unique pleasure that comes from giving *all* the money to the farmer, who usually gets only a small fraction of each dollar we spend on food, yet without whom there would be no eats. A special gratification clings to transactions that involve only the producer and the consumer, unassisted by food processors, advertising agencies, strings of middlemen, and two or three long-distance truckers.

In fact, between the superior quality of the vegetables and the moral high ground of buying them directly, shopping at the farmers' markets would be a bargain even if it were expensive. But it isn't, of course; it's cheap. And it's exciting, too, since farmers' market offerings do not have the boring uniformity of mass-produced produce. Instead you find special surprises: giant lettuces like cabbage roses, just about to bolt, huge leaves of Swiss chard, home-garden varieties of squash and beans and potatoes, bouquets of old-fashioned country flowers — nasturtiums, calendulas, cosmos. If you keep an open mind, you can fill your basket without emptying your wallet — and satisfy more than one appetite in the process.

Vegetable Freezing

The number of manuals, textbooks, etc., that will tell you how to properly blanch, cool, dry, and freeze garden produce is nothing short of awesome, as is the detailed nature of the instructions they contain. The reality they fail to address is that, these days, between the root cellar on the one hand and the worldwide food imports that reach to the tiniest hamlet on the other, there is almost no occasion when you want to eat frozen vegetables. Not *plain* frozen vegetables, anyway.

When you come to the end of a long, hard day in the midst of the cold, cold winter, you are most unlikely to exclaim, "Oh, goody, goody, oh joy entire, frozen string beans!" — whereas you might indeed feel jolly to the point of exclamation when you know that a steaming bowl of Full-Dress Minestrone awaits, like Sleeping Beauty, in the freezer. Minestrone, rich with flavor, light as sunshine, a harvest symphony in every spoonful — and all you have to do is heat it up and spoon it down.

To a lesser extent, this is true of just about every vegetable it's worth the bother to freeze, or indeed put up in any way. Canned beets are ho-hum, but pickled beets are fun; frozen green peppers are flabby and dull, as are frozen squash and corn, while frozen Colache, a Mexican stew of squash, beans, and corn (recipe on page 156) is delicious in the extreme. There is no trick to making big vats of harvest delights to freeze for later, but it *is* important to undercook them slightly, since freezing breaks down tissues and reheating won't help things either.

The only exceptions to the "nothing just plain" rule are plain yellow crookneck squash stewed in butter, which holds the fresh taste of summer very well and is infinitely better than the "fresh " yellow summer squash sold in the off-months, and tomatoes, for further disquisition on which see the "Leslie's Autumnal Minuet" chapter on page 159.

✱ Full-Dress Minestrone

Every region in Italy has its own version; this is (loosely) based on the one from Milan. Ingredients and amounts are highly variable — no minestrone recipe worth its pesto should really call for teaspoons and tablespoons — so regard the instructions below as general guidelines.

There are only 2 important things to remember: (1) The seasoning mixture that starts the soup should not be omitted, as it flavors all that comes after, and (2) not too much cabbage.

For about 1½ gallons, approximately 12 to 14 servings

⅓ pound lean salt pork
2 or 3 large cloves garlic
½ cup parsley leaves, flat-leaf parsley preferred
¼ cup olive oil
Finely grated zest (thin, colored outer rind) of 1 lemon
1½ cups thinly sliced onion, about 1 medium
3 quarts water (This is mentioned in the ingredients list because quality is so important. Buy spring water if your tap water's lousy.)
2½ to 3 cups mixed root vegetables — carrots, potatoes, turnips, parsnips (not beets, on account of they bleed), cut in roughly 1-inch chunks
1½ cups fresh shell beans or almost-cooked dried beans (Fresh are much better. Don't forget scarlet runners.)
½ cup medium thin–sliced celery
2 cups sliced (about ¼ inch thick) summer squash or zucchini
½ to 1 cup snap beans, cut into 1-inch lengths
2 cups ripe tomatoes, peeled, seeded, and chopped (Use good canned tomatoes or frozen ones from last year unless the fresh ones are really first rate.)
2 cups fresh peas or diced sugarsnaps, if available (Do not substitute frozen.)
2 cups shredded green cabbage (Savoy is best; do not use red.)
⅓ cup long-grain rice, covered with boiling water, then drained
⅓ cup each minced fresh parsley and basil
Salt to taste

Cut the salt pork into 1-inch cubes, dump into a large pot of boiling water, and turn off the heat. Let sit 5 minutes, then drain. This will remove excess salt.

Combine the pork with the garlic and ½ cup parsley and chop the mixture until it resembles fine hamburger. A processor makes this super-easy, but people have been doing it with sharp knives since time out of mind, and that's not so hard either.

Put the olive oil in a large soup kettle over medium-low heat and add the pork mixture. Stir in the lemon zest and cook, stirring often, until the meat looks melted and the fat is running free. This will take about 20 minutes, toward the end of which it will take all your strength to resist just scooping the stuff out of the pot, spreading it on bread, and wolfing it down.

When the mixture has achieved this attractive state, stir in the onion and cook, stirring, until it is golden — no browner. Add the 3 quarts of water and raise the heat to high. When the liquid boils, add the root vegetables and shell beans, lower heat to a fast simmer, and cook 15 to 20 minutes.

Add the celery, squash, snap beans, and tomatoes and give it 20 minutes more. Now add the peas, cabbage, and rice and cook 20 to 30 minutes more over very low heat. The soup is done as soon as the rice is. Stir in the minced herbs and let them barely wilt, correct the salt, and serve hot, cold, or — an Italian favorite that makes a lot of sense once you get used to it — at room temperature, with plenty of grated Parmesan on the side.

NOTE: I freeze this in 1-quart plastic yogurt containers, leaving about 1 inch for the soup to expand as it freezes. Each container provides 2 servings.

AUTUMN

NEW POTATOES

THE NEIGHBORS have interrupted their daily constitutional to stroll over and watch me dig the potatoes. "*I* really love them just plain," she says, "no butter or anything, just some salt. *He* [a contemptuous nod] likes lots of butter and sour cream on *his*. People think potatoes are fattening, but they're really a very nutritious food and . . ."

At this point she wistfully trails off, giving me the opportunity to leap right in there and say, "Yes, you're right, they *are* great plain. But what I really love is plenty of grease — deep-fried potatoes, crusty potato pancakes sautéed in chicken fat, mashed potatoes with butter and sour cream. Lots of butter and sour cream." I finish with a kind of hideous relish: "I could go for a whole vat of 'em right now."

Okay, so I was feeling mean. I was also, nevertheless, admitting the central dilemma of potato consumption: most delicious and most healthy have little in common. But I take heart from the fact that this dilemma, although central, is not absolute. There are a number of ways to enjoy potatoes that are not ruinously fat-laden, and fall is the perfect time to enjoy them, because fall is new potato time.

New potatoes — even new baking potatoes — are sweet and dense. That light and starchy quality doesn't develop until potatoes have been stored for a while. This means new potatoes are best suited for steaming and boiling and braising, rather than mashing or sautéing. Being very moist, they do not take a crust well and are almost impossible to deep-fry. I like to think this is because a beneficent Providence has arranged things so that apple pie and homemade French fries will not lay their invidious snares in the same season.

Apple pie time is the time for little red new potatoes steamed in their jackets, so sweet and moist they need very little beyond a light spicing of salt and herbs. Hot, they want only the lightest gilding of butter or splash of sweet cream. Cold, they make terrific salads, dressed vinaigrette, not with mayonnaise. For maximum nutrition with minimum calories, consider the application of a curried low-fat yogurt sauce.

My friend Scootch, who was born in Idaho, has the minimalist approach par excellence: She actually enjoys (or appears, at any rate, to enjoy) eating potatoes raw. I must say I do like them plain, with salt, when they have been cooked and cooled. But I must also say that when I am neither in a raving hurry nor on a diet, I'd really rather they were jazzed up a bit.

My Father's Omelette

That gentleman's culinary specialties are few; as a rule he stays out of the kitchen. But this, also (more widely) known as *Omelette Paysanne*, has his name on it in my memory. It was prepared only occasionally, when for whatever reasons he decided to shine at the stove, and it was prepared with what may have been, in retrospect, a somewhat disproportionate amount of ceremony, but it *was* (credit where credit is due) extremely tasty. It still is.

For 2 omelettes, which will serve 4

¼ to ⅓ pound thick-sliced bacon
2 or 3 tablespoons unsalted butter, plus butter for the eggs
4 cups thinly sliced onions, about 3 large
Approximately 1½ pounds new potatoes, cut in ½-inch wedges
Salt and pepper to taste
6 eggs

Fry the bacon crisp, drain it thoroughly, crumble, and reserve. In a large, heavy skillet, slowly melt 2 tablespoons of butter, giving it time to soak into the pan. Add the onions and cook, stirring occasionally, until they are a rich gold-brown with dark brown edges. This will take quite a while; don't try to rush it or you'll miss out on that all-important caramel quality engendered by the slow cooking.

Steam the potatoes over simmering water about 5 minutes, or until they are half-cooked. Spread them out on paper towels to dry. When the onions are ready, remove them from the pan with a slotted spoon and reserve them. There should be enough fat left in the pan to keep the potatoes from sticking; add a tad more if it looks necessary. Then add the potatoes and cook until they are the same color as the onions. This will not happen instantly, but it'll go faster than the onions did.

When the potatoes are tender, add the onions and cook just long enough to reheat them. Add a bit of salt and pepper, remembering that the bacon is salty, and use the mixture to fill a pair of 3-egg omelettes, made according to your own recipe, which is undoubtedly (like my father's untranslatable one) the only right way to make an omelette. Garnish the omelettes with the reserved bacon and serve at once. Alternatively, you may prefer to turn the whole thing into a . . .

🍂 Frittata

Frittatas are essentially omelettes with the filling cooked in instead of folded among. They're a bit drier than omelettes, and a bit less fussy in the timing department, and many people find them easier to make.

To make a frittata of the ingredients in the preceding recipe, prepare the filling as described above. Use a flat spatula to push everything to one side and check out the bottom of the pan. If it looks pretty clean, fine. If it's sporting those crusty bits that announce stickiness, plan to use a new pan for the frittata.

If using the filling pan, just pour in the well-beaten eggs, stir gently, cover, and cook over low heat until the eggs are almost set — about 3 to 4 minutes. Uncover the pan, then slide it under a preheated broiler for about 2 minutes more, to set and brown the top.

If the filling pan is sticky, heat a generous film of butter in a clean one over medium-low heat. Pour in about half the beaten eggs, gently pile on the filling, then add the remaining egg. Stir once or twice, just enough to mix everything up, and cook according to the directions above.

CAUTIONARY NOTE: There is a strong temptation to slip a little cheese in here. It's good with cheese, but it's better without cheese, especially when the potatoes really are new.

🍂 Dumas Salad

According to the *Alice B. Toklas Cookbook*, which is where I got the idea more years ago than I like to remember, the original recipe for this is part of a play called *Françillon* by Alexandre Dumas, Jr. It is also a classic of the

French culinary repertoire, where, for reasons that remain obscure to me, it is known, according to Ms. Toklas, as *salade Japonnaise*. Since it's based on two of Maine's most abundant resources, it might as well be called Salade Down East.

For 6 servings

3 to 4 pounds mussels, picked over, scrubbed, and de-bearded, enough to yield at least 1½ cups meats

Mussel Seasonings: 2 stalks celery, well chopped; 1 branch (several sprigs) parsley, chopped; 1 carrot, chopped; 1 tablespoon minced shallot; and ½ teaspoon whole pepper corns

3 cups light chicken stock

2 pounds waxy new potatoes, as even in size as possible

Approximately ½ cup dry white wine such as Chablis

DRESSING:

½ cup olive oil, the more richly flavored the better

3 to 4 tablespoons tarragon vinegar

½ cup finely minced fresh herbs, parsley predominating, with a little tarragon, thyme, and chive, if possible

Put the mussels and their seasonings in a big kettle and toss well to combine. Cover the pot, put it over high heat, and cook about 10 minutes, or until all the mussels have opened. If fresh, they will produce quite a bit of juice. (See "A Note about Purchased Mussels" on page 89.) Lift out the mussels and strain the stock through cheesecloth, leaving the last sandy bit in the bottom of the pot. You'll need a cup of the stock for the recipe; reserve the remainder to add to fish soup. Pick the mussel meats from the shells and reserve them.

Combine the reserved cup of stock with the chicken stock in a large pan and simmer the whole potatoes therein, stirring occasionally, until they are just tender. (This broth is also useful, though it's too cloudy for clear soups — might as well mix it with the mussel juice, freeze it, and use the whole works for chowder some other day.)

As soon as you can handle the potatoes, while they are still nice and hot, slice them thinly into a large mixing bowl, sprinkling each layer with the wine as you go. If you haven't used a full half cup of wine, pour on the remainder when you get done. Let the potatoes cool, stirring once or twice but not often.

Make the dressing by whisking all the ingredients together. Drain any excess wine from the now-cooled potatoes, pour on the dressing, and mix in the mussel meats. Taste and add salt if necessary, which will depend on the saltiness of the mussels. Chill the salad but don't let it get icy cold. If it has been in the refrigerator, let it warm up a bit before serving, so the flavor can come out.

NOTE: The true Françillon salad is fancier than this one, involving a lot of champagne and truffles. I've never exactly made one — pounds, my dear, of truffles — but I have occasionally topped this off with grilled wild mushrooms (cèpes), and they did indeed make a very tasty contribution. The same cannot be said of cultivated mushrooms, by the way. Adding them is just a waste of mushrooms, energy, and potato salad.

New Potatoes and Green Beans in Hot Coconut Cream

This Indian-inspired preparation really enhances mature, full-flavored green beans. Substantial enough to be dinner's center, it is also delicious served as a side dish beside grilled lamb. The coconut isn't noticeable as such, but you'd miss it if it weren't there.

For 4 main dish or 6 side dish servings

1½ cups medium cream or ¾ cup heavy cream and ¾ cup whole milk
¾ cup unsweetened dried coconut (available at natural food stores)
2 large cloves garlic, coarsely chopped
2 pounds new boiling potatoes, preferably red ones
1¼ pounds fully mature but still tender green beans
2 to 4 fresh hot green peppers (see Note)
2 tablespoons butter
1 heaping teaspoon grated fresh ginger root
2 teaspoons ground cumin
½ teaspoon ground coriander seed
Approximately ½ cup water
About ½ cup lightly piled fresh green coriander leaves, a generous
    handful (optional)
Salt to taste

In a heavy saucepan, combine the cream, coconut, and garlic. Simmer over the lowest possible flame 30 to 40 minutes. While this is going on, wash the potatoes and cut into largish pieces about 1½ inches on the wide face — if you can get potatoes that will be made this size by halving, so much the better. Rinse the beans, cut off the tips but do not tail, and cut into 1-inch lengths. Prepare the peppers (see Note) by mincing into roughly ¼-inch dice. Set vegetables aside.

In a shallow pan large enough to hold everything, melt the butter over low heat, then add the ginger, cumin, and coriander seed. Cook, stirring, 4 to 5 minutes, then add the potatoes and stir until all are coated with the flavored butter. Pour in the water, cover the pan, and cook 10 minutes over low heat; the water should just bubble gently. Add beans and continue to cook, uncovered this time, stirring occasionally, until all the water has cooked away and the vegetables are almost, but not quite, tender, about 10 to 15 minutes more. (Add more water if it cooks away too fast.)

Strain in the coconut-cream mixture, pressing well to get all the liquid. Raise heat to medium and bubble briskly until the beans and potatoes are completely cooked and the cream has reduced to a sauce. Stir in the peppers and coriander leaves and cook just till the peppers turn bright green, about 2 minutes. Adjust the salt and serve at once.

NOTE *about Peppers:* The object is to have a definite bit, but only a bit, of flavor-enhancing hotness. The number of peppers required will depend on your taste and on the nature of the peppers. Jalapeños, especially northern-grown ones, often lose hotness when they are cooked, which cayennes do not. Peppers with the seeds left in are much hotter than the seeded kind. In other words, use your own judgment — just be sure it's "hot but not too hot," whatever that means to you.

SUCCOTASH SEASON

SUCCOTASH, as you remember from grade school, is a corruption of a native American word — *sukqutta-hash, msakwitash,* or *m'siick-quotash,* among others, depending on which native language you're thinking of. There are plenty to choose from, as this famous dish was a staple wherever both corn and beans were major crops, which is to say almost everywhere.

The original, based on field corn and kidney beans cooked in bear grease and/or maple sap, was a great deal heftier than the twentieth-century version, a comparatively bantamweight concoction of sweet corn and fresh green lima beans in cream. They share, however, a common wisdom: Corn and beans, eaten together, create a whole more nourishing than the sum of its parts.

Both corn (a grain) and beans (legumes) contain considerable protein, but those proteins are "incomplete," less nourishing than the protein in meat, eggs, milk, and fish. They are also, however, complementary. Combine them and, hey, presto! Complete protein, just as fortifying, pound for pound, as any hamburger going.

The study of complementary proteins is actually pretty complex (see Note). What it all boils down to, for today's purposes, is that good old succotash, sitting there innocently on one side of the plate (opposite the potatoes, next to the meat) is actually balanced enough to be the center of the meal.

It's certainly delicious enough. Harvest time knows no tastier combination than sweet fresh corn, newly cut from the cob, and the tender baby green lima beans, mixed half and half, lightly seasoned, then drenched with cream. Unless, maybe, it's colache, the southwestern stew made of every good late summer vegetable — not just beans and corn, but squash and tomatoes as well.

Fresh beans and corn are irresistible at harvest, but the beauty of this nourishing pair is just as striking in wintertime, when dry beans, in the form of chili, and dry corn, in the form of corn bread or tortillas, offer robust charms of their own. Needless to say, mixed marriages are not only possible but pleasant: corn bread can accompany a stew of fresh beans, or corn on the cob can form the first course for a dinner of baked dried beans, with no loss of nutritional benefit or aesthetic gratification.

NOTE: Grains and legumes are the world's primary sources of protein. Eked out with small amounts of meat, fish, seeds, and dairy products, they sustain life in almost every culture except those of the industrialized West. But because individual vegetable proteins do not contain the full range of amino acids necessary for human nutrition, they must be combined so that the strengths of one make up for the weaknesses of the other. The best practical guide to this alchemy has for many years been Francis Moore Lappé's *Diet for a Small Planet*. Not only does it offer a detailed explanation of the way complementarity works, but it also provides plenty of helpful charts for those who wish to devise their own recipes and plenty of recipes for those who do not.

September Bean Stew

This dish is at its best in early September, when the fresh shell beans have first come in and the snap beans are still nice and tender.

For 4 main dish servings

1 large yellow onion, chopped small
3 tablespoons butter or bacon drippings
4 cups fresh shell beans, mature but not yet dried — lima, French horticultural, cranberry, etc. — 3½ to 4 pounds in the pod (Frozen beans may be substituted if necessary, but do not use cooked dry beans.)
2 tablespoons snipped fresh oregano or 2 teaspoons dried
2 cups light chicken broth or water
2 cups snap beans cut in 1-inch lengths, about 1 pound
1½ cups peeled, seeded, chopped tomato, about 3 large
½ cup minced fresh parsley
Salt to taste
½ cup sour cream or yogurt, for garnish
1 large lime, cut in wedges, for garnish

In a large, lidded saucepan, cook the onion in the fat over medium heat until it is golden brown. Stir in the shell beans and oregano and turn until all are well coated with fat.

Pour in the broth and bring it to a boil, then lower the heat to medium and cover. Simmer 15 to 20 minutes, or until the beans are almost but not quite tender.

Add the snap beans and tomato and cook, uncovered now, another 10 minutes, or until the snap beans are just tender. The tomato should still be recognizable. Stir in the parsley. When it wilts, taste and add salt as necessary — if you add it sooner, it toughens the beans. The stew is now done. Serve it garnished with dollops of sour cream and lime wedges. There is a lot of liquid in this. That's so you've got something to dip your corn bread in.

Double-Corn Bread

For 6 generous servings

Heavy 10-inch pan, such as a cast-iron skillet
Butter or drippings for the pan
1 cup all-purpose flour

1 cup yellow cornmeal, preferably stone-ground, which, still
   containing the germ, is much more flavorful
4 teaspoons baking powder
1 teaspoon salt
1 heaping tablespoon sugar (optional, but it does bring out the corn
   flavor)
½ teaspoon ground cumin
¼ teaspoon ground cloves
2 eggs, well beaten
⅞ cup milk
⅓ cup butter or meat drippings, melted
¾ cup uncooked corn kernels, about 1 large cob's worth

Preheat the oven to 450°F. Generously grease the pan and put it in to preheat after the oven warms up.

Combine the dry ingredients in a big bowl, stirring thoroughly with a wire whisk. Set aside. Mix together the eggs, milk, and melted fat. Have the corn cut and ready.

When the pan is hot, dump the liquid ingredients onto the dry, then add the corn. Now stir, as briefly as possible, just until the dry ingredients are dampened — maybe 10 strokes. Turn the batter into the preheated pan and return it at once to the oven.

Bake the corn bread 20 to 25 minutes, or until a toothpick comes out clean. The quick cooking at high temperature makes a light bread with a crisp crust, which will be very brown on the bottom. It might be only lightly browned on top, however. Be sure not to overcook it by waiting for the top to color.

VARIATION: Jalapeño corn bread, prettily speckled with bits of hot green pepper, is an instant favorite with almost everyone who tries it, even those who do not ordinarily like hot food. Just add 2 tablespoons to ½ cup seeded, deveined jalapeño peppers, cut into ¼-inch dice. Mix the peppers with the corn kernels first to be sure they're evenly distributed.

✸ *Colache*

Like most harvest stews, colaches are as various as the produce in southwestern markets and the cooks who combine it. This version is more highly spiced than most Mexican ones would be, and except for the fat, which adds considerable flavor, contains no meat. Just about any smoked pork is good, if you do want some meat in it, and crabmeat, stirred in at the very end, is a delicious addition for those who prefer aquatic protein.

For 6 generous servings

3 tablespoons lard, bacon fat, or vegetable oil
1 large onion, cut in rough chunks, about 1½ cups
2 tablespoons snipped fresh oregano or 2 teaspoons dried
1 teaspoon ground cumin
½ teaspoon ground coriander seed
1 pound yellow summer squash, in the approximately 6-inch size, mature but not yet seedy and watery, cut into 1½-inch chunks
1 cup fresh shell beans, about 1 pound in the pod — horticultural, cranberry, scarlet runner, lima
1 cup fresh snap beans cut in 2-inch lengths, about ½ pound
2 large red or green bell peppers, cut in ½-inch cubes, about 1½ cups
¼ to ⅓ cup finely diced fresh hot green chilies — jalapeños, ideally — with some seeds if you want it hot, without if you want it only slightly hot (optional)
Enough ripe tomatoes, peeled and chopped, to make 2½ cups
5 cups corn kernels, plus juice scraped from the cobs, about 8 ears' worth
1 bunch finely sliced green onions (scallions), including an inch of the green part, about ⅓ cup
¼ cup minced fresh coriander
Salt to taste

Put the fat in a large saucepan or shallow kettle over medium heat. When it sizzles, add the onion and cook, stirring often, until it is golden and starting to brown. Stir in the oregano, cumin, and coriander seed, then the squash and beans. Pour in about ⅓ inch of water, just enough to keep the vegetables from burning, cover the pan, and simmer about 10 minutes, or until the vegetables are half-cooked.

Add the snap beans, peppers, chilies, and tomatoes and cook, uncovered, about 15 to 20 minutes more, or until everything is well cooked but not falling apart. Stir in the corn, green onions, and fresh coriander and give it 3 to 4 minutes more, just enough to heat through. Add salt to taste and serve with corn bread, over rice, or, for gala occasions, in a small (roughly 6-pound) pumpkin or winter squash.

To prepare the squash, cut a lid and remove the seeds and enough flesh to make a container, being sure to leave a shell at least 1½ inches thick. Smear the inside with butter and bake in a 350°F. oven about an hour. (Bake it on a table-presentable pan so you don't have to lift and risk breaking it once it's cooked.)

Half-Breed Beans
(Half Chili, Half Boston Baked)

These are both hot and sweet, better with tortillas or corn bread than traditional Boston brown.

For 8 generous servings

4 cups small white beans (pea beans)
½- to ¾-pound slab of lean bacon, the more heavily smoked the better
1 large onion
3 whole cloves
2 to 4 small whole dried red peppers (see Note)
3 tablespoons tomato paste
2 large cloves garlic, crushed
1 medium onion, chopped fine, ¾ to 1 cup
1 tablespoon ground cumin
2 teaspoons dried oregano
1 teaspoon cracked black pepper
¼ teaspoon ground cloves
⅓ cup maple syrup
Garnishes: shredded sharp Cheddar or mild Jack cheese, minced sweet
   red onion, shredded crisp lettuce, sour cream

Put the beans in a kettle and cover generously with boiling water. Put the bacon in a heatproof bowl and similarly cover it. Let all sit until cool, then drain. This will make the meat less salty and the beans less gassy. Set aside the bacon.

Stud the large onion with the cloves and bury it in the beans along with 1 pepper. Cover with cold water to come 2 inches above them and bring the liquid to a simmer. Simmer, partially covered, adding hot water if necessary to keep the beans under the liquid, until they are half-tender, cooked to the point where the skins split if you blow on them. This will take 1 to 3 hours, depending on how long those beans have been sitting on the shelf. Drain them, saving the liquid and discarding the onion and pepper.

Cut the rind from the bacon in a single piece and use it to line the bottom of your bean pot or other heavy, nonmetallic, small-mouthed cooking vessel. Rind side should face into the pot. Cut enough thin slices from the wide face of the meat to blanket the opening of the pot and chop the remainder into roughly ⅓-inch pieces.

Combine the chopped bacon and drained beans with the remaining ingredients except garnishes and turn the works into the pot. Pour in enough of the reserved cooking liquid to barely float the top layer of beans, arrange the bacon slices on top, and cover the pan. Bake in a very low (250°F.) oven 6 to 8 hours, or until beans are very tender, adding more bean liquid (or water) if they look like they're drying out. Uncover the pot for the last 1½ hours to crisp the crust.

NOTE: Whole peppers contribute flavor with minimum heat. The hotter you want the beans, the more broken up (and plentiful) the peppers should be. Use all 4, thoroughly crushed, if you want to lean to the chili side and make your eyebrows sweat.

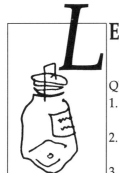

*L*ESLIE'S AUTUMNAL MINUET

QUESTIONS:
1. How did that whole inexplicable business about "the frost is on the pumpkin" get started?
2. Why is an ant better than a grasshopper?
   a.   b.   c.
3. "How doth the little busy bee _____?"
4. How much longer do you think you have to fool around before frost?
5. How long before it starts snowing?
6. How long until spring?
7. What are you going to do about it?

Lois's Tomato Trick

I don't suppose Lois can actually have invented this, but Lois is the one who, confronted with a plethora of perfectly gorgeous ripe tomatoes and the usual dearth of time that besets summer people in autumn, decided to ignore all the rules and just throw the damn things in the freezer. Oh, she did wipe 'em off, and she did put 'em in plastic bags, but that was it.

Well, of course, they didn't hold their shape or texture. What emerged from the freezer indistinguishable from billiard balls became, upon thawing, a bunch of mighty dejected-looking collapsifications — still red as red can be, lying at the bottom of a bowlful of clear yellow juice. Yet while definitely not much in the looks department, Lois's tomatoes did turn out to retain all the fresh flavor even the fussiest could desire.

They're ideal for soup, do fine in stews, and make a lovely, very nearly instant tomato sauce so successful I sometimes freeze tomatoes at the height of the season and thaw them the next day just for that purpose. No recipe is required. Just allow some frozen whole tomatoes to thaw and carefully pour off the juice (it does have some flavor and vitamins and probably should be saved for soup). Put the tomatoes through a food mill set loose so you get a rough purée without any skins or ground seeds in it. Heat some butter — about 2 tablespoons for each cup of purée. Add the purée and cook just long enough to heat it through. Add salt to taste and serve with pasta, grilled eggplant, baked fish — anywhere a light, rich-flavored tomato sauce might go well.

The Best Way I Know to Put Up House-Ripened Tomatoes

Peel, seed, and chop them into big chunks. Cover the bottom of a wide (not iron or aluminum) soup pot with a thin layer of olive oil, butter, or both. Heat the fat to sizzling and add enough of the prepared tomatoes to fill the pot one-third full.

Bring them to a boil, lower the heat, and simmer about 3 minutes. If you want to add fresh greenery — parsley, chervil, dill, or coriander — add it after the tomatoes are off the heat.

Let them cool at room temperature, then pack, leaving plenty of head space for expansion, and freeze. They'll stay fresh tasting until April if the power doesn't go off. It is in the context of these frozen preserves that the formerly vast appeal of stewed tomatoes is finally understood.

The continuing vast popularity of green tomato mincemeat can be attributed only to how many it uses up. Dilled green tomato pickles are much better, and much easier, although they are less efficient. Put a grape leaf in the jar to give its flavor and keep the pickles crisp. This is an ideal use for green cherry tomatoes, since they are about all the green tomato pickle you would want at any one time. All else failing, you can put them in your martinis and start a trend.

✳ *Fried Green Tomatoes*
(Southeastern-Style, with Bacon and Cheese)

Cut the tomatoes crosswise in slices about ⅓ inch thick and let them drain 5 to 10 minutes. Dip them in milk, then flour, then milk again, then cornmeal seasoned with lots of pepper but no salt. Let dry on a cookie sheet in a single layer for 10 minutes or so, then repeat the milk, cornmeal, and drying stages.

Meanwhile, try out two slices of bacon per tomato in a big, heavy black iron skillet. Drain the bacon, saving the fat. Leave a ⅓-inch layer of fat in the pan and put it over medium-high heat. When it's good and hot, add tomato slices in a single layer. Fry them about 3 minutes per side, or until well browned. If you're doing a lot, keep the first batches warm in a low oven, in a single layer on a brown paper–lined sheet.

Sprinkle grated sharp Cheddar cheese over the hot tomatoes just before serving so the rich, golden brown crust is jeweled with the freshly melted shreds.

The bacon goes along, too, of course, and so do the biscuits, the honey, and the Frank's Louisiana Hot Sauce.

On Putting Up Herbs

I dried my own for years, in spite of the difficulty of achieving, on the fogbound Maine coast, that famous dry, breezy, dark attic universally called for in the homesteading manuals. Now, however, so many capable serious farmers, herb growers, and similar specialists offer very good dried herbs I seldom bother.

And, of course, fresh herbs are now easier to get. Season extenders make my own available for nine months or so, and the expanded market among my fellows has encouraged local storekeepers to offer them as well. Nevertheless, the desire to squirrel up all that green and lovely flavor stubbornly persists, as a result of which plenty of herbs do too, largely in the form of pesto and herb butters, largely in the freezer.

You will notice I have made no mention of plain old good-for-about-six-weeks frozen herbs, whether chopped, made into ice cubes, or tenderly blanched, chilled, dried on six thousand paper towels, and wrapped in individual portions in little plastic bags. From the tone of the preceding, you know why.

Freezer Pesto

The thing to remember when making pesto for the freezer is that it is the oil and cheese, which, having absorbed it, are saving the basil flavor. The actual mashed-up basil itself is, after the manner of frozen herbs, incapable of remembering much after the first couple of weeks. For maximum basil-flavor retention, it is important to be sure the pesto is very thoroughly puréed, even if you prefer it chunky under other circumstances.

The other even more important thing to keep in mind is that garlic often behaves strangely when frozen. Sometimes it intensifies, sometimes it fades away to nothing, and sometimes it acquires an unpleasant sweet/acrid flavor about which it is unnecessary to speak further. Leave it out, therefore, when preparing pesto to freeze, and add it fresh, after thawing, right before you put the pesto on whatever you're putting it on.

Herb Butters

These can be made of single herbs — delicate ones such as chervil, for instance, are better saved in this than any other way — or combinations. Allow 1 cup of salted butter for each loosely packed cup of herbs.

Chop the greenery very fine, put it in the corner of a tea towel, make the towel into a bag, and squeeze mightily to remove all possible juice. Beat the butter until it is soft, then beat in the purée.

Spread the mixture in an even 1-inch layer on a piece of plastic wrap, cover it with another piece, making sure the fit is snug, and freeze solid. Use a sharp serrated knife to cut the frozen sheet into 1-inch cubes, rewrap securely, refreeze at once, and use within about 6 months. The cubes equal about a tablespoon each and are quite strong in flavor, designed to be used for their seasoning power. One or two cubes is about right for a cup of cream sauce, as an example. If you want to make the kind of herb butter used as an instant sauce, use 1½ cups butter for each cup of herbs or blend each cube with half its volume again in butter at serving time.

Concerning the Canning Kettle

The most important thing to remember is that very few people need anywhere near as many pickles as most pickle recipes (and cucumber plants) would have the unsuspecting believe.

They don't need as much jam, either. Ditto jelly, preserves, conserves, marmalade, and chutney. Even if you eat jam every blessed morning of your life, even if your offspring subsist largely on peanut butter and jelly (in which case they probably prefer the sort from the store), even if you always put jam in the birthday cakes — that still only works out to maybe fourteen pints a year, say sixteen if you're piggy.

"But jam makes such wonderful *gifts*," you are saying. "Always ready when a small house present is needed or a birthday comes up unexpectedly." Well, yes and no. The truth is that the people who like making preserves tend to hang out with the same sort of people. These people, being overloaded with assorted jams of their own, do not really need or want any of yours, though they will, of course, be polite.

FINAL NOTE: I hate to mention it just now, when the upshot of summer is so much with us in the preservation department, but the truth is that apples are almost as seasonal as strawberries, and though they will be *available* in February, they won't be very good. If you want first-rate applesauce right through the winter, you'd better put some by pretty soon.

R OAST PIG REVISITED

WHAT, IF ANYTHING, comes to mind when you hear those famous names Bobo and Ho-ti? Do they, I hope, make you think of Charles Lamb's famous "A Dissertation Upon Roast Pig"?

Having just reread the plausible tale of how Bobo, that "great lubberly boy . . . fond of playing with fire," inadvertently invented the art of cooking meat, and having found both stirring narrative and masterly culinary musing as good as they ever were, I hereby heartily recommend that you go forth and do likewise.

If for some reason your local library has, as mine does, more books about Lamb than by him, look for the dissertation in English textbooks of the old-fashioned sort, or in one of those portmanteau popular chestnut compendia of which we hear so little lately.

These latter are treatlike, Lamb or no Lamb. The one in which I finally found the essay, for instance, is a wonderful collection of ancient wheezers called (I swear) *A Treasury of the Familiar.*

Where else could the nostalgia-prone reader find gathered Oscar Wilde's "Requiescat" (set right before the Roast Pig) and William Ross

Wallace's "The Hand That Rocks the Cradle Is the Hand That Rules the World" (immediately post-Porker)?

In this truly gem-studded treasury, "Over the Hill to the Poorhouse," twenty-one stanzas worth, is followed by a paragraph from Lincoln's first annual message to Congress (1861), then "The Lost Sheep," Luke 15:4–7, then a snippet concerning prayer lifted from *Idylls of the King*, and *then* a bit of "Why I Went to the Woods," by Henry David Thoreau. Exhilarating, to say the least.

To return to our piggies:

"There is no flavor comparable, I will contend, to that of the crisp, tawny, well-watched, not over-roasted, *crackling*, as it is well called — the very teeth are invited to their share of the pleasure at this banquet in overcoming the coy, brittle resistance — with the adhesive oleaginous — O call it not fat — but an indefinable sweetness growing up to it."

The crisply roasted outside of a proper suckling pig is indeed incomparably delicious, but hardly a dish for every day. The crisply roasted outside of a properly done pork roast, on the other hand, is not only far from awful, but it's also quite easy and cheap (comparatively speaking) to achieve, and fall, I would like to point out, is an excellent time to seek good pork that has been locally grown. Increasingly, rural entrepreneurs are raising meat as well as vegetables and selling it to those who'd like a break from the chemical-laced, growth-forced meat of the supermarket.

Here in Maine we have the excellent "Producer to Consumer" brochure listing direct sources for meat, vegetables, and all manner of farm products. Other states have similar guides, pamphlets, and miscellaneous directories, available through the marketing departments of the bureaus of agriculture. The classified ads are also likely sources, and the more rural the district, the easier it all is.

Not all of it is wonderful, of course. Caveat emptor applies no matter where the buying is done. One fellow I know raised a whole gang of hogs on rather more fishmeal than he ought, producing pork that, while indisputably organic, was a bit more flavorful than anyone had bargained for. Home-raised meat is generally pretty good, however, and if it isn't, there's somebody to complain to. (To me, the "meat" sections of the supermarkets are now tied with the "breakfast food" aisles for the title "Most Surreal in Store." I particularly like the slice of ham with the picture of the slice of ham on it.)

Complaints duly registered, alternatives duly emphasized, we can return to the pleasures of cooking the stuff. Pork is one of the easiest meats to cook well, adaptable to all manner of preparations, from the simplest to the most elaborate, difficult to overcook unless you really try. Don't forget an internal temperature of 137°F. has been found to be sufficient to kill any *trachinae*, so cooking to 150°F. or 160°F., still far less than old-fashioned cookbooks recommend, should give you an ample margin of safety. If you follow those outmoded instructions and wait until it's 175 degrees in there, you might as well just cook up your shoes and be done with it.

 Crisp-Skin Roast Pork
(Old-Fashioned, with Mushroom Stuffing)

For 6 generous servings (Make dinner for 4 and save some; it's delicious cold.)

A 4- to 5-pound pork loin roast*

STUFFING AND PREPARATION:
12 ounces chopped mushrooms, enough to make 3½ cups
½ cup minced shallots, about 4 large
⅔ cup dry bread crumbs, fine but not powdered
Pinch of ground saffron (optional)
1 cup lightly packed parsley tips, minced fine (measured before mincing)
½ teaspoon salt
1 egg
1 tablespoon brandy
2 tablespoons dried thyme leaves (Do not use powdered.)
Approximately ¼ teaspoon freshly grated nutmeg
Kitchen string
Pepper, salt, flour

BROTH AND SAUCE:
1 medium onion, outer skin removed, dirty root cut off, otherwise unpeeled, stuck with 4 cloves
1 large carrot, peeled
2 to 3 inner celery stalks, with leaves
6 peppercorns
1 small bay leaf
⅔ cup strong red wine such as zinfandel
2 tablespoons flour

---

*Our passion for all things lean means most pork roasts have had their outer fat layer trimmed to a mere suggestion. If you want the crisp crackling of which Lamb so eloquently speaks, be sure to ask for one with the fat layer intact.

Making the stuffing and broth base for the sauce takes quite a while. Feel free to do these things a day in advance.

Begin by boning the meat (many butchers will do this for you). Put the bone in a shallow pan with the onion and carrot and roast in a 375°F. oven about 1 hour, or until richly browned.

While the bone is cooking, wipe the mushrooms for the stuffing with a damp towel, then cut off the stems flush with the caps. Save the stems. Open up the pork and cut out all easily removable lumps of fat from the interior. Put a few of the lumps in a wide skillet over low heat and cook until they've shed a generous layer of fat, then discard them.

Chop the mushroom caps into roughly ½-inch pieces. Add them to the skillet, and turn up the heat. Fry the mushrooms, stirring with a flat spatula, until they have shed all their moisture, reduced to about a third of their former volume, and started to turn a rich brown. Lower heat once the liquid has boiled off, so they don't burn.

When the bone has browned, transfer it and the vegetables to a small kettle or large saucepan. (Save the roasting pan with the fat in it and you'll be all ready to make hotel roast potatoes to go with the meat.) Add the celery, peppercorns, bay leaf, and reserved mushroom stems to the bone pot. Pour in enough cold water to cover the bone completely and cook the broth over medium-low heat 2½ to 3 hours, or until the flavor has been extracted from the solids. Strain the broth, put it over medium-high heat, and reduce to about 1 cup of liquid. Reserve.

Meanwhile, the mushrooms are, of course, done. Add the shallots, stir well, and cook, stirring, over low heat, just until they wilt. Transfer the mixture to a bowl and add the bread crumbs, saffron, parsley, and salt. Stop here if you're preparing in advance; otherwise add the egg and mix well.

When ready to roast, allow the meat to come to room temperature and preheat the oven to 350°F. Roll up the meat to see which outside part will be tucked under and remove all fat from that part. Score the remaining fat into diamonds, cutting down to but not into the meat.

Turn the roast fat side down and open it up on the work surface. The interior will be of uneven thickness. Holding a sharp knife blade parallel to the work surface, level with the low point of the roast, slice outward through the thicker parts of the meat so they open like a book. Do not cut all the way through to the edge. The sheet of meat will still not be even, but it'll be flatter and more level than before.

Sprinkle the brandy over the meat. Rub the thyme to powder and sprinkle that on, then the nutmeg. Rub everything in well. If you haven't already done so, add the egg to the mushroom mixture and spread the stuffing over the surface of the meat, pressing it in well, then fold the cut parts back together and roll up the roast. Tie securely in several places.

Grind a generous dusting of pepper over the fat, sprinkle with salt, dredge with flour, then rub the flour into the cracks. Position a rack over a shallow roasting pan and pour in just enough water to keep the juices from catching and burning — about ¼ inch. Put the meat on the rack, fat side up, and roast 25 minutes per pound, or until a meat thermometer registers 150°F. Be sure the thermometer is in the meat, not the stuffing.

Remove the meat to a platter and keep it warm. The pan will now contain mostly fat. Pour it off and reserve, leaving any meat juices behind in the roasting pan. Pour the wine into the pan and set it aside.

Measure 1½ tablespoons of the fat into a saucepan and stir in the 2 tablespoons flour. Cook, stirring, over medium heat until the mixture is lightly browned, then stir in the reserved bone broth. Add the wine from the roasting pan, scraping to get all the tasty bits. (If there are juices under the fat in the cup, discard the fat, then add the juices.) Raise the heat slightly and bubble the sauce, stirring frequently, until it is thickened and smooth.

Remove the string, carve the meat in ½-inch slices, and serve with the gravy on the side.

VARIATION: This is delicious with wild mushrooms in the stuffing, especially *cèpes* (*porcini, Boletus edulis*, and relations). Just substitute fresh for cultivated ones cup for cup in their season. Out of season, use a handful of dried ones to boost the flavor of cultivated mushrooms. Cut those back by about a cup, and add the chopped, soaked dried mushrooms toward the end of the cooking. Mushroom soaking liquid should replace some of the water for the bone broth.

 Basic Pork Scaloppini

For each portion, you will need a ¼-inch-thick slice of boneless meat, cut from a section that is wide and smooth, with no connecting membranes that will divide it when it is pounded. This could be loin or leg (fresh ham) or the wider end of a butt roast.

Trim off any fat from the edges, then put the meat between 2 sheets of waxed paper or plastic wrap. Pound it gently with a meat-pounder or rolling pin, working from the center outward, until it is approximately ⅛ inch thick. It must be uniform to cook evenly, and it must be thin to cook quickly, but exact measurements are not important.

When the required number of scaloppini have been pounded, they can be cooked at once or refrigerated, separated by sheets of plastic wrap, for up to a full day.

To cook, choose a heavy sauté pan or skillet large enough to hold the meat in one layer (if necessary, use 2 pans). Heat a film of fat in the pan, using half unsalted butter and half refined vegetable oil (to keep the butter from burning). As soon as the fat is hot, dust the scaloppini lightly with flour and slide them into the pan. Turn the heat to high and fry about 3 minutes, then turn and give the other side the same length of time. (Keep the heat high; they must cook quickly or they will be tough.)

That's it. As soon as they're cooked through, they're done. And very tasty, too, served with nothing more than a wedge of lemon and a sprinkling of chopped parsley.

Pork Scaloppini Piccata

This recipe takes about 30 minutes, start to finish. Served with French bread and a big salad, it's light, elegant, and fast, fast, fast.

For 2

2 large boneless pork chops cut ¼ inch thick (see recipe on page 167), about ½ pound
Grated zest (thin, colored outer rind) of 1 large lemon
¼ cup flour
4 tablespoons unsalted butter
1 tablespoon olive oil
¼ cup white wine or water
Juice of the lemon
1 tablespoon minced capers (optional, use 'em if you've got 'em)
Pepper

Make the chops into scaloppini as described in the recipe on page 167. Combine the lemon zest and flour, then use the mixture to flour the meat. There will be some flour left over. Fry as in the previous recipe, using 2 tablespoons of the butter and all of the olive oil.

When the meat is cooked, put it on prewarmed plates. Pour the wine or water into the pan and cook over low heat, stirring, until the browned bits are loosened. Add the lemon juice, capers, and remaining butter. Stir to combine, then pour over the meat. Grind a bit of pepper over each chop and serve at once. Good cold too, especially as sandwich material or part of a composed salad.

✿ Pork Sate with Peanut Sauce

In Indonesian cooking, a sate means grilled meat cooked on skewers.

For 4 to 6 servings

Lean cut of pork (loin, leg, shoulder), allowing 8 to 12 ounces per person
1 pound salted crunchy-style peanut butter (freshly ground, without extra oil)
½ cup dry sherry
⅓ cup tamari or other aged soy sauce
¼ cup brown sugar
3 to 4 cloves garlic, crushed
Pinch of powdered ginger
1 teaspoon to 2 tablespoons crushed red hot pepper (to taste)
Thin bamboo skewers

Remove all removable fat and cut the pork into 1½-inch cubes, allowing 8 to 10 cubes per person. Bring a large kettle of lightly salted water to a boil and add the pork cubes. Turn off the heat and let them sit 1 minute. Drain the meat and spread it out to cool, lightly covered.

To make the sauce, put the peanut butter in a deep bowl. Work in the sherry (mixture will be stiff). Stir in the tamari, then add the brown sugar, crushed garlic, ginger, and hot pepper (2 tablespoons will make it extremely hot). Mix the cooled pork cubes with the sauce, making sure each piece is coated. Marinate in the refrigerator overnight, up to 2 days.

Make a charcoal fire that will provide a good bed of coals. Soak the bamboo skewers in cold water for about an hour, then thread the pork cubes onto the skewers, about 4 cubes on each one. Catch any marinade that drips off and combine it with the marinade left in the bowl, adding enough water to make a sauce you can spoon over the meat as it cooks (the sauce should have the consistency of thick applesauce). Put the grilling rack about 6 inches above the fire, let it get hot, then lay on the skewers. Cook 5 minutes, then turn over. Cook another 5 minutes, until the underside is quite brown, then turn again and start basting with the sauce. Keep turning and basting 10 to 15 minutes longer, until the juice from a cut piece flows clear and the crust of peanut sauce is firm.

*T*HROUGH THE CIDER MILL

HARD CIDER is such a delicious beverage — so piquant, so luscious, so thirst quenching — it's easy to see why fermented apple juice was the most popular drink of Colonial times. Right up to the turn of this century, cider was plentiful and cheap everywhere around the country. In many parts of rural America, it was as common as water and, quite often, a great deal safer to drink.

But hard cider *does* have alcohol in it — from 3 to 8 percent and sometimes (though not often) more. Naturally, it has been a major target for prohibitionists from the earliest days of our history.

Starting in the 1830s, whole orchards were felled by teetotalers seeking to destroy the demon at its source. And where prohibitionists failed, progress has often succeeded. Some of America's finest cider orchards once were in Newark, New Jersey. One way and another, by the time the "Great Experiment" failed, native cider was nearly extinct.

Nearly, but not quite. Cider is still the do-it-yourselfer's dream. Whole books have been written, detailing every step of the process, from planting the right apple trees to proper aging procedures.

For those with modest ambitions, it's easy to get an approximation — all it takes is some unpasteurized, natural apple juice, commonly called sweet cider. Procure some of same, put it in the refrigerator, and keep your eye on it. At somewhere between two and seven weeks, depending on how old it was when you bought it, the age of the apples when they were pressed, etc., the cider will start to ferment. Little bubbles will start rising, and a slight whooshing will be heard when the cap is unscrewed.

Unscrew the cap, very slightly, just enough to let a bit of the gas escape (thus preventing explosions), and let the process continue until you like the taste. At first you will have "fizzy cider," about 4 percent alcohol. Next you will have hard cider, about 8 or 9 percent alcohol. And then, almost before you know it, you will have vinegar. Drink it up, therefore, as soon as it's ready.

This is not, I need hardly add, a very sophisticated product, but it's a lot better than most of what's being sold as hard cider at the moment. Although one or two small cider makers are trying to revive the industry, the native article effectively does not exist commercially — unless you want to count things like apple wine, which I'd rather not, thank you. On the other hand, the imported stuff from France, England, and Canada is neither as tasty nor as natural as it would be in a better world. Furthermore, the imports tend to be expensive, while cider should be an everyday drink, as affordable as beer.

The refrigerator routine works well enough, but it isn't instant and it does take up a lot of space. Impatient types and those with small refrigerators may prefer to fake it by mixing pure, unsweetened apple juice half and half with dry white wine. The result is a drink of sprightly fruitiness and low alcoholic content, which, if it doesn't much resemble the hard cider of our forebears, does serve well enough for both quaffing and cooking.

 Mulled Cider

The tastier the cider, the fewer spices are needed, so there's no recipe that shouldn't be changed to suit the ingredients on hand. Cooking will change the flavor of both cider and spices, and long cooking will make the whole works taste stale. Be sure to make several small batches if you're serving mulled cider over a long period or keep it warm over very low heat indeed.

For 1 quart, 4 to 6 servings depending on mug size and possibility of embellishment with alcohol

1 quart sweet cider (pure apple juice) or hard cider
4-inch cinnamon stick
1 teaspoon allspice berries
½ teaspoon whole cloves
Either a 3-inch piece of vanilla bean *or* ½ teaspoon cardamom seeds *or* 2 roughly 4- by ½-inch lengths of orange peel

Combine everything in a heavy, narrow pan that is impervious to acid. (Some Teflon-type coatings absorb odors, by the way. Be sure if you use one that it's been thoroughly cleaned, with baking soda if necessary.) Put the pan over low heat and cook, stirring occasionally, just until bubbles begin to rise around the edge. Serve at once, with or without rum, applejack, or bourbon to fuddle the senses further.

This produces an agreeably spicy, still strongly apple-flavored drink. If you want the spice flavor stronger, combine apple juice and spices an hour or so in advance of heating.

Hot Buttered Cider with Rum

For 6 to 8 servings

Ingredients for Mulled Cider (recipe on page 171)
Dash angostura bitters
1 cup light rum
¼ cup dark rum
Approximately 2 tablespoons butter

Proceed as described in Mulled Cider recipe. When the cider is hot, add the bitters and take the pan from the heat. Stir in the rums, pour the mixture into heated cups, and top each with a roughly ¼-inch pat of butter.

Cider Syrup for Pancakes and Pies

This is a thick, sweet syrup useful just about anywhere maple syrup would be — on waffles and griddlecakes, over ice cream, etc. — and it's great instead of corn syrup in the making of pecan pie. Like maple syrup, it will mold if kept at room temperature but lasts indefinitely when refrigerated.

For about 1 pint

1 quart pure apple juice
¼ to ½ cup sugar

Taste the apple juice for sweetness, remembering it will be concentrated, and decide on sugar proportion according to your taste for sweet. Don't forget you can always add a bit more at the end.

Combine the juice and sugar in the heaviest possible acid-resistant pan (see Mulled Cider recipe on page 171 for Teflon caveat). Cook, stirring occasionally, over the lowest possible heat until the sugar has completely dissolved and the liquid has reduced to about 2 cups. That's it. If you can it, you can keep it at room temperature until it's opened, and, of course, it will be fine in the freezer.

Braised Short Ribs and Apples in Cider Sauce

For 4 servings

2½ pounds lean, meaty beef short ribs
Flour to dust, about 2 tablespoons
2 tablespoons unsalted butter
1 tablespoon vegetable oil
4 cups chopped onion, about 2 large
2½ cups hard cider or 1¼ cups each pure apple juice and dry white wine (see page 170)
1 large carrot, cut in fat coins, about ½ cup
2½ cups firm, tart apples, cut in 1-inch chunks, about 2 large
2 tablespoons flour
1 teaspoon coarsely cracked black pepper
Salt to taste

Trim all outside fat from the short ribs and dust them with flour. In a deep, noncorrodible stew pan, heat the butter and oil over medium heat until they are almost smoking. Add the meat, turn the heat as high as you can get it without burning things or scorching the fat, and brown the meat, turning it frequently with tongs.

Remove and reserve the meat. Pour off and save all but a thin layer of the fat. Put the pan over medium heat, add the onions, and sauté until they are well browned.

Return the meat to the pan, add the cider, and turn the heat to medium-high. As soon as the liquid simmers, reduce heat to low and cover the pan. Cook the ribs 1½ hours, then add the carrot and cook 1 hour more. Add the apple.

In a cup or small bowl, combine 2 tablespoons of the reserved fat with the 2 tablespoons flour. When the mixture is perfectly smooth, thin it with some of the cooking liquid, then pour the whole works into the stew and stir well.

Cook, uncovered, about 20 minutes more, or until the sauce is smooth and slightly thickened and the meat is completely tender. Add the pepper and salt to taste. There will be a lot of sauce. You need it for the mashed potatoes.

QUESTION: What do Old Foxwhelp, Engleton Styre, Handsome Norman, Black Taunton, and Spreading Redstreak have in common?

ANSWER: They are all the names of old English apples considered especially fine for cider making.

S AVING A SAVORY HEIRLOOM
The Sauerkraut Story

JUDGING FROM the amount of play it gets lately, I fear sauerkraut may be about to slip into the mists of history. Where once this deliciously pickled cabbage was a staple food of winter, locally manufactured, if not homemade, everywhere in the northern two-thirds of the country and consumed weekly, if not daily, in all but the haughtiest households, it is now thought of (when it's thought of at all) as a minor relish adjunct for frankfurters, eaten almost inadvertently on the street or at the ballpark.

What a comedown! Mostly it's due to the wide range of fresh vegetables now available year-round. There's no more "six weeks' want" between Christmas and springtime, when even the root cellar is running bare and sources of vitamin C are in short supply. We don't *need* salt-cured cabbage these days, any more than we need salt-cured meat. Ham, however, shows no signs of fading into oblivion, and neither would kraut, I can't help feeling, if the well-made article could just get wider attention.

Well-made — ah, there's the rub. All too often what currently passes for sauerkraut is a mushy, acid imitation of what should be a crisp, bright-flavored, and highly refreshing pickle. Neither excessively salty nor unpleasantly sour, fresh unpasteurized sauerkraut is an excellent tonic, especially for those who have been eating a diet rich in meat and dairy products.

Further, unprocessed kraut is a living product, like natural cheese and wine, in which the organisms that converted the fresh material to the pickled are still present. Though most of the bacteria natural to sauerkraut cannot survive in the human intestinal tract, some health experts believe eating unpasteurized kraut (or miso or yogurt) after taking a course of antibiotics will help restore the internal balance undone by these powerful drugs.

For aesthetics, therefore, for utility, for the sake of posterity, if it comes to that, eschew canned kraut and buy the fresh, unpasteurized product, which can still be found at any reputable delicatessen and not a few supermarkets (look in the refrigerator case). And once you get it, treat it with respect. All kraut should be briefly rinsed with cold water to rid it of excess salt, but no kraut should be endlessly soaked, cooked forever, or otherwise abused. One does not think of it as delicate, but it is. Good, too.

Old-Fashioned Slow-Cooked Sauerkraut with Apples and Onions

This is usually served with fatty meat such as pork chops, goose, or sausage, but it is also delicious with fish, a classic accompaniment to pike in Hungary and Poland, countries where sauerkraut is still a national treasure.

For 4 to 6 servings

3 tablespoons butter or meat drippings (goose fat is particularly tasty)
1 large onion, chopped coarse, about 1½ cups
2 large carrots, chopped coarse, about ¾ cup
2 large cooking apples, peeled, cored, and sliced into wedges, about 2 cups
2 pounds fresh sauerkraut, briefly rinsed in cold water and drained
¼ cup plus 2 tablespoons gin
Cheesecloth
1 bay leaf
3 or 4 large, well-branched stalks parsley
10 peppercorns
5 cloves
1 cup chicken broth

Heat the fat in a heavy skillet over medium heat. When it sizzles, add the onions and carrots and sauté until they are wilted and just starting to brown. When vegetables are cooked, combine them with the apples, sauerkraut, and ¼ cup of the gin and transfer to a presentable shallow casserole, roughly 1½ quarts. Make a little bag from the cheesecloth. Put the bay leaf, parsley, peppercorns, and cloves in the bag and tie it up. Bury it in the middle of the casserole, pour the broth over everything, tightly cover the pan, and bake in a 350°F. to 375°F. oven 1 to 1½ hours. It's not really fussy. The important thing is to let it sit in a warm place about 5 minutes after it comes out of the oven, to reabsorb some of the juice. After this rest period, sprinkle it with the remaining gin and serve at once.

 Hot-and-Sour Noodles
(A One-Dish Dinner)

Though most sources credit the ancient Romans with inventing sauerkraut, there is substantial evidence that, as so often happened, the Chinese were there first. This fragrant, filling variation on a northern Chinese peasant classic is easy, speedy, inexpensive, exotic, low in calories and cholesterol . . . just about perfect, in other words, though not for the faint-hearted. To be at its best it should be coarse, both garlicky and hot.

For 2 full meal–sized servings

6 ounces fresh sauerkraut
4 stalks celery, about 1 cup prepared
1 large bunch scallions (green onions), about ½ cup prepared
1 small green pepper, about ¾ cup prepared
2 tablespoons peanut oil or bland vegetable oil
4 or 5 small dried hot red peppers, each broken into 3 or 4 pieces
1 tablespoon Szechwan peppercorns (brown pepper, flower pepper)*
2 large cloves garlic, minced coarse, about 1 tablespoon
8 ounces fresh Chinese egg noodles* or 5 ounces dried
3 ounces boneless lean pork, about 1 large chop's worth
1½ cups warm chicken broth
3 tablespoons hoisin sauce*
1 tablespoon dark sesame oil*

Put on a large kettle of water to boil for the noodles. Rinse the kraut briefly in very cold water and drain thoroughly, then transfer it to a mixing bowl. Cut celery into match sticks and add. Slice scallions very thin, including about 2 inches of the green part. Reserve about 3 tablespoons for garnish and put the rest in the mixing bowl. Slice the green pepper on the diagonal into the thinnest possible shreds and add. Toss the vegetables together until they are completely mixed, being sure the

---

*Ingredients available at specialty and Oriental groceries

strands of kraut don't remain clumped up. Fingertips are the best mixing tool.

Put a wok over medium-high heat, add the 2 tablespoons oil, and warm to sizzling. Add the hot pepper, including the seeds, and the Szechwan pepper. Cook, stirring constantly, until the red pepper has turned a deep mahogany brown, 1 or 2 minutes at the most. At once lower the heat to medium, stir in the garlic, and cook, stirring, until the garlic starts to change color. Turn off the heat under the wok, remove the solids with a slotted spoon, and stir them into the vegetable mixture.

By now the noodle water is boiling. Put in the noodles and leave to cook, allowing about 6 minutes for the fresh ones and 9 to 10 for the dried. The noodles are done as soon as they are tender. While the noodles are cooking, put the serving bowls on the back of the stove to warm and slice the pork on the diagonal into the thinnest, broadest slices you can get.

About 4 minutes before the noodles are set to be done, reheat the wok over high heat until the oil is almost smoking. Add the pork and fry, stirring constantly, until it is completely cooked. Stir in the broth and hoisin sauce, then the vegetable mixture.

Drain the noodles and toss them with the sesame oil. By the time the noodles are coated with the oil, the sauce mixture should be boiling hot. If it isn't, keep them warm until the sauce boils. Divide the noodles between the warmed bowls and ladle the sauce over them, making sure each portion gets it share of the soup. Garnish with the reserved scallions and serve at once.

*T*HE PEAR PERPLEX

"ALTHOUGH IT IS already a good long time ago, I well remember. . . . Our meal that evening was composed of a cream of pumpkin soup with little croutons fried in butter, a young turkey roasted on the spit accompanied by a large country sausage and a salad of potatoes, dandelions and beetroot, and followed by a big bowl of pears cooked in red wine and served with whipped cream."

That's "the king of chefs," Auguste Escoffier, writing, in 1912, about an early November vacation in the French countryside, being quoted (in

1960) by Elizabeth David, and proving that some things don't change. The marvels of modern food transportation notwithstanding, gastronomy is still a seasonal art —if pumpkins come, can pears be far behind?

In my experience, pears are not usually what one might call an exciting fruit — widely available throughout fall and winter, yes; inexpensive, yes; tasty, yes. But not exciting. Yet in my experience, often enough to keep me buying and hoping, pears are one of the most thrilling fruits in existence.

You know how it happens: People will be standing around in the kitchen, just being casual, and somebody will start to eat one of the pears that is lying there in the fruit bowl the way pears usually *are* lying there in the fruit bowl at this time of year, and the person's face will suddenly assume this peculiar yet familiar look of beatitude and disbelief. If the person is of a kindly, sharing disposition, they will say something like, "Wow, taste this pear!" If they are, on the other hand, tenacious of their pleasures, they will veil their eyes, say nothing, and munch on in meditative silence. I, for one, can scarcely blame them. A perfectly ripened pear, be it Bartlett or Comice, Anjou or Bosc, is well worth hoarding.

Getting Good Pears

Although they are closely related to apples, pears are a much fussier fruit. The trees are less adaptable than apple trees, and the pears themselves are more delicate — easily thrown off their ripening stride and very vulnerable to bruising as soon as they are anywhere near edible. Still, if there were any justice, almost all pears on the market would be good ones, because pears are one of the very few fruits that must be picked while still green and ripened off the tree if they are to reach perfection.

There are two reasons for this. Most important is the avoidance of grit cells, which mar the buttery texture with tiny lumps closely resembling sand. Grit cells are mostly formed in the latter stages of the fruit's progress; pick it at the moment it has reached maturity, when ripening is inevitable though not yet achieved, and you will head most of those grit cells off at the pass. Additionally, pears tend to ripen from the inside out, a characteristic that makes judging ripeness difficult, and tree ripening accentuates this process.

What all this means is that the key to good pears is patience. Buy the ones that are still firm and unripe, as soon as possible after they have come from storage. They will ripen just as well at your house as at the greengrocer's, and they will get handled a whole lot less along the way. When you get them home, put them in a brown paper bag with a few air holes in it, or in one of those fruit-ripening domes, or in a fruit bowl with some bananas (they give off ethylene, a natural ripening gas). Put them somewhere where the temperature is between 65°F. and 70°F., if possible. In any event, keep them away from extreme temperature changes and out of the sun.

Wait. Each day, press gently at the stem end. As soon as there's a bit of give, the pears are ripe. Either eat them at once or put them in the refrigerator to slow down the ripening. The cold won't really hold things up much, and it's not great for the flavor, so try to enjoy them as soon as possible. Be sure to serve them at room temperature; cold suppresses their fragrance.

Reasons why the pears weren't so great even though you conscientiously did all of the above: They might have been picked too soon; they might have been exposed to extremes of temperature during shipping and/or storage; they might have been afflicted as children with brown-core disease; or they simply might not have been all that great to begin with. I should add here the happy observation that, unlike our most common commercial varieties of apples, our common commercial varieties of pears (Bartlett, Anjou, Comice, Bosc, and Winter Nellis) are all good ones, fully capable of nobility when at their best.

Dessert vs. Cooking Pears

Cooking pears such as Seckel and Bosc are delicious eaten raw when they are fully ripe, but dessert pears such as Comice and Anjou do not respond well to cooking even when still slightly green. Best bets for all-purpose pears are Boscs and Winter Nellis, both of which are good either way, large, firm, and reliable — or, at least, reliable as pears go.

 ## *Pear-Macaroon Pudding*

Just juicy pears baked under a rich almond topping. Serve slightly warm or at room temperature for maximum pear flavor. For gala occasions, top with ice cream and a splash of *poire* (clear pear brandy).

FILLING:
Butter for the pan, plus ½ cup
1 cup confectioners' sugar
Finely grated zest (thin, colored outer rind) of 1 lemon,
    about 1 tablespoon

1 cup (6 ounces) almonds, finely ground
2 eggs
1 egg yolk
¼ teaspoon almond extract
5 or 6 large barely ripe cooking pears, preferably Bosc, about 2½ pounds,
    enough to pave the baking pan with halves

TOPPING:
1 egg white
¼ cup sugar
½ cup (3 ounces) sliced almonds, coarsely chopped so you have flakes

Preheat the oven to 350°F. Butter a table-presentable baking dish about 8 by 10 inches and set aside. Prepare the filling: Cream the butter, beat in the confectioners' sugar a little at a time, then beat in the zest and the nuts. Add the eggs, one at a time, the yolk, and the almond extract. Set aside.

Peel, halve, and core the pears and arrange them, cut side down, on the bottom of the pan. They should pretty much cover it, but a few small gaps are okay. Distribute the filling over the fruit, spreading it as evenly as possible. There probably will be a bit of pear showing.

Make the topping: Beat the egg white to stiff peaks, slowly beat in the sugar, then fold in the almond flakes. Spread the topping over all, covering any still-exposed fruit. You should be able to get a very thin coating over everything. Bake 35 to 45 minutes, or until the top is a nice warm brown and a toothpick inserted in a pudding pocket comes out clean.

Mousse of Pears with Kiwi

Very light and fruity, this pale, creamy, intensely vanilla-flavored pear mousse makes a perfect foil in taste and texture, as well as appearance, to the cool, green kiwi. Light, crisp cookies, such as almond wafers, may be served for further textural contrast but aren't really necessary.

For a 2-quart mousse, 6 to 8 servings

4 large, barely ripe Bosc pears, about 2½ pounds
1½ cup plus 3 tablespoons water
½ cup sugar
2½- to 3-inch piece of vanilla bean, split 2 or 3 times the long way
2 tablespoons unflavored gelatin (2 envelopes)
1 teaspoon lime juice

1 pound kiwis, 6 to 8, enough to make 2 cups of thin slices
1 cup heavy cream
3 egg whites

Peel the pears, dropping them into a large bowl of ice water as they are finished to prevent discoloration. Combine the 1½ cups water, sugar, and vanilla bean in a large saucepan and cook, stirring often, over medium-low heat 5 minutes. Quarter and core the pears, dropping the sections into the hot syrup as they are prepared.

When all the fruit is added, stir well, lower heat to low, and cook, stirring from time to time, until pears are very tender. Remove the pan from the heat and let the fruit cool in the syrup.

Put the 3 tablespoons cold water in a small saucepan, sprinkle on the gelatin, and set aside to soften for 5 minutes or so. Drain the pears, remove the vanilla bean, and measure the syrup. You should have ⅔ to ¾ cup. If necessary, reduce it by boiling over medium-high heat. Combine the syrup with the softened gelatin and cook, stirring, only until the gelatin is completely dissolved. Purée the pears, stir in the lime juice, combine the purée with the syrup, and chill the mixture until it's very thick, almost set. Stir from time to time so it doesn't separate.

While the purée is chilling, peel, cut crosswise into thin slices, and drain for 10 minutes on paper towels enough of the kiwis to line the bottom of the mold . Rinse a 2-quart mold with cold water, drain off all the water, and use some of the kiwi slices to line the bottom.

When the purée is ready, beat the cream until it forms floppy peaks and fold it in. Quickly beat the egg whites until they form stiff but still shiny peaks and fold them in. Carefully turn the mixture into the mold, cover with plastic wrap, and chill at least 12 hours.

At serving time, peel, slice, and drain enough of the remaining kiwi to pave the top. Remove the plastic, pave the surface with kiwi, and loosen the sides of the mold with a thin-bladed knife. Put a serving platter against the mold and reverse the works. If the mousse doesn't drop out by itself, jerk downward sharply. Any slices that stick to the mold can be easily pressed back against the mousse, along with any remaining slices you wish to use to decorate the sides. Serve at once, as it won't stand up long.

WARNING NOTE: Like pineapple juice, kiwi juice will both tenderize meat and discombobulate gelatin. The amount in the paving slices here is too small to be a problem, but the fruit must be heated briefly to neutralize this quality if you want to use it as the basis for something like a bavarian cream.

Wine-Baked Pears with Raspberry Sauce

These should be cooked in a very low oven (about 300°F.), one in which you are already braising a daube of beef, for instance.

For 4 servings

4 large cooking pears, neither hard green nor ripe but about halfway
 between
1 lemon
2 cups not-too-dry white wine, such as German Riesling
3 tablespoons light brown sugar
¼ teaspoon powdered ginger
2- to 3-inch piece of vanilla bean, split 2 or 3 times
1 package (10 ounces) frozen raspberries, or 1½ cups of your own
1 tablespoon clover honey, or more to taste
1 tablespoon raspberry jam
1 tablespoon finely shredded lemon zest (thin, colored outer rind)
2 tablespoons rum, or to taste
1 cup heavy cream, whipped, or 2 cups vanilla ice cream

Peel the pears, rubbing each with a cut piece of lemon as soon as it's done so it doesn't darken. Combine the wine, sugar, and ginger in a small saucepan and heat, stirring, until the sugar dissolves.

Put the pears in a noncorrodible pan just big enough for them and the wine, tuck in the vanilla bean, and pour in the liquid. Cover the pan tightly and bake in a low oven, 300°F. to 325°F., about 3 hours, or until pears are very tender when tested with a knife point. Halfway through the cooking, turn them over and add more wine if necessary (it shouldn't be). If the pears were riper than you thought, they will already be mush. See note for what to do.

When the pears are cooked, lift them into a heatproof glass or china dish just big enough to hold them comfortably. Put the cooking liquid over high heat and boil until it is reduced to a thick syrup, then pour it over the pears. Let cool, then chill. Keep turning them and ladling syrup over them whenever you think of it.

Make the sauce by puréeing the berries through a mouli or sieve to remove the seeds, then mixing them with the honey, jam, lemon zest, and rum. At serving time, let the pears come to cool room temperature, stand them (on the ice cream, if you're using it) in individual serving dishes, and pour a bit of the syrup around them. Carefully spoon on just enough of the raspberry sauce to make red streaks and serve the remainder of the sauce separately. If you're using whipped cream, beat it quite stiff and pipe a bit on each pear, then pass the remainder separately. I prefer the whipped cream because it is less sweet, but you can play around with the sweetness of the sauce and cooking liquids, too, until you find the balance you prefer.

NOTE: Mush? No problem. Strain out the seeds and cores, replace vanilla, cook, uncovered, stirring almost constantly, until the purée is very thick. Let it cool, then remove the vanilla bean, measure, and chill well. At serving time, measure purée and fold in one-half its volume of stiffly whipped cream. Add up the total volume produced and fold in 3 tablespoons of the raspberry sauce per cup. You now have a sort of loose mousse–pear fool creation, which should be served in stemmed glasses, with the remainder of the raspberry sauce and some crisp cookies such as gingerbread or amaretti.

*H*ALLOWEEN
A Harvest New Year

PUMPKIN PIE is a favorite, of course, with its echoes of the headless horseman and the light grinning jack-o'-lantern. Devil's-food cake can be included purely on nomenclatural grounds. Those who are willing to do such things more than once a year will be making roll-and-cut cookies in appropriately spooky shapes. And yet it all has a forced, almost greeting card quality. These foods have only the slightest connection with a holiday that was originally the most important day on the pre-Christian Celtic calendar, a New Year's festival called Samhain.

Samhain (pronounced SAH-ween) was a harvest celebration marking the end of the agricultural year. It was also a fire festival and a time when the spirits of the dead made their way to the underworld. Sound familiar? Christian missionaries did their best to wipe out Samhain by creating an alternate holiday, All Saints' Day (Allhallows), that just happens to fall at exactly the same time of year. What they mostly accomplished was to push Samhain more firmly into the nighttime, where the rituals involving bonfires and wandering spirits became the appropriate celebration of All Hallows' Eve, otherwise known as Halloween.

"Trick or treat" is the descendant of one of Samhain's most important aspects, the propitiation of wandering spirits by offerings of food and drink. But though several sources discuss these edible offerings, nobody has spent much time telling us just what these foods *were*. (One may assume that possibly evil spirits were not propitiated with just any old thing that was lying around in the cellar.)

Whatever it was, it cannot have presented the problems raised by today's small trick-or-treaters. Open the door and there they are, the little monsters, loot bags outstretched, eagerness shining through the crayon on every upturned face. The parade is somehow very endearing (even when the costumes come straight from the five-and-dime) and what the hell do you give them?

If you give them candy, you rot their teeth, ruin their health (or at least their dinner), and probably contribute to a bad case of indigestion. If you give them money, they will go out and spend it on candy and war toys. If you give them a nice shiny red apple, they will, quite rightly, consider you a fink.

Homemade treats do come to mind. They are usually fun to make and much tastier, at least to adults, than the store-bought kind. Several are quite quick and easy. A few, O precious popcorn balls, are quick, easy, and cheap — important if you live in a populous neighborhood. Homemade treats do have to be made, though. If you haven't the time and can't arrange to be out of town on Halloween, the best course probably is to go out and buy cookies. Things like fig newtons and animal crackers, molasses cookies and gingersnaps, while not exactly healthy, are a lot better than the traditional candies, at least in part because they come in natural colors.

Children love above all things bright red candy, neon blue candy, poison green candy . . . candy in every color that makes sensitive adults quail. The adults are squeamish for good reason, since many of those colors come from coal-tar dyes, dyes that first came into use in the nineteenth century and have been consistently proved unsafe ever since. Which doesn't, unfortunately, mean they've ever gone completely out of use. The profit motive being what it is, each individual dye is considered safe until somebody gets around to doing a sufficiently careful study and raising a fuss. Then, a fair amount of the time but not always, the offender is banned. (The otherwise forbidden red dye used in maraschino cherries has been slated for complete removal from the approved list more than sixty times. But as of this writing the cherry manufacturers have managed successfully to plead economic hardship.)

If you're so determined to be healthy about this that even cookies are out, try nuts in the shell and plain dried fruits such as dates and apricots. There are lots of ways to grind up the fruit and nuts and mix them with honey and spices and wheat germ to make more or less healthy candy. It tastes, to children, adults, and probably dogs, exactly like more or less healthy candy. Why make work for yourself? The fruits and nuts are tasty enough as is, and they hold up well when tossed about for hours as the loot bag is swung to and fro.

This does not, of course, solve the problem of what to feed everybody else when you are longing to make something apposite to Allhallows. Consider making something with symbolic decorations, such as the briochelike, lightly spicy Mexican Bread of the Dead, traditionally festooned with tears and bones made of dough. Or, should you be feeling apprehensive about the things that go bump in the night, why not make a dish redolent of garlic, which is well known to keep vampires at bay? On the other hand, it may well be that pumpkin is calling. Many of us have many of them at this time of year. If that's the case, why not make Squashkes, a welcome change from the sweet uses to which that rather bland vegetable is usually put? They are rich in squash flavor, crisp outside, and soft but not mushy within, made the same way you make *latkes* —jewel of the Jewish kitchen — the all-time potato pancakes. That is how they got their name — that and the fact I am mightily disinclined to call them pumpkin patties, which, more or less, they are.

Browned Garlic and Pine Nut Sauce

Though this rich, nutty sauce is delicious with pasta, it was designed to be served with big, flaky baked potatoes. It's also good with plain steamed vegetables such as broccoli and cauliflower, to say nothing of roast chicken, so there's your easy Halloween dinner — no fuss, no muss, and plenty of antivampirical flavor.

For 2 or 3 servings

½ cup pine nuts (pignoli)
3 tablespoons butter
1 tablespoon olive oil
5 large cloves garlic, chopped fine but not mashed

2 egg yolks
½ cup heavy cream
½ teaspoon salt

In the top part of a double boiler set directly over medium heat, simmer the pine nuts in the butter until they are well browned. Remove them with a slotted spoon and reserve. Lower the heat, add the olive oil to the butter, then cook the garlic, stirring almost constantly, until it is barely golden but no browner. You want it to get toasted gently. Scorching will make it bitter, so be careful not to let it brown overmuch.

In a small, heatproof bowl, beat the egg yolks with the cream until they are thoroughly combined. Beat in the garlic with its buttery oil and return the mixture to the unwashed pan. Cook over barely simmering water, stirring almost constantly, until the sauce has thickened, about 5 minutes. Do not let it boil. Stir in the salt and the reserved pine nuts and use the sauce at once.

Squashkes

It takes more than a minute to peel and shred the pumpkin, but once the mixture is made up, these cook very quickly. Since, unlike shredded raw potato, squash doesn't turn black on contact with air, the whole thing can be prepared a few hours in advance and the squashkes fried at the last minute so they are at their transcendental best. Like latkes, they do reheat, but not very gracefully.

Measurements are approximate — the mixture might take a little more flour if the pumpkin is juicy, a little more egg if it is dry. If you have a 5-cup hunk of squash, use a slightly smaller onion and forge onward; this recipe can survive quite a bit of bending.

For about ten 5-inch squashkes, ½ inch thick (5 side dish or 3 main dish servings)

6 cups peeled, coarsely shredded, raw pumpkin or winter squash, about 3 pounds untrimmed
1 medium-sized onion, grated on the large holes of a grater , about ⅔ cup
2 eggs, beaten
1 tablespoon flour
1 teaspoon salt
Butter or light vegetable oil for frying, about 2 tablespoons

The easiest way to deal with the squash is to cut it into wedges about 1½ inches wide. Then you can use a sharp paring knife to dispatch the insides and peel off the outer skin, all without having to deal with bumps. Grate the squash — in my experience a hand grater is faster than a processor, but then my processor, though powerful, is old. Mix everything except the fat together. Heat a very thin film of fat over high-medium heat in a heavy skillet. When a shred sizzles, make an experimental squashke, a pancake about 2 inches across, ½ inch thick. Fry about 2 minutes a side, or until the crust is crisp and the filling cooked through. If necessary, make adjustments, adding egg if the mixture falls apart or flour if it's watery and won't get crisp. That's it. Fry 'em up and eat 'em up; it couldn't be hard.

In fact, it's so easy you might want to play around a little. As with batter-based pancakes, you can stir little bits of other stuff into these to vary the effect. Herbs, both fresh and dried, are good, as are shredded vegetables of sturdy character like that of the pumpkin. Little bites of meat or shellfish or a few crumbs of cheese also work well. If you season the mixture with fresh ginger, soy sauce, and garlic, then fry the squashkes in bland oil, they will taste a great deal more Japanese than Jewish, and if you season them with a bit of ground cumin and fresh coriander, then serve them with Pumpkin Seed Sauce (see recipe on page 207), you will be eating a combination of foods that has been popular slightly south of here since about the beginning of agriculture and quite possibly even before.

 Pan de Muerto
(Bread of the Dead)

The bread must rise in the refrigerator overnight, so plan accordingly.

For 2 loaves

2 teaspoons anise seeds
1 tablespoon shredded orange zest (thin, colored outer rind)
¼ cup lukewarm water, plus ½ cup
1 tablespoon dry yeast (1 envelope)
Approximately 6 cups bread flour
½ cup sugar, plus sugar for sprinkling (the latter pink or red if you
**   want to be authentic)**
1 teaspoon salt

3 eggs
6 egg yolks
¼ cup orange flower water (available in specialty stores)
¾ to 1 cup unsalted butter, allowed to become very soft, plus butter for
the pans and bowl

GLAZE:
2 egg yolks
1 teaspoon flour
Scant ¼ cup water

In a small saucepan, combine the anise seeds and orange zest with the ¼ cup water. Bring the mixture to a simmer, cover, and cook over low heat 4 to 5 minutes. Strain the mixture, pressing on the solids, and reserve.

Dissolve the yeast in the ½ cup water in a small bowl. Beat in about ¾ cup of the flour, enough to make a soft, sticky dough that just leaves the sides of the bowl. Cover with plastic wrap and set aside to rise.

In a large mixing bowl, thoroughly combine 4 cups of the flour with the ½ cup sugar and the salt. Beat the eggs, yolks, orange flower water, and 3 tablespoons of the anise-orange infusion together until the mixture is liquid and smooth, then stir it into the flour mixture, alternating with the softened butter. The dough will be crumbly, then very sticky and stiff. Be sure to use a strong-handled spoon.

By now the yeast mixture will have risen double. Stir it down and beat it in, then work in about 1 cup more flour, or enough to make a soft dough that leaves the sides of the bowl. It will still be sticky.

Turn the dough onto a lightly floured (stable) work surface and start kneading with one hand — the stronger one. Stickiness will acquire new meaning. Do not try to get your hand out of the dough or the dough itself off the surface; just keep pushing and pulling in a more or less kneading motion, lifting handfuls of the dough from time to time, scraping what you can from the edges into the center.

In what will seem like an eternity but is actually only about 6 to 8 minutes, the dough will start leaving the board and stop sticking to your hand. Once it's on the road to smoothness, you can use both hands to finish the job. Knead vigorously. Lift the dough and smash it down, being careful not to send bits flying. Before very long it will be satiny.

Put the dough in a clean, lightly greased bowl that will fit in your refrigerator, cover tightly, and refrigerate at least overnight, as long as a full day.

To make the glaze, beat the yolks with the flour, then beat in the water. Set the glaze aside.

Lightly butter 2 small, flat baking sheets at least 9 inches across — the bottoms of springform pans work well. Divide the dough into slightly unequal thirds — 2 larger pieces for the loaves, a small one for the decorations. Keep the small piece refrigerated while you shape the larger ones into flattish rounds like fat (¾-inch-thick) pancakes and put one on each sheet.

Use the reserved dough to make decorations. The bones are made by rolling walnut-sized pieces into short cylinders, then lengthening the midsections; tears are made by rolling small balls and pinching out the ends. A simple ball traditionally crowns the cake, with a cross of bones arranged around it and tears sprinkled in the spaces. Press firmly so decorations adhere, then brush with glaze.

The loaves should rise covered, but anything placed directly on them will stick to them. I invert mixing bowls over the pans; a damp towel draped over several tall, strategically placed glasses also would work. Let the loaves rise until almost double, usually about 2 hours, then place in a preheated 375°F. oven. At once lower the heat to 350°F. and bake 30 minutes. Working quickly, brush each loaf with glaze, sprinkle lavishly with sugar, and return to the oven. Bake about 10 to 15 minutes more, or until the bread is richly brown and completely set. Cover with foil if necessary to prevent overbrowning. Cool on wire racks.

*A*PPLES

CONNOISSEUR'S LAMENT, with Ray of Hope: Though the indestructible tomato* is usually assigned the role, no fruit could be a more telling indictment of agricultural malpractice than the modern American apple.

The biggest seller by far is called the Delicious, an Orwellian appellation if ever there was one. Red or yellow, these triumphs of the apple breeder's art are above all things durably handsome, remaining shiny and blemish-free through long storage and much punishment. But beauty is indeed skin-deep; the flesh of this popular fruit is insipid, oversweet, and flat as commercial sherbet. The texture resembles cotton wool, and the aroma is too vague to be compared with anything.

Delicious apples are about one-fifth of the total produced and sold in America, which is the largest apple grower in the world. Most of the rest are McIntosh, with a few Jonathans, Rome Beauties, Cortlands, and Granny Smiths thrown in. This is especially staggering when you remember that at this writing there are about twenty commonly cultivated varieties, still widely referred to in cookbooks and occasionally available, if a little bit hard to get; and those are over and above the literally hundreds of experimental, rare, and "heirloom" types still growing and producing.

Discounting farm stands in apple-growing areas, the likeliest place to get something besides the big three is — O, irony of ironies — the fancy greengrocer's, where Newtown Pippins, Gravensteins, Wolf Rivers, and Northern Spies sit shoulder to shoulder with mangoes, kiwi fruit, and assorted exotic chilies. What a fate for such a homespun product.

---

*See "Tomatoes in Snowtime" on page 247.

Still, it's better to get them that way than not to get them at all. Keep asking for your favorite apples, especially at this time of year when you just might get them, and maybe suppliers, from orchards to supermarkets, will get the hint.

Best Apples for Cooking

Rome Beauty, early season Cortland, Macoun, Newtown Pippin, Rhode Island Greening, Northern Spy, York Imperial, Wolf River, and Granny Smith. The Golden Delicious is often recommended because it doesn't darken and holds its shape very well, but even cooking (with or without sugar and butter and lemon and spices) can't make it taste very good.

Other Uses for Apples: Softening brown sugar (put a wedge in the tightly closed sugar jar); keeping cookies tender (put an apple wedge in the tin); being the centers of pomanders (impale all over with whole cloves); and helping the pears get ripe (like bananas, apples give off ethylene gas — the stuff they use to turn tomatoes red — and will hasten the ripening of any fruit stored with them).

The Skin Question

Used to be, if you were for health and nutrition, you left the peels on whenever possible, both to take advantage of the roughage and to avoid losing the vitamins and minerals stored right under the skin. Nobody ever pretended that the peels, which are usually both tasteless and tough, contributed much in the way of gustatory pleasure, but at least eating them made you feel virtuous. These days, those apples have been doused with so many insecticides, fungicides, and beautifying waxes they're as unwashable as Lady Macbeth's hands. Supposedly, they're perfectly okay to eat or the government wouldn't allow them to be sold. The skeptical may prefer to err on the side of safety, especially since the sacrifice is so small.

Applesauce

Consider the famous dictum "less is more." Cook peeled, cored apples very slowly in a covered pan, with just enough water or pure apple cider to keep them from sticking and scorching. Stir frequently. When the apples are falling apart, purée the sauce if you like the smooth kind. Now taste the sauce and add flavoring — sugar, a pinch of salt, a squeeze of lemon if the apples are bland.

While all the classic "pie spices" do complement apples very well, there are probably children growing up in America who think exposing apples to the heat of the stove automatically makes them taste like cinnamon. If you are able to get decent apples, the sauce will be delicious with only a pinch of salt, a pat of butter, and perhaps some sweetening to smooth things out.

Norman Rabbit

For 4 servings (Recipe may be either halved or doubled, if desired.)

2 large, tart cooking apples such as Northern Spies, Cortlands, or
    Granny Smiths
3 to 4 tablespoons butter
1 fryer rabbit, approximately 2 pounds, cut in 8 serving pieces
Flour to dust the rabbit
6 large shallots or 1 small onion, minced fine
¾ cup hard cider or "fizzy" natural cider (see Note) or ½ cup natural
    apple juice plus ¼ cup white wine
1 large clove garlic, peeled and stuck on a toothpick
¾ cup heavy cream
Salt to taste
1 bunch watercress

Peel and core apples and cut into rings about ⅓ inch thick. Melt 2 tablespoons of the butter in a heavy skillet over medium heat and fry apple rings until well browned on each side. Save 4 of the prettiest rings for garnish and chop the rest. Set aside.

Dust the rabbit pieces with flour and fry in the same pan, adding butter as needed, until the meat is well browned on both sides. Stir in the reserved chopped apple and the shallots, then pour in the cider. Bury the garlic in the middle, cover, and simmer 20 minutes. Heat cream in a small pan to just below boiling and stir it into the meat. Turn the meat and continue cooking over low heat, partially covered, until just tender, about 30 minutes more.

Remove the rabbit and keep it hot. Discard garlic and purée the sauce through a food mill or in a blender. Reheat and add salt to taste. Pour the sauce over the meat, garnish with the reserved apple rings and serve at once, wreathed around with watercress.

NOTE: "Fizzy" cider is pure apple juice that has just started to ferment — no longer sweet but still fresh-tasting and only slightly alcoholic. See "Through the Cider Mill," page 170.

$\mathcal{O}$ Intense Double-Apple Cake

Honesty compels me to admit this is a real bowl-dirtier, intense but not instant. It is, however, extremely easy, very pretty, moist, luscious, fruity, and, as a bonus, rather large.

CAKE:
1 cup raisins
¼ cup dark rum
2 cups sifted cake flour
1 teaspoon baking soda
1 teaspoon cinnamon
½ teaspoon baking powder
¼ teaspoon ground cloves
¼ cup brown sugar
½ cup granulated sugar
½ cup butter, plus butter for the pan
1 egg
1½ cups thick, lightly sweetened applesauce
½ cup coarsely chopped pecans
½ cup coarsely chopped walnuts

TOPPING:
3 medium-sized cooking apples, peeled, cored, and cut in eighths
2 tablespoons dark rum
½ cup flour
3 tablespoons brown sugar
3 tablespoons butter

Combine the raisins with the ¼ cup rum in a small, lidded saucepan and simmer, covered, over medium-low heat until the liquid is all absorbed — about 5 minutes. Let the raisins cool.

Combine the topping-apple wedges with the 2 tablespoons rum and set them aside. Mix the topping flour and brown sugar thoroughly, then cut in the butter until the mixture resembles coarse crumbs. Set aside.

Generously butter an 8- by 12-inch rectangular baking pan and preheat the oven to 350°F. Sift together all the dry ingredients for the cake except the sugars and set aside. Cream the butter with the sugars, then beat in the egg. Stir in the dry mixture, which will take some doing. You'll end up with a sort of soft dough.

Working quickly now, beat in the applesauce, then stir in the raisins and nuts. Spread the batter in the prepared pan.

Arrange the topping apples, rounded side up, in 3 rows, pressing them lightly into the batter as you go. They can be close but shouldn't touch. Sprinkle the topping mixture over the apples and set to bake. The cake will be done in about 45 minutes to an hour, when a toothpick inserted in the cake part comes out clean. Let the dessert partially cool on a rack and serve warm. It's also perfectly tasty cold, of course; the apples do shrink and sink a bit, but not objectionably.

 Apple-Apricot Crumb Pie with Sour Cream Custard

CRUST:
1¼ cups all-purpose flour
¼ cup whole-wheat flour
Scant ½ teaspoon salt
3 tablespoons lard or solid vegetable shortening such as Crisco (see Note on page 123)
7 tablespoons butter (see Note on page 123)
¼ cup ice water
1 tablespoon lemon juice
1 egg white

FILLING:
½ cup dried apricots, cut in ¼-inch dice
⅓ cup Triple Sec or other orange liqueur
7 or 8 medium-sized Cortlands, Granny Smiths, Newtown Pippins, or Macouns, peeled, cored, and cut into wedges ¼ inch wide at the fat point
2 to 4 tablespoons sugar, depending on apples
1 heaping tablespoon flour

CRUMBS:
4 tablespoons sugar
½ cup flour
¼ cup butter
½ cup walnuts, broken into small pieces

CUSTARD:
¼ cup sugar
2 egg yolks
1 cup sour cream

Make the crust: Thoroughly combine the dry ingredients in a large, shallow bowl, then use your fingertips to rub in the 3 tablespoons lard or shortening until it has completely disappeared. Switch to a pastry blender or 2 knives and cut in the butter until it forms lumps the size of peas. Mix the ice water with the lemon juice, then dribble in the liquid a tablespoon at a time as you toss the dough together. As soon as the dough will hold together, it's done; you might not need all the liquid. Gather the dough into a ball, flatten slightly, wrap tightly in plastic, and chill at least an hour, as long as overnight.

Allow the dough to return to room temperature, then roll it out ⅛ inch thick between two pieces of waxed paper. It might be crumbly at first but should come together as you roll it out. Fit it carefully into a deep 10-inch pie plate and build a high, decorative rim. Chill the shell. Right before filling, beat the egg white just enough to mix and paint the inside of the shell with it — most of it will be left over and can be fed to the dog.

Make the filling: Combine the apricots with the liqueur and let marinate at least an hour, as long as overnight. Drain them, reserving the liquid. Taste an apple wedge and decide on the sugar needed, remembering that the crumbs and custard also have sugar in them. Toss the apple wedges with the sugar and flour, then toss in the apricots.

Make the crumb mixture: Combine the sugar and flour, then pinch in the butter until it forms coarse crumbs. Stir in the walnuts and set aside.

Put the rack in the upper third of the oven and preheat to 425°F. Pile the filling in the prepared shell — you don't have to be superprecise about setting the wedges in there, but you must have them lying more or less flat or they won't all fit. Aim for the flattest top you can arrange so the crumbs, which come next, don't fall off. Using one cupped hand as a barrier/crumb-catcher at the outside rim of the pie, dribble the crumb mixture in a wide band around the edge. Leave an uncrumbed hole in the center about 3 inches in diameter.

Bake the pie 20 minutes, then remove it, turn the heat down to 350°F., and move the rack to the center.

Make the custard: Beat the sugar and egg yolks, then beat in the sour cream and the liquid drained from the apricots. Transfer to a pitcher or spouted measuring cup. Slowly pour the custard through the uncrumbed bull's eye, using a wide-bladed knife, such as a table knife, to depress the apples so the custard flows in smoothly. Return the pie to the oven and bake 40 to 60 minutes longer, or until custard is set, apples are tender, and both crust and crumbs are well browned.

*P*OT ROAST TRIUMPHANT

IMAGINE. (WELL, WHY NOT? The days are getting cooler and there is a somewhat greater chance of getting everybody together for Sunday dinner.) Imagine a perfect pot roast, perfectly tender, perfectly juicy, neither stringy nor gray. The meat carves into beautiful slices, the fluffy mashed potatoes await the abundant, flavorsome gravy, and all around the table faces shine with happy anticipation of this most comfortingly homelike of gustatory pleasures.

Okay, now imagine that this dandy dish is not, as you've probably been thinking, a hunk of beef, but is instead a plump, well-stuffed chicken, breast and thigh equally well cooked with no trace of the fattiness that mars so many modern birds. The long, slow, moist cooking has guaranteed juiciness; a bit of attention to pot size and turning assured there would be plenty of gravy and an evenly done bird; preliminary browning gave an appetizing color (and more flavor for the gravy); and making the whole business was as easy as, or easier than, the more familiar stuffed, roasted chicken of the magazine illustrations.

This is not, I hasten to add, some marvel of the new cuisine. It is, in fact, the chicken in every pot that France's King Henry IV desired, so quotably, so long ago. "I want," said the king (in French, of course), "there to be no peasant in my kingdom so poor that he is unable to have a chicken in his pot every Sunday." The king died in 1610, while the words above are from a history written in 1681, so they may not have been his *exact* words, but they were certainly the general idea. (The king was an earthy type from the Béarn, where babies' lips were rubbed with garlic and wine when they were born, and I've always imagined him a somewhat more pungent speaker, but you never know.) In any event, in the pot was the place for the chicken then, and it still is today.

In France, both the stuffing in the chicken and the other items in the pot vary with the circumstances of the cook and the importance of the occasion. Often, the chicken is but one ingredient of a *pot au feu* that also contains a big piece of beef, some meaty bones, and a grand assortment of vegetables. In this case, a lot of water is used, and the resultant soup is eaten separately. Instead of being served with a gravy made from the cooking juices, the meat will be accompanied by an independent sauce, usually a sharp one involving capers, tomatoes, vinegar, or some such variation on the sour-accent theme.

Alternatively, the chicken will be the star of the show, cooked with a smaller assortment of vegetables in just enough liquid to provide the basis for a sauce. In either case, the stuffings will be made from what is handy as well as what is traditional. Like American stuffings, they will usually be based on bread crumbs, accented with herbs, often studded with mush-rooms or olives or nutmeats, and bound with egg. But French stuffings are usually denser than ours, with a high proportion of uncooked sausage, ground pork, and/or liver. This results in a juicier bird, basted from the inside by its filling, and a denser, more pâté-like stuffing of which a small portion is plenty.

All of this is in aid of saying that the recipe on page 199 should be regarded as a general set of instructions rather than a detailed prescrip-tion. Use it as a base from which to take off in your own creative direction. The method is the message when it comes to pot-roasted chicken; the specifics are up to you and your larder.

The chicken gets first mention here because, although my family is not at all French, it was pot-roasted poultry of the sort just described that I learned to love first. Not for me the excellent sauerbraten that so frequent-ly graced my mother's table, though that tender beef in its spicy gravy was a model of its kind. Not for me the pot roast that *means* pot roast to most people. And why? The usual tacky Freudian reasons. It was all my fa-ther's fault.

Being an informal, home-loving sort who was forced for business reasons to travel a lot and eat out almost incessantly, he developed a fondness for pot roast that was almost obsessional. Pot roast, specifically sauerbraten, was the welcome-home meal he craved above all others, the meal we duly had, more often than not, upon his frequent returns.

What I wanted was something a lot more special than plain old pot roast, no matter how deliciously it was prepared. What I wanted was a treat worthy of the occasion, something like roast beef, or maybe steak, or, best of all, *dinner out* in a fancy restaurant.

Thus it was that that splendid sauerbraten fell upon a deaf tongue. It took me years ('twas ever thus) to acknowledge my father's wisdom and come to the conclusion sensible people never doubt: Sauerbraten is where it's at.

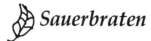 *Sauerbraten*

For about 6 servings, with a few leftovers (maybe)

5-pound chunk of stewing beef, the squarer the better (Fattier cuts
such as brisket and blade chuck are traditional, but even lean items
such as bottom round will work.)

MARINADE:
2 large onions, sliced thin
1 large carrot, cut in thin rounds
2 quarter-sized pieces of fresh ginger root
2 or 3 thick slices of lemon, seeds removed
Zest (thin, colored outer rind) of 1 small orange
10 peppercorns
3 to 4 good sprigs of fresh thyme or 2 teaspoons dried
1 small bay leaf
Approximately 2 cups dry red wine
1½ cups mild red wine vinegar
1 cup water

TO COOK THE ROAST:
Flour to dust meat
2 or 3 tablespoons rendered beef fat or bland oil
1 cup finely chopped onion
½ cup finely chopped carrot
4 or 5 gingersnaps, crushed to powder
Salt to taste
Sour cream to accompany

Combine the meat with all the nonliquid marinade ingredients in a
big glass or china bowl. Heat the liquids just to a boil, let them cool to
lukewarm, and pour them in, too. The meat should be at least one-half to
two-thirds covered; add more wine if it isn't. Cover the bowl with plastic
wrap, refrigerate, and let marinate at least 2 days, up to a week. Stir and
turn at least once a day, more often if the marinating time is short.

Remove the meat from the marinade, brush off any flotsam, and pat
the surface dry with paper towels. Strain the marinade and reserve it,
discarding the solids. Dust the meat generously with flour, rubbing it in
well, then brushing off any excess.

Heat the fat over medium-high heat in a heavy, noncorrodible pan
such as a Dutch oven. (The ideal pan is one that holds the meat comfort-

ably with a small amount of room to spare. This pan does not exist.) Brown the meat thoroughly on all sides.

When the meat is browned, lever it up and put the onions and carrots underneath it. Pour in enough of the marinade to come about one-third of the way up the side of the roast and bring the liquid to a bare simmer. Cover the pan tightly and gently cook the meat over very low heat or in a very low (275°F. to 300°F.) oven 3½ to 5 hours, depending on the tenderness of the cut and your version of low heat. It's ready when fork-tender but not yet falling apart. Check the liquid level from time to time and add heated marinade if necessary to keep it constant.

When the meat is ready, carefully remove it (two wooden spoons work well) and keep it hot. Strain the gravy into a tall, narrow container and purée the vegetables. Skim as much fat as you can from the liquid. Put the crumbs in the unwashed pan and slowly stir the liquid into them. Add the puréed vegetables (there won't be much; by this point they'll have mostly disintegrated). Heat the gravy, stirring, and cook over medium heat until it is smooth and slightly thickened — the thicker you want it, the more gingersnaps you should use.

Taste the gravy and correct the salt. Slice the meat onto a heated platter, annoint with some of the gravy, and put the rest of the gravy in a sauce boat. Serve the sour cream on the side, next to the big platter of potato pancakes, or, if you're a pantywaist, the egg noodles.

NOTE: Before you go thinking of those gingersnaps as low-rent, just one step away from putting marshmallows on the sweet potatoes, bear in mind that rolled toast and powdered crumbs are old and honorable thickening media. Archaic, even, might be the word, since their use was already more historical than common by the beginning of the nineteenth century.

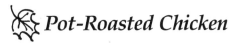 *Pot-Roasted Chicken*

For 6 generous servings

5½- to 6-pound roasting chicken
1 lemon
2 tablespoons olive oil, or slightly more
1 tablespoon butter
1 large onion, chopped into roughly ¼-inch pieces
1 large or 2 medium-sized carrots, peeled and chopped into roughly
    ¼-inch pieces

1½ cups dry white wine
2 tablespoons cornstarch
¼ cup Madeira, tawny port, or other medium-sweet, fortified wine
Salt to taste

STUFFING:
1½ cups coarse dry bread crumbs, preferably from unsweetened
   French or Italian bread of some substance
⅓ pound ground pork, just a tad less fatty than sausage meat
½ cup fresh parsley leaves and tender stems, minced fine
5 or 6 sprigs fresh thyme, minced fine, or 1 tablespoon dried,
   crumbled (Do not use powdered.)
2 large cloves garlic
2 tablespoons Madeira or substitute (see above)
Finely shredded zest (thin, colored outer rind) of 1 lemon
½ teaspoon salt
Pinch each of nutmeg, ground cloves, and white pepper
2 eggs
Heart and liver of the chicken, plus 1 or 2 extra livers if available
Trussing needle and string

Remove giblet bag and any loose pads of fat from the chicken. Grate off the lemon zest and set aside for the stuffing. Halve the lemon, squeeze gently to release juice, and rub the entire inside of the chicken with it. Set the chicken aside and make the stuffing.

Combine all the stuffing ingredients through the eggs, mixing vigorously to ensure even distribution of the seasonings. The stuffing should be on the mushy side, far looser than that for a roasting bird but not actually runny. Add a bit of milk if it's dry or a few more bread crumbs if (most unlikely) it seems dangerously liquid. Cut the heart and liver(s) into small dice and stir them in.

Retrieve the chicken. Insert a heavy knife point where the tail meets the body and press hard to break the bone — you want to be able to truss up the tail into the cavity. Balance the bird on the neck end and spoon in the stuffing. Most of it should fit, but don't pack it in — it needs plenty of room to expand and cook thoroughly.

Bend the tail up, tuck it in, and sew up the opening, being a bit more thorough than is necessary with a roasting bird. If there's room for stuffing at the neck (and the stuffing to put in it), by all means take advantage of the fact. Otherwise, just sew the neck closed so the skin protects all the meat. Truss legs and wings close to the body.

Choose a deep, heavy pan just big enough for the chicken to fit comfortably. Put in the olive oil and butter and put the pan over medium heat. When the fat sizzles, add the chicken and brown it, turning (without piercing) from time to time until all surfaces are well colored. This will take 20 to 30 minutes.

The more ideally shaped the pan, the more difficult it will be to turn the chicken, as the two spoons you are probably employing persist in slipping. Especially at this early stage, the easiest way around the problem is to protect your hand(s) with paper towels and just grab the wretched thing.

When the chicken is well colored, pour off all the fat that remains in the pan. (It can be either discarded or saved for frying potatoes, making soup of the leftovers, or other worthy purposes.) Scatter the onions and carrots around the bird; pour in the wine and enough water so the liquid level comes about a third of the way up the bird. In the best of all possible worlds, this is about 1 cup, but don't worry if your particular pan takes more. Lever up the chicken so the liquid runs underneath and the bird is resting on its side.

Bring the liquid to just under a boil, then turn the heat as low as it will go. Cover the pan tightly, employing tinfoil if the lid is loose or nonexistent. Let the chicken cook 45 minutes, then turn it (paper towels still helpful) on its other side, cover, and give it 45 minutes more. Again uncover, turn the chicken on its back, re-cover, and let cook until thoroughly tender, 30 to 45 minutes once again.

Remove the chicken to a serving platter — this time it's too tender for much hand holding, but a strong, flat skimmer usually lifts it. Strain the liquid into a wide, shallow pan, pressing to get all the juice. Put the pan over high heat and boil until the liquid is reduced to about 2 cups. Dissolve the cornstarch in the Madeira, stir it into the liquid, and cook the gravy, stirring constantly, over medium heat, only until it is nicely thickened. Correct the salt.

I usually carve the chicken in the kitchen so I can steady things with my hands without anyone freaking out, but you can carve at table if you prefer the effect. Do remember in the latter case to remove the trussing string and thread before serving.

HATING RUTABAGAS

"WHAT'S THAT you're peeling there, then, hey?" I asked, knowing full well what the round, purple-splotched, pale orange object actually was. It was a rutabaga, beyond a doubt, and a really prize specimen, too. Furthermore, no sooner was the question put than everyone in the room turned around and began to chant, "Rutabaga, rutabaga, rah! rah! RAH! RUTabagaRUTAbaga, sis, boom, BAH! ROOTABAYgah, ROOTABAAYGAHH YAYYY!"

Locally, my aversion is both famous and unique. On the occasion just described, six people ate mashed rutabagas while I confined myself to the potatoes. But I don't care, 'cause I know the wider world is rich in fellow rutabaga haters.

According to the *Larousse Gastronomique*, a rutabaga is a "turnip with yellowish flesh, edible but seldom used in France as foodstuff." No recipes are given, though the *Larousse* is otherwise thorough enough to provide nine different recipes for camel meat. Sometimes the French know what they're doing.

Why anyone, of any nationality, would willingly eat a simultaneously harsh and insipid, watery, stringy root that manages to combine the almost chemical sweetness of cabbage grown too slowly with the rank bitterness of elderly turnips and the least fortunate perfumes of them both is beyond my comprehension. Yet people do.

Nice people. Sweet, generous, smart people. People, furthermore, who usually cook and eat not only wisely, but if anything, too well.

My friend Sharon, for instance, she of the splendid green tomato relish, once confounded me utterly by surrounding, with peeled and quartered rutabagas, one of the most tempting roast legs of lamb I've ever yearned for.

Fortunately, the inside of the meat remained unsullied, all pink and luscious as good roast lamb can be. But the savory, spicy marinated crust and wine-rich gravy that should by rights have gilt this golden item were inedibly rutabagafied.

This is not, alas, the only instance of such madness. When I stopped at my neighbor's house the other day, innocently intending to unload a bag of green tomatoes pregnant with incipient rot, I smelled again that ominous, boarding-house smell, that smell I have dedicated an entire career to eradicating from the homes of decent people everywhere. Sure enough, he was cooking rutabagas for supper.

Here is a man whose spacious garden flourishes like the green bay tree, whose home and freezer bulge (his cavalier approach to harvest notwithstanding) with unimpeachable private produce — principally squash — a man whose bank account permits him endive, if he'd buy his food, and what has he done? He has gone to the supermarket and purchased, actually *purchased,* one or more rutabagas. Which he is currently boiling in a beautiful copper saucepan and which he will presently employ his Cuisinart to mash.

He had the grace to turn pale when he saw me coming and could defend his perversion only by offering the most reliable of classic excuses, the only excuse that makes sense when a person gets caught in rutabaga delicto: "With all the butter and maple syrup I put on it, how could it taste bad?"

How, on the other hand, could it taste good? Especially when autumn is so rich in other yellow vegetables, principally squash, on which people will be putting butter and maple syrup often enough as it is.

Because my squash crops tend to do well and the blessed things keep forever, I have had plenty of opportunity to observe that although eternity is famously defined as "two people and a ham," "two people and a whole bunch of winter squash" is also a pretty serviceable description. Yet whether they're neatly lined up on newspapers in a cool attic or piled in an Aztec pyramid at your neighborhood grocery store, they are inescapable, as much a staple of the winter table as potatoes, cabbage, and celery. The differences in flavor between types do provide some variety, but there's no denying a certain sameness starts creeping in after a while.

Humorist Will Cuppy, a man of old-fashioned tastes, once said, "You can bake, boil, or steam pumpkins, but they were originally intended for pie, and I see no reason to go against nature." The other squashes can't seem to go against nature either. Whatever the variety, if it's *good,* it will be pielike — dense and sweet and soft — and orange (which seems somehow the wrong color for a vegetable, carrots notwithstanding).

Actually, orangeness is highly desirable and the oranger the better, since orange signals the presence of provitamin A, changed by the body into vitamin A itself. And there's nothing really wrong with dense and sweet, either. It's just that for squash to be an enjoyable vegetable on a regular basis, one must work *against* the pie effect, seasoning with things such as onions and cheese, avoiding additions such as honey, maple syrup, and brown sugar.

Choosing a Good Squash

As with melons, this is, to some extent, a lottery, since the quality of the squash is largely dependent on how ripe when picked, how long it's been stored, and under what conditions. Once you get beyond the basic and obvious injunctions to avoid fruits that are bruised, moldy, shriveled, etc., there's little to go on except color, which varies widely, and weight. A good one will heft heavy for its size.

Another classic test is knocking on the rind and listening for a hollow tone. I always knock, the squash to my ear and an intelligent, concerned expression on my face. Sometimes it sounds hollow, sometimes not. Millions swear by this method, however, so you might as well give it a try.

An Abbreviated Squash Directory

ACORN: This dark green, deeply ribbed, acorn-shaped type, though available all winter, is at its best freshly harvested. Though it doesn't rot, flavor and texture deteriorate rapidly, and acorn is just about worthless once it's been in storage for a while. Popular because of its small size (1½ to 2½ pounds) and its sweetness when fresh. Occasionally available in gold, as Jersey golden acorn, bred to be especially rich in provitamin A.

BUTTERCUP: A turban squash bred down to a flat cylinder with a knob on it. Size varies greatly, from miniatures of only about 1½ pounds to the tastier, larger 4 to 6 pounders. These are different varieties, by the way, not simply different stages of the same squash. Skin is dark green with gray, occasionally warty, sometimes with a yellow or orange flush. Sweet and moist, an excellent keeper, and the most reliably good squash commonly on the market.

BUTTERNUT: More or less club shaped, an even tan, as variable in size as buttercup, and like buttercup better in the larger versions. Very popular, intensely squash-flavored, but more inclined to fibrousness than some others.

BLUE HUBBARD: An elongated, bumpy, blue/green/gray teardrop usually sold in chunks, since even the small types weigh 10 to 15 pounds. A reliable old favorite, this is the usual foundation of commercial pumpkin products, including pies.

RED KURI: Shaped like a blue Hubbard, but squatter, smaller (5 to 7 pounds), and bright orange. Though not too good a keeper, it is growing in popularity because of its beauty and good flavor.

DELICATA: A creamy green flat-ended torpedo shape with dark green stripes, it gradually turns to orange over long storage. Called sweet potato squash for its sweetness and rich texture, the fruits range from 2 to 4 pounds and are somewhat variable in quality. At their best, they're exquisite, so be sure to try again if your initial encounter with delicata was disappointing.

Concerning Pumpkins

Pumpkins, like acorns, are generally lumped with winter squash, *Cucurbita maxima* and *C. moschata*, although from a botanical point of view they are more closely related to summer squash, *C. pepo*. This being the case, pumpkin should, from a purely logical perspective, be light flavored, delicate, and juicy — like its fellow *pepo*, zucchini, for instance.

And sure enough it is. Except that with pumpkins, "light flavored" really means "bland," and juicy — well, watery might be closer to the mark. This is one reason the makers of canned pumpkin, pumpkin pies, and other pumpkin items actually *make* most of those items from winter squash — Hubbard, more often than not.

This is not to say good pumpkin doesn't exist. New England pie pumpkin, also known as sugar pumpkin, is the one to look for if you seek a squash that combines the lightness of *C. pepo* with the sweetness and more filling quality of *C. maxima*. The only problem is that unless you're able to do the looking in your own garden, the chances of finding a New England pie pumpkin are pretty small. This, as you may have guessed, is because about 98 percent of the fresh pumpkins on the market are sold not to be eaten but to be made into lamp shades. That is the best use for them, as you will rapidly discover if you decide to get old-timey and make pumpkin pie from scratch, employing the interior of your jack-o'-lantern for the raw material.

Pies made from the insides of big, round, orange pumpkins are why a lot of people eat pumpkin pie only once a year. That and, of course, the problem of its being pumpkin, in the end, even when it's good — tasty enough, and nourishing, but not, how shall we put it, sexy. This being the season when recipe writers feel compelled to mention the subject, pumpkin lovers can rely on current periodical literature to provide plenty of recipes for pies, cakes, pancakes, muffins, quick breads, ice creams, cheesecakes . . . There is, fortunately, a largish number of places where some custardy, vaguely fruitlike material can be safely introduced.

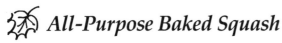# All-Purpose Baked Squash

Simplicity itself. Put the whole, well-washed squash in a shallow baking dish. To avoid explosion, slit it in several places with a knife so steam can escape. Bake in a 350°F. to 400°F. oven 45 minutes to 1½ hours, depending on size. It's done when a fork will enter easily. Peel, seed, and serve with butter, yogurt, hot sauce, etc.

Japanese squashes such as red kuri (described on page 204) and green Hokkaido (a pale green balloon with a pointed stem end, not yet widely distributed) are sometimes rather bitter in the seed cavity. These types should have seeds and assorted inedible center parts removed *before* they are cooked. Halve, scrape out the interior, and bake with cut side against a lightly oiled flat pan.

VNI (Very Nearly Instant) Squash Soup, Southwestern-Style

A sort of liquid taco, hearty enough for a full supper. Prepare the last-minute additions while the soup itself is heating, and the whole thing shouldn't take more than about 20 minutes.

For 4 generous servings

SOUP:
2 tablespoons butter, lard, or bacon fat
2 teaspoons ground cumin
1 teaspoon dried oregano
1 clove garlic, pressed
⅓ cup diced sweet red pepper, about ½ large pepper
2 cups plain puréed cooked winter squash
Approximately 2½ cups milk

ADDITIONS:
1 small sweet red onion, cut into little dice, about ½ cup
2 hot green peppers, minced, about 2 tablespoons (optional)
Salt to taste
½ cup very finely shredded crisp lettuce, 2 large leaves romaine
½ cup crumbled mild white cheese (*queso blanco*) or shredded Jack or
    Muenster, about 2 ounces
Crisp tortilla chips

Melt the fat in your soup pot over medium heat. When it foams, add the cumin, oregano, and garlic. Stir well and turn off the heat. Let sit 5 minutes, then turn the heat to low-medium. Stir in the pepper and, as soon as they are coated with butter, the mashed squash. Stir until all is thoroughly combined, then slowly stir in enough milk to make a smooth, creamy soup texture. Cook, stirring occasionally, only until hot through. Do not let it boil. Stir in onion (and hot pepper) and cook just long enough to remove the onion's raw taste, not enough to make it soft (about 1 minute). Add salt to taste, stir in lettuce, sprinkle with cheese, and serve at once, with the tortilla chips on the side.

Pumpkin Seed Sauce for Vegetables

This tastes rather like a peppery, nutty mayonnaise and is good on most of the things mayonnaise is good on. Though not exactly slimming (pumpkin seeds are a high-calorie item), it's not as fat-making as some sauces I could mention.

For about 1¾ cups

1 cup raw pumpkin seeds (*pepitas*), available in natural food stores
   and Latin groceries
1 cup water
10 whole allspice berries
10 peppercorns
2 whole cloves
1 small clove garlic
1 large fresh jalapeño pepper, seeded
Salt to taste

Spread the pumpkin seeds in a shallow pan and roast in a 300°F. oven about 8 minutes, or until they pop and a sample tastes toasted. Try not to let them brown. Let them cool. In a small saucepan, combine water, allspice, peppercorns, and cloves. Simmer, half-covered, over medium-low heat 30 minutes. Strain and measure; you should have about ⅔ cup liquid.

In a processor, blender, or large mortar, grind the garlic and pumpkin seeds to paste, then grind in the jalapeño pepper. Add the liquid in a thin stream, combine thoroughly, taste, and adjust the salt. If the sauce seems thin, simmer, stirring constantly, over very low heat for just a minute or two — it'll thicken right up. In fact, it will become solid if left to its own devices, so keep your eye on it.

HANKSGIVING

EVERY YEAR, as the day officially consecrated by Mr. Lincoln approaches, periodicals are filled with articles on the "larger meaning" of Thanksgiving. Every year we are reminded, often at length, that Thanksgiving is not just stuffed turkey and cranberry sauce but a celebration of gratitude for American Abundance.

This is all very well and good, but at my house Thanksgiving *is* largely a matter of stuffed turkey and cranberry sauce. For me, as for most folks I know, these ritual foods are so saturated with meaning that no more needs to be said. Now is no time for clever variations and brilliant new recipes. Using the *old* recipes is pretty close to the whole point. Once you know how to make good bread stuffing, that's *it*, the flavor of Thanksgiving for the rest of your life.

The best, in fact the only, turkey is a fresh turkey. There's no point in going to that much bother over a second-rate bird. Turkey does not freeze well even under ideal conditions, never mind the conditions that usually obtain. Other things being equal, a fresh turkey will always have juicier meat and crisper, more tender skin than its frozen counterpart. The flavor of cooked turkey, however, survives freezing very well.

If you can spare the money and freezer space, a very large turkey (eighteen to twenty-five pounds) is almost always a better buy than a six to eight pounder. The giants are usually cheaper per pound, yet they carry more meat in proportion to bone and are likely to have better flavor as well.

Assuming, that is, that they are commercially grown turkeys. Farmyard birds of such imposing size may very well be elderly and tough, but feedlot gobblers, like battery chickens, don't stay around long enough to get old and don't move around vigorously enough to develop the muscles that might make them tough. They've been so thoroughly hybrid for big breasts and small legs that they can barely stand up.

Still, they can be very tasty, if they are fresh and unprocessed. Regrettably, an ever-larger percentage of commonly sold turkeys have been brutally violated. Either they're impaled with a plastic button that supposedly leaps up and shouts "I'm done!" at the appropriate moment, or they've been invaded and embalmed, or both.

You can remove the button if it offends you, neatly leaving a largish hole so the juices can run out, but don't, in any event, listen to it. By the time the tissue has shrunk enough to force the flag out, the turkey is overcooked. If you eat a turkey inoculated with sodium phosphates, hydrolyzed vegetable protein, soy and coconut oils, glycerin, polysorbate 60, and artificial flavor and color, you deserve whatever you get.

Assuming that what you get and cook is a properly fresh turkey, there will come a time to serve it. Before you do, consider the classically laden plate of Thanksgiving dinner. It holds: turkey, stuffing, mashed potatoes and/or sweet potatoes, squash or carrots or turnips, broccoli or Brussels sprouts or something else more or less green, plus gravy, plus cranberry sauce. At the very least. Even if you use one of those old-fashioned dinner plates with compartments for keeping things separate, eating a mouthful of food that has been so cosily presented is about like eating a mouthful of Persian rug — heavy and busy and not really a lot of fun. Unlike the rug, it will probably also be cold.

The best way to avoid that overwrought quality while still observing all the rituals is to stretch out the courses. Serve the vegetables first, while the turkey is re-collecting its juices and the gravy is mellowing. Allow everyone to enjoy the freshly cooked, simply sauced fruits of the earth, *then* pass the turkey and stuffing and gravy, along with another round of the vegetables. This second pass will take care of those who crave gravy on their potatoes and those who wish to intersperse bites of meat with something that's sweet and orange. The cranberry sauce, bread and butter and such may simply rest on the table throughout, for application as needed.

Once the noble bird has been dispatched, a little wisp of salad should make its appearance. Though yet more food might seem inappropriate, something clean-tasting is needed. This is to clear a path for the dessert, which will be too much of a muchness if it follows at once upon the heels of the richest course in the dinner.

Actually, the nicest way to deal with dessert is not to serve any until several hours later. In my family, we have the main meal in the late afternoon, around four or so, and we serve the pumpkin and apple pies with coffee (and hot cider for those who prefer it) at the close of the festivities, around nine or ten at night.

Even with this careful modulation, there's no doubt some flavors get lost. The cranberry sauce, for instance. Though absolutely essential to the production, its role is a small one, and niceties of its composition are usually lost in the multiflavored melee. Come the reruns, however, when the stuffing and gravy are long gone and it's just you and the cold turkey, that's when the relish really shines.

When, at last, it *is* time to deal with the leftovers, the first thing on the agenda is to *remember to de-stuff that turkey or you will die!* Maybe, anyway. You'll certainly improve your chances of getting at least mildly sick. When scientists want to culture poisonous microorganisms under the best possible laboratory conditions, they make a big roast turkey with meat-studded bread stuffing and put it in the refrigerator without taking out the stuffing. The dense layers of meat and bread insulate the interior, which never gets cold, and keep air out, to improve growing conditions further.

You don't have to employ a vacuum cleaner, as some food writers imply; just be sure the cold can get next to the whole turkey and don't re-create a turkey interior by tightly packing a deep, wide, heavy china bowl with stuffing.

The meat will stay most moist if it is packed for the freezer in large chunks, wrapped first in plastic and then in foil. Wide, flat packages both freeze and thaw more quickly than fat, square ones.

Mustard Fruit

This rich, seed-crunchy concoction of apricots, pineapple, pears, and chestnuts was originally suggested by the famous *mostarda di Cremona*, a mustard oil–flavored, syrup-bound condiment composed entirely of candied fruit. In the version below the pears are fresh and the other fruits are dried. This is partly for a change of flavor and partly to avoid the preservatives and dyes present in almost all candied fruit. Besides, why try to duplicate the unique? Genuine *mostarda* is widely available in gourmet and specialty stores. This is a sauce of a different relish.

For 2 pints (one for now and one for Christmas)

1¼ cups sugar
2¼ cups water
3-inch cinnamon stick, broken in 2 or 3 pieces
12 whole cloves
½ teaspoon whole mace blades
12 peppercorns
Cheesecloth
9 ounces fresh chestnuts in the shell

1 pound slightly underripe Seckel pears, the smaller the better, 5 to 8, depending on size
6 ounces dried apricots, about 1 cup
4 ounces dried pineapple, about 1 cup lightly piled half circles
2 ounces currants, about ½ cup
1 tablespoon dry mustard
¼ cup whole yellow mustard seeds

Dissolve the sugar in the water over low heat in a large saucepan. Tie the cinnamon, cloves, mace, and peppercorns in a small square of cheesecloth and put the spice bag in the syrup. Allow to simmer very slowly about 15 minutes.

Cut a cross in the flat side of each chestnut and roast on a cookie sheet in a preheated 375°F. oven about 10 minutes. They should be *barely* cooked; a little on the raw side is better than overdone. Peel the chestnuts, trying to keep them whole, then set aside. You should have about a cup.

Peel, halve, and core the pears, dropping them into the syrup as soon as they're prepared. Cook over low heat, stirring occasionally, until they are semitranslucent and tender when pierced with a toothpick. This will take 20 to 30 minutes, depending on size and ripeness. When the pears are cooked, remove them with a slotted spoon and reserve.

Stir the apricots, pineapple, and currants into the syrup and continue to simmer 30 to 45 minutes, or until the fruits are fully plumped and the liquid is substantially reduced and thickened. Stir, but not too often. Remove the spice bag, return the pears to the pan along with the chestnuts, and cook, stirring carefully and infrequently, only enough to mix the fruits and prevent sticking and scorching, 10 minutes more. Turn off the heat.

Put the dry mustard in a small bowl and dribble in only enough cold water to stir up a smooth paste the texture of heavy cream. Let it sit 10 to 15 minutes to mature, then combine it with some of the fruit syrup before stirring the whole works together.

Put the mustard seeds in an ungreased heavy skillet over low-medium heat and toast, shaking the pan constantly, about 3 minutes, or until the seeds have popped. They will quickly turn gray and taste toasted. Do not let them scorch. Turn the toasted seeds into the fruit mixture, stir one more time, and that's it. Needless to say, the stuff can be "put up" in sterilized jars, but it probably would keep until Easter anyway if it were refrigerated and nobody ate it up.

Crisp Root Relish

If Mustard Fruit is an embellishment, almost medieval in gaudiness, this is a refreshment, modern as tomorrow in its clarity of flavor, integrity of ingredients, and paucity of calories. A sort of instant Oriental pickle, it's an ideal contrast to the rest of the Thanksgiving fare.

For 8 to 10 small servings

1 pound small white turnips, peeled and cut in match sticks, about 3 cups
¾ pound parsnips, about 3 large, peeled and cut in match sticks, about 2¼ cups
1 tablespoon salt
¾-inch chunk of fresh ginger root, peeled and grated fine
Pinch of sugar
⅓ cup rice vinegar or other mild (4 percent) vinegar
1 cup mixed small sprouts — alfalfa, radish, mustard

In a corrosion-resistant bowl, combine the turnip and parsnip match sticks with the salt. Stir thoroughly. Allow to marinate at least 1 hour, up to 1½ hours. Stir when you think of it. Drain liquid, rinse briefly, and drain again.

Combine grated ginger, sugar, and vinegar and pour this dressing over the salt-wilted vegetables. Marinate, stirring now and then, at least 30 minutes at room temperature. Refrigerate, tightly covered, at least long enough to chill. The relish may be prepared up to this point as long as a day in advance. At serving time, toss the sprouts with the vinegared vegetables. Present this relish on small side dishes, if possible, so its sharp flavor doesn't get mixed up with anything else.

Sort of Scandinavian Turkey

This would be called "a nice luncheon or supper dish" in a Victorian cookbook. In the Victorian manner, it is on the heavy side. Not only is there a lot of cream sauce, but you also will want a lot of starch — mashed potatoes or noodles or rice or crusty bread — to sop it up. Wisdom suggests waiting at least a few days after the holiday before attempting it.

For 4 generous servings

4 tablespoons butter
1 teaspoon peanut oil

2 large cloves garlic, crushed but left whole
1 large onion, diced small, about 1½ cups
2 cups chopped mushrooms (see Note)
1 tablespoon minced shallot, about 2 small
½ cup vermouth
3 tablespoons Dijon mustard
½ teaspoon sugar
½ teaspoon freshly grated nutmeg
Generous handful, about ½ cup, minced fresh dill tips
3½ to 4 cups cubed cooked turkey meat (up to 1 cup could be ham or
    crabmeat if you are running low on turkey)
2 cups sour cream
½ cup heavy cream
Salt to taste

Combine the fats and garlic in a large skillet over low heat. When the butter melts, turn off the stove and let the mixture sit about 20 minutes. Remove and discard the garlic, turn the heat to medium, and add the onions and mushrooms. Fry them, stirring often, until they are a rich brown, about 10 minutes. At first they'll suck up all the fat, but they won't stick if you keep stirring.

When brownness is achieved, stir in the shallots, lower the heat, and cook until they are just softened, 2 to 3 minutes only. Add the vermouth, raise the heat again, and cook, stirring often, until the liquid is reduced by about one-half.

Add the mustard, sugar, nutmeg, and dill. Stir to combine, then add the meat and continue cooking only long enough to heat it through. While this is going on, put the sour cream in a bowl and beat it with a whisk to thin and de-lump it. Beat in the cream. Keeping the heat low, slowly stir the cream mixture into the meat. Continue cooking and stirring, always over low heat to prevent curdling, until the sauce is smooth, slightly thickened, and hot. Correct the salt and serve at once.

NOTE: This is very tasty made with wild mushrooms, especially chanterelles. At post-Thanksgiving time they will undoubtedly be dried or frozen (canned are not recommended). Frozen ones can be used as is; dried should be reconstituted by soaking in boiling water, with the liquid then strained and boiled down to a few tablespoons. Add the wild mushrooms when the onions are almost done; add the mushroom liquid with the wine. You'll need about 1½ cups frozen or ½ cup dried mushrooms; the latter will need about 1¼ cups boiling water. Either way, the wild ones won't add as much bulk as fresh mushrooms, so throw in a few roasted chestnuts or a bit more meat if there seems to be too much sauce.

✳ *Turkey Tacos*

This is basically a recipe for sauce. The more of the classic taco embellishments you set out for people to garnish it with, the further it will go. Don't forget that cold items such as sour cream and lettuce right from the refrigerator make it tough to assemble a hot taco, no matter how fast you are.

I am still waiting to meet a frozen corn tortilla good enough to just wrap in foil and heat up the way you can the flour ones, as a result of which I usually serve flour tortillas even though I prefer the taste of the corn. When ambition and diet admit of deep-frying, it's corn every time.

For 4 to 6 servings

¼ cup lard (yes, lard, not butter or vegetable oil, although bacon
    drippings or chicken fat is marginally acceptable)
1 large onion, chopped medium-fine, about 1½ cups
4 or 5 large cloves garlic, pressed
2 teaspoons dried oregano, crumbled
2 teaspoons ground cumin
1 teaspoon ground coriander seed
¼ teaspoon ground cloves
1 small bay leaf or half a big one
¼ cup (not a misprint) paprika (Be sure it's nice and fresh.)
1 cup puréed tomatoes, canned preferred once it's post-Thanksgiving
1 bottle (12 ounces) flat beer
2½ to 3 cups bits and odds and ends and shreds and miscellaneous last
    crumbs of the turkey
Plus, for assemblage: tortillas; finely chopped sweet onions; grated
    Jack, Muenster, or other mild cheese (mozzarella, though
    inauthentic, is tasty if it's truly fresh); chopped black olives;
    shredded lettuce; sliced avocado; sour cream; Tabasco or other hot
    sauce of choice

Melt the lard in a large skillet and slowly fry the onion over low-medium heat until it is transparent and golden but not brown. Stir in everything up to the tomatoes, turn off the heat, cover the pan, and let the seasonings "sweat" about 5 minutes.

Uncover and return the pan to the heat, add the tomatoes and beer, and bring to the boil. Stir in the turkey, lower the heat to medium-low, and simmer, stirring more and more frequently, about an hour, or until the turkey has almost disintegrated and the sauce is very thick.

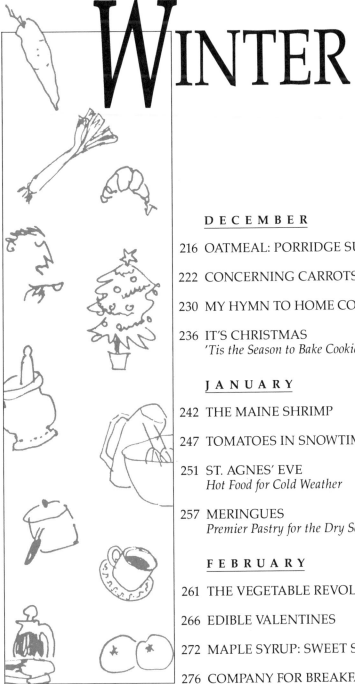

WINTER

*O*ATMEAL: PORRIDGE SUPREME

THERE WAS a time when oatmeal was the keystone, if not the capstone, of every hearty breakfast worth the name. It was the very meat and meaning of hot cereal; a foodstuff *worthy* of Ceres, grain's good goddess; a guarantee of nourishment, warmth, and homey substance in general. But though it may still support the Scots, it no longer enjoys much of a reputation here.

Friends are prone to snicker if you talk it up in their hearing, and house guests give you funny looks if you so much as offer it. Its much vaunted nutritional value has been debunked by expert dieticians, and the same outfit that merchandised it to its former American eminence now manufactures porridge so instant you merely pour the loathsome powder into your matinal bowl and pour the boiling water thereon. Then, presumably, if you have even a grain of sense, you pour it out.

I have no intention of railing at further length on the subject. I ask only that when morning comes you look earnestly into your heart, toward the place where your moral sense abides, and ask yourself, "What do I know, deep down in my very bones, will be the most comforting, fortifying, satisfying breakfast this cold and stormy day?"

Making *Good* Oatmeal

Is essential. The Fall of Oatmeal is undoubtedly in part attributable to the resemblance of ill-made oatmeal to the glutinous gruel confected by the devil for the breakfast of the damned. There's nothing to good oatmeal but oats, salt, and water; technique is everything. The water should be lightly salted, to help keep the grains firm and separate. The grain should be added so slowly the water never stops boiling, for the same reasons. Stir as you add, then turn the heat to medium-low and keep cooking, stirring often, about 4 minutes. Cover the pan tightly and let it sit in a warm place 3 to 4 minutes more. (These directions are for rolled oats — plain old rolled oats, the flaky type of oatmeal. True "Irish" (!) oatmeal is coarsely cut grain that will not cook tender in this amount of time. Cover with cold water the night before, drain, and follow these directions, using the soaking water, in the morning; or plan on taking about a half hour to cook the stuff.)

Correctly made oatmeal will vary in thickness with the preference of its maker, but it will always be a deliciously warming mixture of slightly nutty, chewy grain in a flavorful, rather creamy sauce. Butter and/or cream will make the sauce even more unctuous. I like sweet and salty oatmeal buttered and brown-sugared. Scots, a rugged bunch if ever there was one, traditionally opt for simple milk and salt, or sometimes just salt, milk being a "Sassenach," or English frippery, as far as old-timers are concerned.

Some (benighted) people put preserves or raisins on or in; more sensible ones use maple syrup. Honey is okay but not great; it's hard to get a pleasing balance of flavors without oversweetening the oatmeal. Spices are, in my opinion, a poor idea, as they overpower the nutty taste of the oats.

Don't forget to heat the bowls.

Plan on ⅓ cup oats and a scant cup of water with a pinch of salt for each serving, and go from there. Half oats and half water produces porridge that'll stand a spoon. A few additional oats can be used to thicken weak oatmeal at any time up to the pan-covering part, and you can add more water if the cereal is too thick. Just remember to use hot. Cold water and hot porridge make oat glue.

Cold water and hot sticky foul old impossible oatmeal pan, however, when given an hour or two of soaking time, make cleanup easy.

RAY OF HOPE DEPARTMENT: Although oatmeal is on the "out" list, as far as food fashion is concerned, there is a related star new-shining on the horizon. That star is oat bran, currently regarded as a miracle food, supposedly so potent it will help prevent cancer while lowering your cholesterol level, thus preventing heart attacks as well.

"Soluble fiber" is what oat bran provides — gums and pectins, to be precise, two of the five or more kinds of available dietary fiber, *all* of which we should be eating more of if the nutrition experts (speaking for once pretty much in concert) are to be believed.

Scotch Collops with Spiked Onion Sauce

Originally, "collops" were boneless slices of something. It's from the same root that gives us the French *escalopes* and the Italian *scaloppine*. In Scotland nowadays, "collops" usually means minced meat — more like hash than hamburgers, though this varies, but definitely not slices. This recipe is for the old-fashioned kind of collops, in a rather new-fashioned preparation. The chappit 'tatties (mashed potatoes) classically served with haggis go well here, and if you wanted a suitably Scottish green vegetable, you couldn't do better than kale. Serve ice cream with butterscotch sauce for dessert and the haggis eaters will have nothing on you in the chauvinistic eats department.

For 4 servings

1½ cups finely chopped onion, about 1 large
1 tablespoon plus 1 teaspoon butter
1 cup plus ⅓ cup lamb broth or chicken broth, divided
⅓ cup cream
1¼ pounds lean, boneless lamb slices, from the leg or loin, cut about ⅓ inch thick
Approximately 4 tablespoons oat bran (look in the health food or gourmet section if it's not in with the cereals) or finely ground oatmeal (not rolled oats)
Approximately 2 tablespoons bacon fat, beef drippings, or mixed butter and oil, for frying
⅓ cup or a bit more Scotch whisky (see Note)
1 heaping tablespoon cornstarch
½ teaspoon cracked black pepper
Salt to taste
¼ cup minced fresh parsley

In a heavy saucepan, sauté the onion in the butter over medium heat until it is thoroughly cooked and a light golden brown. Add 1 cup of the lamb or chicken broth and the cream and set the mixture to simmer over medium heat.

Pare from the meat as much fat as possible. Sandwich the pieces between sheets of waxed paper and pound gently but firmly until the meat is flattened to ¼ inch or a bit thinner. Sprinkle the collops on both sides with the oat bran to make a very light, even coating. Press it in with your fingers.

Heat a generous layer of the frying fat in a wide skillet over medium-high heat, then quickly sear the prepared collops about 2 minutes a side, just long enough to brown them and cook to a pinkish rare. Do not crowd the pan; fry in two batches if necessary. Remove the meat to a serving platter and keep it warm.

Pour the Scotch into the skillet and stir it with a flat metal spatula to get up all the browned bits. It will bubble away rapidly to only a few tablespoons. Before it vanishes completely, add the onion-broth mixture.

Dissolve the cornstarch in the remaining ⅓ cup broth and pour the result into the sauce, stirring as you do so. Add the pepper and continue to stir until the sauce liquid has thickened slightly. Taste, adjust the salt, and add a bit more whisky if that seems necessary. Then pour the sauce around the collops, garnish with the parsley, and serve at once.

NOTE: Any old Scotch whisky you happen to have lying around will do, but unblended (single malt) Scotch is particularly effective because it is so flavorful. The malts are what give blended whiskies their distinctive tastes; everything else is nearly neutral spirit added to bulk things out and calm things down. The single malts are so intense they're usually compared to cognac. Like cognac they should never be mixed or iced, and like cognac they are very expensive. They're worth it, though, as a special treat.

✳ *Oat Nut Sourdough Bread*

This is a singularly satisfying bread, very nutty flavored, with an indefinable tart edge contributed by the sourdough. If you don't have your own starter, try to find a friend who does, since that is much the nicest way to get one. Failing that, it's off to the health food or gourmet store, where instant sourdough starter mixes are sold.

For 2 loaves

SPONGE:
1½ cups firm cooked oatmeal
½ cup milk
¼ cup water
1 cup batter-strength sourdough starter
1½ cups bread flour

BREAD:
2 teaspoons dry yeast dissolved in ¼ cup tepid water
1 beaten egg
½ cup butter, melted, or even better, ⅓ cup duck, goose, or chicken fat, melted, plus enough to grease the pans

¼ cup mild honey
2½ teaspoons salt (less if the oatmeal is salty)
⅓ cup lightly toasted, unsalted cashew nuts, chopped fine
¼ cup sesame seeds
1 tablespoon anise seeds (optional)
6 to 7½ cups bread flour (Don't use more than 1 cup whole-wheat or
 the bread will be heavy and coarse.)
Oat flakes for the pans

GLAZE:
1 egg, beaten
2 tablespoons cream or milk
Cinnamon

Start the night before you want to bake. Beat sponge ingredients together in the order given in a very large bowl and cover tightly with plastic wrap. Allow to rise at cool room temperature 8 to 10 hours, or until very light and bubbly. If your sourdough is very lively, the sponge may rise so much it collapses. That's okay.

Beat down the sponge and add all the bread ingredients except the flour, mixing all well. Then start stirring in the flour. When you have a soft dough that leaves the sides of the bowl, turn it out on a well-floured board, cover it with the overturned bowl, and let it rest 5 to 10 minutes. Uncover and start kneading in additional flour until you have a smooth bread dough that is still slightly — very slightly — sticky. Return it to the bowl, cover with plastic wrap or a dampened tea towel, and let rise until fully double, usually about 3 hours.

Generously butter 2 standard loaf pans and sprinkle the buttered surfaces with oat flakes. Knock down the dough on a lightly floured board, reknead briefly, form loaves, and put 'em in the pans. Again cover and let rise, this time until just a tad shy of fully double.

Preheat the oven to 400°F., put in the bread, and turn heat down to 375°F. Bake 40 minutes, then brush with the glaze, which you have confected by beating together the egg and cream. Sprinkle loaves with the cinnamon. Return them to the oven and bake 5 minutes more, or until the glaze is set and they test done by your favorite testing method — I tap and listen for hollowness. When in doubt I always overbake, but then I really love crust.

Big Oatmeal Cookies with Dates and Nuts

For thirty 3½-inch cookies

¾ cup butter
¾ cup brown sugar
½ cup granulated sugar
2 eggs
¼ cup milk
1 teaspoon almond extract
2 cups all-purpose flour
1 teaspoon cinnamon
1 teaspoon allspice
½ teaspoon baking powder
½ teaspoon baking soda
½ teaspoon salt
2½ cups rolled oats (not instant)
1 cup dates, cut in ¼-inch dice
1 cup coarsely broken walnuts
¼ cup sweetened shredded coconut
¼ cup sesame seeds

Cover a flat baking sheet with parchment if possible, tinfoil if necessary. If you use tinfoil, butter it generously. Preheat the oven to 375°F.

Cream the butter with the sugars until light and fluffy — the sugar needn't be completely dissolved, but it should be very well mixed in. Beat the eggs with the milk and almond extract until the mixture is foamy. Sift the flour with the spices, baking powder, baking soda, and salt. Make sure all the embellishments are ready.

Using a wooden spoon, work about half the flour mixture into the butter and sugar. Add the milk and egg mixture and combine well. Then add the rest of the flour mixture and, as soon as the dough is smooth, the oats, dates, nuts, coconut, and sesame seeds. Give each addition about 2 stirs before adding the next, but don't wait until each is well mixed. Stir only enough to ensure proper distribution of the goodies at the end.

Put golf ball–sized dollops of the dough on the lined baking sheet, spacing them about 8 inches apart. Use a knife blade to flatten and spread the dough into 3½-inch circles (which will spread a bit in the oven). Be sure they aren't more than about ¼ inch thick.

Bake the cookies 8 minutes, then reverse the sheet so they brown evenly and lower the heat to 350°F. Bake another 5 to 8 minutes, or until the cookies are nicely browned and a broken one is dry in the center. They will be soft when they come out of the oven, but will become chewy, with crisp edges, as they cool. Cool on a wire rack.

HINTS FOR SUCCESS *(actually these are pretty hard to mess up):*

1. Parchment paper is ideal for baking this kind of sturdy cookie. The bottoms are less likely to burn, there is no fear of sticking, and the browning is very even. Plus you don't have to grease the pan (or wash it either).

2. If you dip the ends of a pair of scissors in cold water before using them to cut up the dates, life will be less sticky.

3. There is a strong temptation to experiment in the fruit and nut department, which should be indulged. Remember that dates are very sweet — if you substitute dried apricots, for instance, increase the sugar a little bit. Also, that small sprinkle of coconut has a marked textural effect; cookies without it will be less chewy. Cookies with more will be very chewy indeed.

4. The salt really enhances the flavor and should not be lightly discarded.

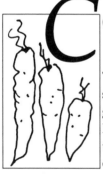ONCERNING CARROTS

THE THING ABOUT carrots is that they're so . . . well, so *there*, so commonplace, so taken for granted, so long given but limited use that one's response to them is Pavlovian. Say the word and the mind dutifully registers "good for you," "see at night," and, if one is of a certain age, "makes curly hair." What does the mind picture? Carrot sticks, the dieter's friend, faithful standby of the relish tray; glazed carrots, staple vegetable of childhood; frozen carrots, in little dice, with fat, flat-tasting green peas.

There's been a bit of an improvement lately. Those under the age of thirty seem to associate carrots primarily with cake, which may not be healthy but is at least not dispiriting. Yet how many think of *Potage Crécy*, the classic French carrot soup? Of carrots browned in butter and showered with dill? Or of *gajar halva*, the silver leaf–topped Indian sweet, rich with pistachios and rose water, that is made of carrots cooked with milk into a silken fudge?

And how many think of standing in the sunny late spring garden, pulling one of the first small carrots, wiping off the dirt with the feathery tops, and tasting that incomparably fresh, juicy, aromatic pleasure that is a *good* carrot?

Alas, far too few. Carrots might, like potatoes, have been doomed by their durability. Storage carrots are less wonderful than fresh carrots, but if they were good to start with, they'll stay pretty tasty (when properly kept) for a very long time. As a result, nobody thinks of them as a seasonal specialty. They are at their best when freshly harvested, though, from late winter through late spring and again in the fall.

Right now, carrot-consciousness is at about the place lettuce-consciousness used to be before the produce-mad eighties, when almost everybody ate iceberg except the gourmets, who ate romaine. There are still only two basic varieties of carrot being widely sold, out of a possible four, and that's just counting orange carrots. They also come, albeit not to market, in yellow and purple and white.

Kinds of Carrots

IMPERATOR: This is the only kind most consumers ever see, the most commonly sold type of "fresh" carrot. Rather pale in color, long, tapering to a point at about eight inches, Imperators grow easily and uniformly, with strong, substantial tops that make them easy to pick. They also store well, holding a fresh flavor and texture for considerable periods. Though quite tasty, especially if very fresh, they are by no means the be-all and end-all of carrot-hood, as their ubiquity would lead one to suppose.

DANVERS: Long and pointy, like Imperators, but fatter, with broad, flat shoulders, these are used extensively in processing. They have a strong carrot flavor, but it isn't very sweet, and the texture tends to be a bit tough. For these reasons, Danvers isn't much of a fresh market carrot, even though it's one of the easier types to grow.

CHANTENAY *(including the stubby "baby" types)*: These are the championship keepers, holding their bright color and firm texture through many months in storage. The tiny "baby" carrots usually sold in clear plastic bags are actually full-grown minicarrots, hybrids closer to Chantenays than anything else. Whether mini or full-sized, Chantenays are fat, sharply tapered to a fairly blunt end, and comparatively short. Their bright pigmentation and bulky shape make them favorites with processors, and their excellent keeping qualities endear them to home gardeners. They are much tastier than Danvers as long as they have been properly grown, and their darker orange indicates an especially high concentration of the pigment carotene, also known as provitamin A.

NANTES: Almost everything is wrong with these rather pale, mid-sized cylindrical carrots of the sloping shoulders and blunt tips. The foliage is sparse and fragile, so weeds are a problem and harvest is difficult. The roots themselves are brittle, and they do not ship or store well. The only thing that's *right* with them, of course, is their fine eating quality. The texture of Nantes carrots is juicy and crisp; the flavor is full and clean and sweet above that of any other carrot.

Carrots and Health

You probably already know that carrots are an excellent low-calorie source of vitamin A, more of which will be available if you either cook the carrots or drink them as juice. The following, however, from *Jane Brody's Nutrition Book*, might be news: "Scottish researchers showed that eating seven ounces of raw carrots at breakfast every day for three weeks could reduce cholesterol levels by eleven percent and increase the amount of fat excreted by fifty percent." What the psychological effect of a half pound of raw carrots first thing in the morning is likely to be was not discussed.

Shopping for Carrots

Farmers' markets and specialty stores are the only places likely to carry the Nantes type, but no matter what type you're buying, the guidelines are the same. Be sure to avoid "green shoulders," caused by exposure to sunlight during growth. This part of the carrot will be bitter and must be discarded. *Storage* carrots should look wholesome and slime-free, with no signs of sprouting. The roots must use up stored sugars and moisture to support this new growth, so sprouted carrots are flat tasting, limp, and sometimes even mealy. *Fresh "bunch"* carrots are usually sold with stems and leaves attached. Judge their quality by that of the greenery, then cut those leaves off of there so they don't keep drawing goodness from the roots.

Unlike turnip, beet, and radish leaves, carrot tops are too strong and bitter to be useful as greens or in soup, but they are highly ornamental. I have used them successfully in arrangements of roses and lilies, where they looked a lot better than the boresome sprigs of fern and arbor vitae sent along by the florist. And, according to English food authority Jane Grigson, "Ladies of the Stuart court pinned the feathery plumage of young carrots to their heads and on their splendid hats. The leaves drooped down from exquisite brooches on sleeves, instead of the more usual feathers."

Ideally, fresh carrots should be sold "topped," with only a short stub of growth left as proof to the consumer that they were indeed recently harvested. Unfortunately, this sensible though unlovely marketing style has never caught on and is rarely seen.

Preparing Carrots

When they are fresh and sweet and new, the simplest preparations are best. Many vitamins lie right under the skin, so if it is young and cleanable, leave it on. The skin of full-grown carrots, on the other hand, especially of the common type, is rather soapy tasting and should be removed with a carrot peeler. Steam new carrots and serve with a bit of butter, lemon, and either fresh dill or fresh chervil. To enjoy them raw, grate on the fine holes of a grater almost to a paste and mix them with a very gentle, garlic-less vinaigrette.

Hot and Winey Carrots with Garlic and Pecans

For 4 generous servings

½ cup pecans
1 pound mature fresh carrots
1 large onion
2 tablespoons peanut oil or other vegetable oil
2 or 3 small (3-inch) dried hot red peppers, crushed to bits, including seeds
Strip of orange zest (thin, colored outer rind) about ½ by 4 inches
¼ cup water
2 large cloves garlic, minced not too fine
2 teaspoons cornstarch
1 tablespoon plus 1 teaspoon tamari or other soy sauce
⅓ cup Chinese rice wine or medium-dry sherry

Spread the pecans on a shallow pan and toast in a 350°F. oven about 12 minutes, until they smell good and are golden brown inside. Set aside to cool, then chop into coarse crumbs. Peel the carrots if necessary and slice them on a long diagonal into ¼-inch ovals. Slice the peeled onion into 8 wedges and separate the wedges into leaves.

In a large wok or very large skillet, heat the oil over high heat till it sizzles. Add the peppers and orange zest and cook approximately 30 seconds, until they turn dark brown but not black. Dump in the carrots and stir vigorously to coat with the flavored oil. Add the water, lower heat slightly and cook, stirring frequently but not constantly, until the liquid has boiled away and the carrots are tender but still crisp — about 6 to 7 minutes.

Now add the onion leaves and stir-fry until they are almost cooked — still crisp but no longer raw tasting. Add the garlic and cook about 2 minutes more. Combine the cornstarch, soy sauce, and sherry and pour it in. Stir madly, as the sauce will thicken almost instantly to a glazelike coating. Serve at once, garnished with the reserved pecans.

This is a wonderful side dish with roast lamb and a fine repository for leftovers thereof. Add about 1 cup of thinly sliced cooked lamb right before you add the onions and serve with lightly buttered brown rice or whole-wheat noodles for a satisfying one-dish dinner.

Angelhair Carrots with Applesauce

The sweetness of the apple complements the carrot flavor, while masking any of the soapy or bitter overtones storage carrots sometimes display.

For 4 to 6 servings

Approximately 2 pounds carrots, enough to make 4 heaping cups
   prepared
½ cup applesauce, preferably unsweetened
½ cup cider or pure apple juice
1 cup light chicken or vegetable stock
1 large clove garlic, pressed
1 tablespoon tamari or other aged soy sauce
Tiny pinch of cinnamon
2½ tablespoons butter
Salt to taste
Fresh minced parsley for garnish, about 3 tablespoons

Begin by preparing the carrots; you want long, thin strips about the size of fat spaghetti. Depending on the age and type of the carrots, it might be necessary to cut the flavorful outer carrot flesh from the cores before you start cutting the strips.

Cut off the tip, stand a carrot on end and slice down to get four slabs of outer carrot; set aside and taste the core. If it tastes good, the rest of those in the same batch probably will be fine. Regrettably, in the case of commercial storage carrots, it probably will taste woody if it tastes at all, and you'll have to core the carrots before proceeding. (Well, you don't *have* to, obviously, as almost nobody pays any attention to this nicety when preparing carrots and the world still wags. But if you do, the result will be tastier.) When the carrots are ready, set them aside.

In a wide saucepan, combine the applesauce, cider, and stock. Cook, stirring often, over medium-high heat, until the liquid is thickened and reduced to about a cup. Add the garlic, tamari, and cinnamon and set the sauce aside but keep warm.

Put the carrots in a basket steamer over boiling water in a large kettle and steam about 4 minutes, or until they are tender but still firm. If they are piled deeply in the pan, stir them once or twice to promote even cooking. As soon as they are done, lift the basket, drain the water, and return the carrots to the pan.

Toss once or twice to make sure the carrots are thoroughly dry, then add the reserved sauce and the butter. Swirl the pan around so the butter melts and all is mixed, then taste for salt. If you used canned broth, it is most unlikely that you'll need any salt. (In fact, if you plan to used canned broth, you might wish to use unsalted butter, the better to avoid sodium overload.) Serve at once, sprinkled lightly with the parsley.

❄ *The Quintessential Carrot Cake*

The following is the result of *many* experiments, prompted by the need to make a wedding cake for a carrot cake lover, my fondness for whom was sufficient to overcome a long-standing indifference to the stuff. It wasn't easy — lots of inquiring after recipes, much copying of cookbooks.

They all seemed to be made with oil, which struck me as odd where oil makes such ratty pastry. Still, such unanimity couldn't be wrong; I gave it a try. "First rate," said the various tasters. "Heavy and greasy," said I. Well, why *can't* you make it like a classic butter cake? Dense and dry is why. Too many carrots and it gets soggy; not enough carrots and the thing comes out spongy and bland. This recipe is a lulu.

CAKE:
Butter and flour for the pan
1 cup all-purpose flour
1 cup cake flour
1 tablespoon cinnamon
½ teaspoon each ground ginger, allspice, salt, and fresh grated nutmeg
1 teaspoon baking soda
2 teaspoons baking powder
1 cup plus 2 tablespoons butter
1 cup granulated sugar
¼ cup brown sugar
4 egg yolks
1 cup raisins
¾ cup coarsely broken pecan or walnut meats
2 tablespoons peanut oil
1¾ cups finely grated carrots
5 egg whites
¼ teaspoon cream of tartar

ICING:
½ cup sugar
½ cup water
4-inch length of vanilla bean, split to expose the seeds
11 ounces cream cheese, preferably the fresh, gum-free variety
2 tablespoons unsalted butter
Brandy or rum for the cake

Butter a 10-inch springform pan, dust lightly with flour, and set aside. Set aside 1 tablespoon of the flour and combine the rest with the dry ingredients (down to the butter), sifting or stirring with a wire whisk to make sure they are well combined. Set aside.

In a very large mixing bowl, cream the butter with the sugars until the mixture is very light and fluffy. A bit rubbed between your fingertips should feel just about gritless. When it does, beat in the egg yolks one at a time. Set aside.

Preheat the oven to 350°F. Toss the raisins and nuts with the reserved tablespoon of flour. Beat the butter mixture for a moment, then beat in the peanut oil. Mix the carrots in thoroughly, then stir in the dry ingredients, as rapidly as possible given that this is one heavy batter you bet.

Beat the egg whites with the cream of tartar until they form stiff but still shiny peaks. Stir a third of the whites into the batter to lighten it, then add the next third with a combined stirring/folding motion. Fold in the raisin-nut mixture, then fold in the last of the whites. The flat of your hand works better than a spatula, especially if you have big hands.

Turn the batter into the prepared pan and smooth the top with a couple of fast swipes. Bang the pan straight down, sharply, to dislodge air bubbles and even the surface. Using a sharp, thin-bladed knife, cut a ½-inch-deep groove in the surface about 1 inch in from the edge, all the way around. This encourages the cake to rise evenly, instead of swelling to a majestic hump in the middle.

Bake it in the center of the oven 1 hour 20 minutes, or until a cake tester comes out clean. Let it cool on a rack, in the pan, 10 minutes, then remove the ring, invert the cake on another rack, and remove the bottom. Immediately, before the top has time to stick, invert upright onto the first rack, and let cool completely. You can finish and serve it right away, but like the fruitcakes it so closely resembles, it'll taste better if you let it age, wrapped tightly in plastic, 2 to 3 days.

To make the icing, combine the sugar, water, and vanilla bean in a small, heavy saucepan. Stir over low heat until the sugar melts, washing down crystals from the sides of the pan with a water-dipped pastry brush. Then turn heat to medium and simmer vigorously without stirring until a thick syrup forms. It should register 230°F. on a candy thermometer. Remove from the heat and let cool, then remove the vanilla bean, scraping with a sharp knife blade to get as many seeds as possible in the icing.

Beat the cream cheese with the butter until thoroughly mixed, light, and fluffy. Then beat in the syrup, slowly, until you have a soft, smooth icing (all the syrup might not be needed).

To complete the cake, put it on a level surface and use a long-bladed knife with a serrated edge to slice it in half. Stick in a few toothpicks before you start, to act as guides, and you should get a pair of fairly even layers. Sprinkle both cut sides generously with hooch, then put the lower half, bottom side down, on a serving plate. Spread the surface with a third of the icing, apply the top half of the cake, and spread another third of the icing around the sides. Put the remaining icing in a pastry bag and pipe it decoratively over the top so that the cake is completely covered.

MY HYMN TO HOME COOKING

ACCORDING TO a 1985 *New York Times* story on the subject, the number of different fast-food chains had climbed to somewhere around 340 by that year. They were responsible for the approximately 60,000 fast-food restaurants in America, which did $44.8 billion worth of business. You would think that this would have been enough, already, but, no, "lite" fever and the magic word "upscale" reared their lucrative little heads, and just about then a vast new crop of fast-food outlets began sprouting all over the countryside.

There are fast-food salad bars now, and Chinese places, and gourmet hamburger joints with fancy decor and full alcohol service. There are taco stands and grilled chicken specialists and baked stuffed potato shops that sell corn on the cob. With many of these latter entrants has come either the unspoken implication or the outright claim that fast food, traditional bad guy, is groping its way toward being good food — nourishing, tasty, and still inexpensive, if no longer dirt cheap.

Theoretically, it's far from impossible. All it would take is proper attention to quality and freshness. Steamed asparagus is a fast food — only takes three to four minutes. Boston clam chowder is a fast food — all you do is heat it up, preferably on the second day. Yet the problem is not going to be completely solved even if the food in these places *does* become tasty and nourishing, because the problem isn't just the food. The problem is that something is wrong if your life is so hectic that "fast" is your daily nourishment's first name.

I'm not knocking convenience here, just pointing out that home cooking is an increasingly important source of relaxation in this over-speedy world. Home cooking nourishes the eye, hand, and heart, as well as the belly, whereas a fast-food place, by definition, can only shove the eats at you and run. Good food is so central to daily well-being, why keep it at such a distance? Why stop at just eating it, when there are so many pleasures to be had from getting close to the comestibles *before* you get outside of them?

Fold the raspberry purée into the whipped cream and watch the spreading of that incredible pink, like a wave in a Japanese print. Drop the dark chard in the golden broth and watch the heat intensify its greenness till it glows like grass after a storm. Break back the thick outer stalks of bok choy and rejoice in the perfect miniature heads, tiny sheaves of folded leaves that nestle against the parent stem. Put your palms against the silk smooth bread dough, pliant and elastic, press and knead and form a loaf. The homelike aroma of baking bread is at this point counterfeited in supermarkets, but the fragrance of those loaves while still rising — yeasty, humid, full of promise — is a fragrance only bakers and their families get to enjoy.

In closing this little exhortation I wish to point out that only the home cook, the frequent home cook, has the power to create nourishing, tasty, inexpensive food that is also highly varied; and that chances for personal expression, so essential to mental health, are very easy to come by in the kitchen.

My Mom's Stuffed Meat Loaf

Basically, a juicy hamburger with the bun baked inside, where it can bathe in all the lovely juices. As is generally true of bread stuffings, this one can be embellished by bits of meat, fruit, or extra vegetables, such as celery, green pepper, and mushrooms. Similarly, the herbs can be amplified or downplayed according to your preference.

For 4 to 6 servings

STUFFING:
3 tablespoons butter
1½ cups chopped onion, about 1 large
½ cup walnuts, chopped quite small
Grated zest (thin, colored outer rind) of 1 large lemon, about 1
    tablespoon
2½ cups plain, fairly sturdy bread — French, whole-wheat, or farm-
    style white — either cut into small (not more than ⅓-inch) cubes or
    very coarsely crumbled
1½ teaspoons dried thyme leaves, crumbled
1½ teaspoons dried sage leaves, crumbled
¼ cup minced fresh parsley
¼ teaspoon cracked black pepper
½ teaspoon salt
Approximately ⅔ cup warm milk

MEAT LOAF:
1½ pounds lean ground beef
1 beaten egg

1 large clove garlic, pressed
2 tablespoons catsup
1 teaspoon Worcestershire sauce
Butter for loaf pan
Olive oil and flour for crust, about 1 tablespoon each

Make the stuffing. Melt the butter in a heavy skillet over medium heat and sauté the onion in it, stirring occasionally, until it is wilted, golden, and just starting to turn brown, about 10 minutes. Add the walnuts and cook, stirring now and then, about 8 minutes more, or until they start to smell toasted. Stir in the lemon zest, take the pan from the heat, and at once scrape out all the contents over the bread cubes. Stir thoroughly, then stir in the remaining stuffing ingredients except the milk.

Now start adding the milk, a little at a time, stirring as you go. Pause frequently; you may not want it all, as breads vary widely in the moistness department. You want the stuffing damp enough so it doesn't leach juices from the meat but dry enough so it won't turn to paste when it absorbs all those delicious drippings. Set the stuffing aside.

Combine the meat loaf ingredients, tossing gently with your fingertips or a long-pronged fork so the meat isn't crushed and toughened. Set aside roughly ½ cup of the mixture. Preheat the oven to 350°F.

Set out a sheet of waxed paper about 16 inches long and turn the larger portion of meat out onto it. Patting and smoothing, spread the meat into a flat rectangle about 12 by 14 inches. Spread the stuffing in an even layer over the meat, leaving a ½-inch margin at one end. Press firmly as you go, to bond the meat and its filling together.

Butter the loaf pan. Using the edge of the waxed paper as a helper, turn the ½-inch edge over the stuffing, then roll the loaf up like a jellyroll, pressing and patting as you go. Leave the roll, seam side down, and pat the reserved meat over the top, like icing. Stroke it right into the surface, paying particular attention to the edges so it won't peel up as it cooks. This icing business is to help keep the loaf from splitting on top like a pound cake. Its purpose is purely aesthetic, and its omission will not affect flavor. If you don't feel like bothering, just use all the meat for the roll.

Transfer the loaf, seam side down, to the pan and hand-mold so there's a channel at the sides for juices to collect instead of running over. Rub the top with the olive oil, then sprinkle on the flour — this will form a nice crust — and bake 1 hour, or until the juices run clear.

Let the baked meat loaf cool 5 minutes, then pour off any extra fat. Let sit 2 to 3 minutes more, so the loaf can firm up for easier slicing. As is so often the case with meat loaf, it's even better cold, the next day.

You will notice that there has been no mention of gravy. Of course not; meat loaf doesn't *have* gravy, it has applesauce. There may well be other vegetables — snap beans, corn on the cob, a green salad — but the applesauce is a constant. (And no back talk about how applesauce is not a vegetable. To those of us who grew up with it, it is too.) Don't forget the mashed potatoes.

Simple Cream of Tomato Soup

For 4 generous servings

3 tablespoons butter
1 medium-large onion, minced fine, about 1 cup
2 tablespoons flour
4 cups very light chicken or vegetable stock or broth
2 cups canned crushed tomatoes or tomato purée (see "Getting the Best Canned Tomatoes" on page 234)
1 cup light cream or ½ cup each heavy cream and half-and-half
Salt to taste
Pinch of sugar (may not be needed)

Melt the butter over low-medium heat in a small, heavy-bottomed soup pot and slowly cook the onion until transparent. This should take about 15 minutes, at the end of which the onion should be wilted but not at all brown. Sprinkle in the flour, which is there to bind rather than thicken the soup, and cook, stirring, about 5 minutes. Slowly stir in the broth, then the tomato purée.

Bring the liquid to a simmer, then lower the heat until it barely heaves up a bubble every now and then. Partially cover the pan and let cook at this slow rate approximately 1 hour. Lift the cover from time to time, skim any foam that has risen, and stir the soup to be sure it doesn't catch on the bottom. At the end of the hour, uncover the pan, raise the heat to low-medium, and allow the froth to rise, stirring just enough to prevent scorching. Turn off the heat and remove the froth. Put the finished product through a strainer, pressing to get all the onion flavor but stopping short of actually puréeing the onion into the soup.

Wipe but don't bother to wash the soup pot and heat the cream in it. Slowly, beating constantly with a whisk, add the soup to the cream. The warmth of the cream and the order in which ingredients are being added — possible curdling agent into bulk of curdle-susceptible material, rather than the other way around — help ensure a smooth, indeed velvety, result. Reheat if necessary, being sure the soup does not boil, and add salt to taste. The amount needed to bring out the flavor will vary widely. If the soup seems flat or not tomatoey enough, even after you've put in the salt, try adding a very small pinch of sugar. Tomatoes are, after all, fruit, and the best of them are quite sweet.

Getting the Best Canned Tomatoes

The delicious flavor of home-canned tomatoes is mostly attributable to the higher quality of the tomatoes that went into the can in the first place. Gardeners do get the best tomatoes and there it is. But home-canned tomatoes owe some of their superior flavor to the fact that the "can" is made of glass. For consumers who do not have access to homemade, canned tomatoes are so closely associated with a metallic taste that in one test I read about, a majority of participants actually rejected fresher-tasting products that had been preserved in other ways, preferring the familiar *je ne sais quoi* provided by a *soupçon* of tin.

The acidity of the fruit is what leaches the metal from the can, and it is also the quality that makes tomatoes such an ideal subject for canning, whether of the commercial or home-done sort. They hold their flavor well when cooked, and they are very inhospitable to bacteria, hence quite safe. Just as they are. And for years, that's how they came, with the addition of nothing more than a bit of salt. Now canned tomato products are likely to contain calcium chloride and/or citric acid as well. Neither of these is harmful, exactly, but neither is, how shall we put it, an improvement.

Brands of canned tomato products vary widely — in additive content, flavor, wateriness, intensity of taste. Since they are a staple you can expect to call on quite frequently, shopping around is a justifiable exercise and paying a few pennies more for the best is a justifiable expense.

 Chopped Liver

This delicacy, as straightforward as its title, is one of the glories of the Ashkenazic home kitchen. Rich in flavor, meaty, yet not stodgy, comforting and filling, it is the equal, if not the superior, of many high-priced pâtés. Though not difficult to make, it does require the exercise of one important talent — self-restraint. The temptation to gussy up the chopped liver, to add spices and wine and nutmeats and even, heaven help us, garlic, must be stalwartly resisted. These additions can be used to make a tasty pâté or *mousse de foie*, but they have no place in chopped liver. Even butter should be looked at askance. Chopped liver is supposed to be moistened with schmaltz, the rendered fat of chickens, geese, or ducks, a golden grease that is the very synonym of homely plenty. This being the modern world, in which good schmaltz, like a good man, is frequently hard to find, I am willing to admit the substitution of butter as preferable to no chopped liver at all. But schmaltz, especially goose schmaltz, is infinitely to be preferred.

So is liver from animals that have been "naturally" or "organically" raised. This kind of liver is not yet exactly common, but it can be found. Natural and gourmet food stores with good lines of frozen foods are likely spots to try, as are fancy butchers that feature prime meats and kosher butchers whose sources of poultry are necessarily different from those of the supermarket.

For a pint of chopped liver, which serves from 1 to 6, depending on how long it's been since they've had any

1 pound calves' liver or chicken liver, whichever is better quality at your store
4 to 6 tablespoons schmaltz or unsalted butter, soft but not melted
1 medium onion, chopped fine, a scant cup
2 hard-boiled eggs
Salt and pepper to taste
1 or 2 tablespoons minced onion (optional)

Preheat the broiler and grill the liver quite close to the heat about 5 minutes a side, or until it is lightly browned and barely cooked through. It should still be very slightly pink inside. Allow it to cool.

Melt a thin film of the fat in a small skillet and sauté the onion over medium heat just until wilted; it should retain some sharpness. Set aside.

Trim the liver of any veins, membrane, etc. Chop it — *do not grind it* — until it is reduced to rice-sized or slightly larger pieces, then add the boiled eggs and keep chopping until you have a coarse paste with even coarser lumps in it. Chicken liver is softer than calves', so it will make a smoother finished product. The important thing is to avoid baby food.

Transfer the liver to a bowl and stir in any cooking juices, the sautéed onion, and enough of the fat to make an unctuous spread. Stir in salt and pepper to taste. (Add the minced raw onion for a sharper onion flavor.) Cover tightly with plastic wrap and refrigerate to mellow at least 30 minutes before serving. Chopped liver is best eaten fresh, but it will keep for a day or two if you want to make it in advance for a party.

Chopped liver should be served with rye or pumpernickel bread or toast. Some people serve chopped liver with crackers, to which I can only say it's a free country.

*I*T'S CHRISTMAS
'Tis the Season to Bake Cookies

ALTHOUGH the month of December has its little faults, it's a happy season for everyone who likes to make (or consume) pastry. At no other time of the year does "parade of treats" live so securely as a custom of welcome. No matter what your claims in the ethnicity department, chances are good that it is at Christmas time, more than any other, that the setting out of coffee or tea and sweet cakes comes automatically to mind and hand as soon as the doorbell rings.

Some spoilsports will, of course, argue that the whole business is unhealthy, that the fragrance and flavor of happiness should not be linked to butter and almonds, cinnamon, brown sugar, apricots, honey, and cream. Perhaps you can guess where I stand on the subject, which is (roundly) in favor of seasonal indulgence. As a cook, I can't pass up the pleasure of shopping in spice-fragrant stores, of stocking up on exotic dried fruits, of surveying kitchen cupboards overflowing with the wherewithal — plump, sweet new crop Georgia pecans, pine nuts from Italy, fresh eggs and cream and butter from the organic farm down the road. These items ain't cheap, but with them I am rich almost beyond counting. At my leisure, at my convenience, I can play with them and come up with the true taste of Christmas.

This is, furthermore, about the only way to get that flavor. The Christmas cookie, in its highest and best incarnation, is one of the last culinary ramparts on which the home cook stands pretty much alone, unaccompanied by any but the fanciest caterers. Of course the world is full of second-rate store cookies. Bakeries carry them, tray after tray. Supermarkets devote whole aisles to their dubious charms. There are even take-out shops that purvey nothing but freshly baked, oversweetened, greasy, chocolate-studded invitations to coronary arrest. But first-class cookies are poor candidates for commercial manufacture. They're too fragile, too labor intensive, too reliant on expensive ingredients such as pure butter. They may be emotionally tied to Grandma, they may be quite delightfully easy to make, but however down-home they may appear, their integrity makes them elegant.

Some, naturally, are more elegant than others. I try to offer an assortment — something spicy and something nutty, at least one meringue item, at least one fruit-studded unit, something chocolate, something short-bready, and something (it takes forever, but it's worth it) rolled and cut into trees and reindeer and stars and hearts, decorated with thin tracings of confectioners' sugar icing. Every year I say I'm going to try something different, check out one of the thirty thousand or so cookie recipes that have caught my eye in the course of the past twelve months. And most years that's exactly what I do. One recipe. That's it. By the time I've made all the traditional favorites, I'm too beat (and too poor) to do more.

 ## *Ginger Shortbread*

Candied ginger adds just the right spicy-chewy accent to this Christmas classic. No commercial cookie can touch these for flavor. And *easy*? Oh, boy — one bowl, one pan, and about 5 minutes of very small effort.

Although inclined to crumbliness around the edges, shortbread travels well if you pack it so it can't jostle. I cover cardboard with foil, put the shortbread on that, and then bind the two together with plastic wrap. Thus airtightly cushioned, this is one of the best of all cookies for shipping to distant locations. Kept cool, it will stay fresh tasting about 3 weeks.

For 2 dozen cookies

Scant ¼ cup brown sugar
¼ cup cornstarch
2 cups all-purpose flour
Scant ¼ cup granulated sugar
Pinch each of freshly grated nutmeg, ground dried ginger, and salt
2 ounces candied ginger, the sugar-coated kind, chopped into rice-sized pieces, about ½ cup, loosely piled
½ pound unsalted butter

Combine the brown sugar and cornstarch, which will keep the sugar from sticking to the mesh when you sift or strain the result into a wide, fairly shallow bowl. Sift in the flour, granulated sugar, and spices, then stir with a wire whisk, being sure the dry ingredients are thoroughly combined. Use your fingertips to work in the candied ginger, rubbing the pieces with the dry stuff until they are well distributed and separate. Any overlarge pieces will come to light during this process. Set them aside as you come to them, then chop and work in last.

The butter should be malleable but not mushy; if it's too soft, like butter that's been sitting around in a warm kitchen a couple of hours, the dough will be difficult to work and the final product greasy. If it is too hard, like butter that has just this minute been taken from the refrigerator, the dough will be difficult to work and the final product will be tough. You want something on the stiff side of Play-Doh which will feel just right as soon as you start pinching it into the dry mixture.

This is about like "cutting in butter" for pie dough, the primary difference being that this butter is softer and there is a lot more of it. The dough will therefore come together very quickly. When it begins to clump up, switch from pinching to gentle kneading. As soon as the dough is smooth, it's done. Set it aside for 20 minutes or so to cool off and rest up for being shaped.

Preheat the oven to 350°F. Divide the dough into 3 parts, rolling each into a ball. On one very large or two smaller ungreased cookie sheets, working with one ball at a time, pat the dough out into approximately 6-inch circles no more than ¼ inch thick. As the edges get more heat than the middles, they should be slightly thicker. There should be plenty of space between the circles, and a lonely one should be in the center of its cookie sheet. When all three are formed, use the tines of a fork to prick right through, dividing each circle into 8 wedges.

Bake about 20 minutes, or until the shortbread is cooked evenly, with just the suggestion of brown around the edges. It will be soft. Again prick through while cookies are still hot, then let cool completely before cutting on the dotted lines and removing from the pan.

⚒ Apricot-Ginger Florentines

Classic Florentines are a kind of "lace cookie" — thin, crisp, and sweet, studded with almonds and candied orange peel, glazed on one side with pure bittersweet chocolate. This recipe substitutes apricots and ginger for the peel, making a cookie with a delicate, very different flavor that is delicious on its own and best complemented by white chocolate if you decide to glaze it.

For about thirty 3-inch cookies

½ cup heavy cream (Do not use ultrapasteurized.)
3 tablespoons sugar
½ cup slivered blanched almonds
4 tablespoons diced dried apricots

4 tablespoons diced candied ginger, freed of excess sugar
Pinch of salt
Approximately ¼ cup flour
Unsalted butter and flour for the cookie sheets
4½ ounces white chocolate*

Preheat the oven to 350°F. Combine the cream and sugar and set aside. Chop half the almonds just enough to make pieces the size of the fruit dice and grind the remainder cornmeal fine.

Stir the fruit and nuts into the cream, along with the salt, then stir in half the flour. Continue adding flour by tablespoons until you have a soft dough. Butter a square of foil and make a test cookie, dropping on a tablespoon of dough and gently spreading it out as thin as possible in view of the lumps.

Bake 10 to 12 minutes, or until nicely brown around the edges. The cookie should be very flat and crisp. Add more flour if it ran all over; thin with milk if by some unhappy chance the dough is too thick. Butter and flour two cookie sheets, then form and bake the remaining cookies and cool on racks.

Chop or grate the chocolate so it melts evenly over hot, not quite simmering water. Allow to cool to warm room temperature, then use to paint the bottoms of the cookies.

 *Peppernuts*

These are Christmas par excellence, spicy with every Christmas spice, almost never seen at any other time of year. The recipe makes a lot — they keep and ship well — but you don't have to bake them all at once. The dough can be kept refrigerated for a couple of days if baking the cookies in small batches is more convenient. The nut in the title refers to the texture; they are quite crunchy and hard, perfect for dunking. Though very nearly jaw-breaking when first cooled, they soften again after ripening for a day. The shaped cookies must rest overnight before baking, so plan accordingly.

For about 16 dozen (!) small cookies

3 cups cake flour
2 teaspoons baking powder

---

*You need slightly more white chocolate than you would dark, since it's a bit harder to spread, and you will likely need this amount to coat all of the cookies. I usually just buy a fancy 3- or 3½-ounce white chocolate candy bar and spread it as far as it'll go.

½ teaspoon salt

1 tablespoon cinnamon

1 teaspoon each ground cloves, mace, ginger, nutmeg, and fairly finely ground — but not powdered — black pepper

½ teaspoon ground cardamom

5 eggs

2 cups granulated sugar

1 cup brown sugar, sifted if necessary to remove lumps

3 cups all-purpose flour

Grated zest (thin, colored outer rind) of 1 lemon, about 1 heaping tablespoon

½ cup each blanched almonds and candied citron, minced to tiny pieces

Parchment paper for baking sheets

Brandy or rum

Confectioners' sugar (optional)

Sift the cake flour with the ingredients up to — but not including — the eggs. Use a mixer to beat the eggs and granulated sugar until very thick, expanded, and white; the batter should fall from the beaters in wide, flat ribbons. Then beat in the brown sugar. Slowly beat the cake flour mixture into the eggs. When they are well combined, beat in the all-purpose flour. When it is well mixed in, add the lemon zest, nuts, and fruit.

Knead the dough just enough to be sure it's homogenous, then cover the bowl tightly. Set out several parchment paper–lined cookie sheets and find a sharp knife.

Work with a handful of dough at a time, keeping the remainder covered so it doesn't dry out. Roll into snakes about 1 inch in diameter, then cut into "nuts" at ¾-inch intervals. Arrange the cookies, apart but not widely, in rows on the sheets and set them aside to dry out overnight. (If your kitchen is well heated and winter-dry, *lightly* cover the cookies with plastic wrap so they don't dry out overmuch.)

On baking day, preheat the oven to 325°F. Pour a bit of hooch in a small cup. Turn each cookie over and put a drop (I use a fingertip) of liquor on the soft spot where it was touching the pan.

Bake the cookies as soon as they're turned, about 20 minutes or just until they have "popped" and a broken one is dry clear through. They won't brown much.

Let them cool on the sheets, then store in closed tins to mellow at least a day before eating. Traditionally, they are dusted with confectioners' sugar. This can be done right before they're served for a slightly sweeter effect, or once while they're hot and once after they cool if you want to be really German about it.

Poppy Seed–Parmesan Pinwheel Cookies

Because not all good cookies are sweet.

For about 6 dozen 2-inch cookies

1¾ cups all-purpose flour
¼ teaspoon salt
3 tablespoons poppy seeds
Scraping of nutmeg
¼ cup ice water
1 teaspoon lemon juice
¾ cup butter, plus butter for the baking sheets
¼ to ⅓ pound Parmesan cheese, freshly grated, about 2 heaping,
    lightly piled cups

Thoroughly combine the flour, salt, poppy seeds, and nutmeg. Mix the water and lemon juice and set aside. Cut the butter into the dry ingredients until you have lumps the size of peas — the processor works well — then toss in the liquid and mix gently until you have pie dough. Divide finished dough in half and pat each half into a square, then wrap tightly in plastic wrap and chill.

Roll 1 piece of dough out ⅛ inch thick and sprinkle with half the Parmesan. Cover with waxed paper and roll once more to bind the cheese to the pastry. Roll, not too tightly, as though for a jellyroll. Wrap and chill. Repeat with the second piece of dough.

Preheat the oven to 400°F. and heavily butter the baking sheets. Slice the dough into approximately ³⁄₁₆-inch slices and arrange them, slightly separated, on the sheets. Bake about 20 minutes, or until well browned. If your sheets are thin metal, turn the cookies with a pancake turner about halfway through the cooking.

The cheese will brown faster than the pastry but is pretty slow to burn. The pastry will look absolutely raw until 2 minutes before it gets scorched, however, so keep your eye on it. Remove pinwheels from the pan while they're still hot so they don't stick. Cool on wire racks and store in airtight bags, where they keep quite well for a week or so. Freeze for longer storage.

*T*HE MAINE SHRIMP

THE MIDCOAST of Maine in midwinter is not, generally speaking, what one would call a gastronomic paradise. Our place at the end of the supply line is woefully apparent when "locally grown" means, except in the case of hydroponic lettuce and assorted sprouts, locally frozen, canned, or root-cellared.

There is, however, one stellar fresh product that redeems this icebound season, and that's the shrimp. We are front and center the source for one of the world's finest seafoods, a fact of which we seem to take less advantage than we should, given the cyclical nature of their availability, their almost ludicrous cheapness, and the by no means unthinkable possibility that there won't *be* any, one of these days, if controls are not instituted fairly soon. You can't wipe out the egg-bearing females year after year after year without having an unhappy effect on the size of future generations.

At the moment, supplies are still good. The shrimp are everywhere, available from peddlers and fish markets alike. They can be used in any recipe that calls for shrimp, but their distinctive sweetness sets them heads and eggs above the rest.

Using Maine Shrimp

Most shrimp should not be overcooked because they will become tough and rubbery. Maine shrimp should not be overcooked because they will turn to mush and fall apart. Be sure all ingredients, pans, etc., called for in your recipe are ready before you start. The difference between great and glop is literally a matter of seconds.

All shrimp taste best cooked whole, or at least with the shell on. This isn't always practical, but it is worth remembering when you're precooking the shrimp to be shelled and used in another preparation. The shells themselves make a delicious broth, useful as fish stock in any recipe calling for same or as the base for shrimp bisque, chowder, etc. Shells for stock must be fresh — not more than two days out of the water. If they're older, the resultant broth will be black — unappetizing in the extreme.

Frozen shrimp are easiest to use if they are frozen individually, spread out on trays like blueberries. For the highest quality, on the other hand, they should be frozen in brine. The salt lowers the temperature at which they freeze, helps keep them firm, and prevents enzymatic changes from occurring so rapidly. Simply behead the shrimp and pack them in rigid freezer containers, old yogurt tubs, or the like. Firm the layers as you go and stop about 1½ inches from the top of the container. Pour in strong brine (2 tablespoons salt to 1 quart water), enough to cover the shrimp completely, leaving an inch of head room to allow for expansion in freezing. Attach the lids securely, label and date, and freeze.

According to the experts in these matters, the shrimp should be used within three months. I've enjoyed them all the way through summer, but the quality does start to go down pretty rapidly as time goes on.

To use frozen shrimp, let them thaw slowly in the brine, then rinse well before shelling (unless you plan to boil the thawed shrimp, in which case simply omit salting the boiling water).

A WARNING NOTE: Shrimp to be peeled commercially are soaked for several hours in salt water to loosen the shells. While undoubtedly handy, commercial peeled shrimp is somewhat less flavorful than it might otherwise be. Fish markets also frequently offer headless, rinsed (eggless) shrimp, which keep much longer than their intact sisters. Like the peeled ones, these will be a bit less intensely flavored.

Carol's New Orleans–Style Barbecued Shrimp

"Barbecued" does not mean "slowly smoked in a pit." It means that the sauce mixture is highly seasoned and hot, that the cooking procedure produces burnt ends, and that consuming the finished product is one messy operation you bet.

The shrimp are broiled in their shells, in an aromatic sauce composed primarily of butter and olive oil. Generally you peel and eat them with your fingers, but under ideal cooking conditions you can get them so crisp the shells themselves are a pleasure to eat. Provide plenty of good bread to sop up the buttery, garlicky shrimp juice and a multitude of napkins, and you've got dinner. Purchased sherbet isn't just the easiest dessert, it's also the best now that good all-natural sherbets are on the market.

The following recipe is in the great tradition, which is to say extremely flexible. Its author, who has tried many in her time, says the important points to keep in mind are: (1) Get the freshest shrimp you can. Frozen will work, but it's not in the same league. (2) Use just enough fat to coat the shellfish. It should not swim. (3) Be sure to use plenty of garlic, plenty of hot sauce, and plenty of herbs. (4) The shrimp must be constantly watched and frequently agitated for even cooking. (5) Be sure there is plenty of garlic.

For about 6 servings (see Note)

5 pounds whole shrimp (3¼ pounds headless)
Approximately 3 tablespoons dried rosemary, enough to blanket the shrimp
Coarse-cracked black pepper, several twists of the mill
½ teaspoon paprika, or for hot freaks, cayenne
½ cup butter
¼ cup olive oil, or a bit more
5 or 6 large cloves garlic, pressed
2 tablespoons Worcestershire sauce
1½ teaspoons Tabasco sauce, or more to taste

Choose small shrimp so you won't have to worry about the sand vein and so they'll be tender. Head if necessary, and rinse only if they are muddy. Dry them on paper towels if they are damp. Spread them out in a shallow pan big enough to hold them all in one or two layers.

Rub the rosemary between your palms over the shrimp, sprinkling them evenly. Each shrimp should have a couple of fragments to call its own. Grind on the pepper, sprinkle very lightly with paprika or cayenne, and set the shrimp aside.

Melt the butter, then add the oil, garlic, Worcestershire, and Tabasco. Simmer just long enough to bring out the garlic slightly, then pour the sauce over the shrimp. Shake gently to be sure all are well coated and add more olive oil if they look dry. If there's time, put the shrimp aside in a cool but not cold place and let marinate 30 minutes to an hour. If there is not time, don't worry; the quickness of this dish is part of its charm.

Let the shrimp come to room temperature. Arrange the broiler rack so the shrimp cooking pan will be as close to the heat as it will go without burning down the house — 2 to 3 inches is usually about it. Preheat the broiler. *Thoroughly.* Be sure the rest of the dinner is ready and you are not needed elsewhere. Put the shrimp under the broiler for 2 minutes, then start checking and shaking about once every 20 seconds — really. If the cooking is proceeding at an ideal pace, they will be browning before your eyes. Keep shifting and stirring and broiling and worrying until the shrimp are well browned, probably blackened on the odd tail tip. Total cooking time should be 5 to 8 minutes, depending on the size of the shrimp and the efficiency of your broiler. Some broilers, unfortunately, are not efficient at all. Don't overcook the shrimp in a search for crispness that cannot be achieved. They're still delicious when lightly browned; you'll just have to shell them is all.

NOTE: A large person who loves shrimp and doesn't mind getting dirty could probably finish off most of these solo. "Six servings" allows almost half a pound of cooked shrimp for each person, more than enough from the nutritional point of view though possibly a bit scant if you're talking sensual indulgence.

✳ *East-West Tempura Pancakes*

The pancakes are the Eastern part. Even in Japan they are busy enough to have thought of this particular short cut to the pleasures of tempura. The sauce, however, is a Western one, requiring no specialized ethnic ingredients. "A Few Words on the Frying Part" follow.

For 4 generous servings

PANCAKES:
½ cup carrot or sweet potato, grated on the large holes of a grater
2 heaping tablespoons coarsely grated, peeled fresh ginger root
¾ cup firm vegetables cut in ¼-inch dice (Use peas, snow peas, red sweet pepper, or green onion rather than celery, bean sprouts, or summer squash.)
6 ounces, about ¾ cup, peeled raw Maine or diced Gulf shrimp

BATTER:
1 egg yolk
¾ cup ice water, or a bit more
¾ cup flour
Pinch of baking soda

2 tablespoons dry mustard
⅓ cup cream
1 tablespoon lemon juice, or to taste
1 tablespoon soy sauce
1 teaspoon honey
2 or 3 twists of the pepper grinder
Lemon wedges and soy sauce to pass at the table

Combine the pancake ingredients in a medium-sized bowl. Put the oil on to heat to 370°F. (see note on frying).

Break the yolk into a cup, stir to mix, and measure 1½ teaspoons of it into a small mixing bowl. Whisk in the ice water, then the flour and baking soda, making a thin, lumpy batter. Do not overbeat. Set the batter aside.

Put the mustard in a small saucepan or double boiler. Add water drop by drop, stirring constantly, until the mustard is of conventional mustard paste texture. Beat in the remaining sauce ingredients and set the mixture over very low heat or over not quite simmering water for about 15 minutes. It should warm without actually cooking.

When the fat has reached the proper temperature, combine the batter with the vegetable and shellfish mixture. The result should look drippy-thin. Make the first pancake a test one. Pick up about a tablespoonful of the mixture with a flat slotted spoon or skimmer, allowing excess batter to drip back into the bowl. Holding the spoon close to the surface of the oil, use a knife blade to push the contents in.

You should get a lacy pancake, very loose and open, that fries brown and crisp on one side in about a minute. Turn and brown the other side, then drain on absorbent paper. Taste. The vegetables should be barely cooked, the surrounding batter barely there, not at all doughy and fritter-like. If necessary, thin with additional ice water. If the pancake fell apart, stir in a tiny bit more flour. When adjustments are completed, fry up the rest of the batter by tablespoonfuls, as before. If you use 2 pans, you can probably do all the pancakes in a single batch. There will be batter left in the bowl when you're done.

Serve as soon as they are cooked, with the mustard sauce on the side, and with lemon wedges and a bottle of soy sauce also on the table for those who might wish to add them. Rice, of course, is the starch of choice, and tangerines make a nice dessert.

A FEW WORDS *on the Frying Part:* The best Japanese restaurants use light (*not* seasoning-type) sesame oil. Refined vegetable oil of the all-purpose sort also is fine. The fat need be only 1½ inches deep, but the pan should be 3 times that to allow for bubbling up. Bring the oil up to temperature slowly, starting at low heat and gradually increasing it. This will temper the fat and make it less likely to burn. Be sure to keep skimming out bits and crumbs. If left in the fat, they'll scorch and that flavor will taint everything. If you use 2 pans, it's a lot more oil but a lot less time spent frying.

*T*OMATOES IN SNOWTIME

"TRY IT AGAIN." I tried it again, this time from about four feet above the floor. "I can't believe it. Try throwing it." Not being brave enough to actually wind up and pitch, I settled for a gentle dribbling motion, content, for this round, with applying a measurable downward force instead of simply dropping the object of our investigations.

In case you are still wondering, I will tell you that said object was a standard supermarket long-distance tomato. We started fooling around with it when I discovered, inadvertently, that I could squeeze one — squeeze until my knuckles grew white and the veins in my wrist were blooming like Arnold Schwarzenegger's — without inflicting any perceptible damage.

Damage to the tomato, that is. What this little experiment did to my comfy sense that things were improving in the industrialized vegetables department is, of course, another story. The putative tomato, though it finally began to look a bit fatigued, resisted breach through several additional, ever more forceful rejections; and when at last its iron armor cracked, the wound was utterly bloodless — not a single drop of tomato juice leaked out upon the floor.

Oh, well, you may be muttering, why didn't she buy a fancy, imported (flown direct) Israeli tomato, or a hothouse tomato in a special, pseudowood housing printed with detailed ripening instructions? The answer that comes most readily to mind is that I am not wealthy enough to afford such things, but the *honest* answer is that these high-fashion fruits aren't really that much tastier than the pale styrofoam specials we have all come to know and hate so well.

At this time of year I'd rather eat canned ones, preferably those put up in glass cans by me or someone else who grows interesting types of tomatoes, but failing that any number of (usually Italian) brands of perfectly acceptable canned tomatoes that were picked when ripe, processed correctly, and packed without any additions but salt. Depending on the application, frozen is also an option. Sometimes one might even use sun-dried tomatoes in olive oil, although the danger of overdose is ever present with these. And don't forget, tomato paste now comes in tubes, like toothpaste, rendering that fur-bearing half can at the back of the refrigerator obsolete.

In other words, there is no shortage of excellent sources of tomato flavor in winter — it's just that none of them are fresh fruits. Since most tomato cookery involves cooking, that needn't be any big deal.

Fast Blender Hot Sauce

As its name implies. Worth making because it is much fresher tasting than the currently available bottled hot sauces, with an agreeable chunky texture no processed product possesses. It's great with tacos and such, of course, and for setting out with tortilla chips as a snack. It makes a fine accent on grilled cheese sandwiches — especially old-fashioned rat cheese on whole-wheat — and should not be ignored when pan-grilled pork chops are being served. Nice on baked squash, too.

For about 2½ cups

1 can (16 ounces) of solid-pack peeled tomatoes in juice (not in purée), or come summer, 2 cups peeled, fresh tomatoes, roughly chopped

1 medium onion, cut in rough chunks

2 cloves garlic

¼ to ⅓ cup roughly chopped fresh hot green chilies, preferably jalapeños, with at least a few seeds (The more peppers, the more seeds, the hotter the sauce. But do remove the white membranes on which the seeds are carried. They're not only the hottest part, they're also bitter.)

1 tablespoon lime juice

½ teaspoon salt

¼ teaspoon sugar if the tomatoes are in a metal can (It helps counteract the tinny taste.)

¼ cup loosely packed fresh coriander leaves (optional but irreplaceable; do not substitute)

Put everything in the blender in the order listed. Grind at a fairly slow speed until you have a rough purée the texture of not-quite-done applesauce. You may have to stop once or twice, depending on your blender. A processor will work too, of course; use the pulse option to avoid making baby food. Let the sauce mellow 20 minutes or so before serving, then stir to recombine before setting it out. It will keep, refrigerated, several days, but its greatest charm is its freshness. Try to eat it up as fast as possible.

✽ *Scalloped Tomatoes*

One way and another, this was a country favorite for years. Perhaps the current fashion for that which is old-fashioned will bring it back. It certainly deserves a renaissance. Not only is it an excellent side dish for major protein such as roast lamb, grilled chops, and meat loaves, but it's also quite satisfying served front and center, with a lot of something green on the side, some kind of starch for juice-sopping, and perhaps some cheesecake for dessert.

For 4 to 6 side dish or 3 main dish servings

1 can (28 ounces) solid-pack peeled tomatoes or, in summer, enough
   peeled, fresh tomatoes to make 3½ cups sliced
Olive oil for the pan
1½ cups coarse, stale, dry bread crumbs, preferably from French or
   farm-style bread (whole-wheat's okay but a bit strong flavored)
6 tablespoons butter, melted
1 clove garlic, pressed
1 teaspoon dried basil or marjoram, crushed
1 tablespoon tamari or other aged soy sauce
¼ cup dry white wine (or vermouth, for a more strongly herbal
   quality)
⅓ cup coarsely chopped walnuts or ⅓ cup whole pine nuts (especially
   nice with the vermouth)
2 teaspoons brown sugar

Move the rack to the upper third of the oven and preheat it to 375°F. Drain the tomatoes, saving all the juice, and cut them in thick (about ½-inch) slices. Set them aside. Oil an 8-inch-square, 2-inch-deep baking pan and apply a layer of the tomatoes. Mix the crumbs, butter, garlic, and herb and spread a scant half of the result over the tomatoes.

Make a second tomato layer, which should bring the filling level pretty close to the top of the pan. Combine the reserved tomato juice with the soy sauce and wine and pour it over the top. Mix the nuts and sugar into the remaining crumbs. Use them to form an even, all-covering lid and press it in firmly. Bake 20 to 25 minutes, or until the tomatoes are bubbling up through the well-toasted crumbs. Let cool 5 minutes or so before serving. Like lasagna, it needs to compose itself a bit after baking.

(✱) Tomato-Custard Tart in an Eggplant "Crust"

For a 10-inch tart, 6 to 8 servings

2 very firm eggplants, as oblong as possible
Approximately 2 teaspoons salt
1 can (16 ounces) solid-pack peeled tomatoes
1 tablespoon flour
1 teaspoon dried marjoram, crumbled
Pinch of sugar
⅓ cup finely sliced green onions (scallions), including about an inch of the green part
3 eggs
2 egg yolks
1¼ cups milk
½ cup sour cream
Olive oil for the pans
¼ cup freshly grated Parmesan cheese

Begin with the "crust." Slice the eggplants about ⅓ inch thick, cutting the long, broad way to get the widest possible slices. Layer them in a colander, sprinkling each layer lightly with salt. Put a plate on top and a weight on the plate. Let the eggplant drain about 30 minutes while you turn your attention to the filling.

Drain the tomatoes, chop them up small, and drain them saving all the juices. Set the tomatoes aside and boil the juices until they have reduced to about ¼ cup of very thick material. Be careful not to let it scorch. Combine the tomato meat with the flour, marjoram, and sugar, then stir in the boiled-down juices and the onions. Set the mixture aside.

Beat the eggs until well mixed, then beat in the yolks, the milk, and the sour cream. Set aside.

Preheat the broiler. Retrieve the eggplant and mop off the pieces with paper towels, pressing to remove as much moisture as you can.

Lightly oil a cookie sheet and arrange the eggplant on it in a single layer. Broil until well flecked with brown, then turn with a pancake turner and broil the other side. The eggplant will be, at this point, thoroughly cooked.

Preheat the oven to 350°F. Film a 10-inch glass or other nonaluminum (aluminum darkens the eggplant unpleasantly) pie plate with olive oil and arrange the eggplant slices on it in as near as you can get to an unbroken layer. Cut, piece, and slightly overlap as necessary and press together firmly. (Any leftover eggplant is delicious just as is and also makes a nice addition to a mixed green salad.)

Sprinkle the eggplant with about half the Parmesan and stir the remainder into the custard. Pour the custard into the shell, then at once dump in the tomato mixture, all in 2 or 3 heaps. Use a rubber spatula to streak the two colors partially together as though you were making marble cake, then get the tart into the oven at once.

Bake about 30 minutes, or until a knife blade stuck in about 2 inches from the edge emerges clean. The center should be firm if the tart is to be served right away or still slightly shaky if it will be allowed to cool before cutting. (The held heat will continue to set the custard for quite a while after it leaves the oven.)

VARIATION: This is a good place to use one of the lovely soft fresh goat cheeses that are more and more widely available. Make the custard part by creaming 6 ounces of plain or lightly herbed cheese until it is lumpless and light, then beat in the eggs, yolks, and ¾ cup of milk. Omit the sour cream and Parmesan.

ST. AGNES' EVE
Hot Food for Cold Weather

ST. AGNES' EVE — Ah, bitter chill it was!
The owl, for all his feathers, was a-cold;
The hare limp'd trembling through the frozen grass,
And silent was the flock in woolly fold.

Exactly, Mr. Keats, you've got it just right. Ooph, uph, and similar noises possibly made by said rabbit, and I wish I had a woolly fold or two myself.

January 20 is St. Agnes' Eve. On this night, according to my encyclopedia, "Young girls, in rural districts, formerly indulged in all sorts of quaint country magic ... with a view to discovering their future husbands."

This district is rural enough, but I'll bet *most* of the young girls (along with just about everybody else) are dreaming of less chancy sources of warmth.

A husband is usually only 98.6°F. — all right, I suppose, for those whose rent includes central heating. We who use woodstoves are clinging to them with a far more than spouselike devotion — dreaming of something to warm body and soul all evening long, not just at bedtime.

Something like curry, for instance, which was for me the introduction to food that could actually make you sweat and smile at the same time. Though it seems to have been overtaken in the urge-to-burn sweepstakes by the (marginally) less labor-intensive incendiarisms of Tex Mex, it continues to be, along with the food of Szechwan, among the most delicious ways to use peppers of both the New *and* Old World varieties.

Concerning Curry Powder

Actually, the stuff isn't really as "inauthentic" as its detractors would have one believe. Indian cooks use a number of premixed spice combinations, called *masalas,* which, though often homemade, are traditionally just as likely to be purchased. The problem is that masalas are in daily use, enjoying a fast turnover, whereas curry powder tends to sit around, first at the store waiting to be bought, then in the home, waiting to be used. And all during the wait, those preground spices are exposed to light and warmth, weakening, changing flavor, the original balanced combination getting skewed as some fade faster than others. When fresh, curry powder can be a tasty seasoning, but if you use it often enough so it *stays* fresh, you are going to be mighty tired of the way it makes everything taste the same, before very long at all.

Masalas, on the other hand, are always on hand in the plural — hot ones and mild ones, simple and complicated, as various as the foodstuffs they're designed to season. Making up your own is easy, once you've got the habit — and the spices. One barrier many feel to making their own curry powders is the daunting prospect of buying all those unfamiliar spices, the excess of which they will be stuck with, since they don't expect to use them except for curry.

This fear is exaggerated. Spice stores, co-ops, and specialty groceries sell loose whole spices by the ounce, offering greater variety for less money than prepackaged spices, whether supermarket or gourmet. Being whole, these spices keep quite well, and, of course, almost all of them have many uses beyond Indian cookery.

 Garam Masala
(Hot Mixture)

As explained above, this is but one of thousands. As a rule, commercial curry powders contain large amounts of turmeric, a rhizome related to ginger that provides the characteristic yellow color, and fenugreek, a seed whose aroma is the indefinable "curry-ness" that seems so unfamiliar to Western palates. Both of these spices are at the acrid, bitter end of the seasoning spectrum and must be carefully balanced with other flavors if the end result is to please.

This masala, a simple one, contains neither, both so that it will be a real alternative to commercial preparations and so that those put off by bad experiences with conventional curry powders will be encouraged to have another go. Try adding a bit of turmeric when using this masala with legumes — turmeric *and* fenugreek if you're using it to perk up leftover cooked red meat. Generally speaking, Garam Masala is added near the end of the cooking period so its component spices retain their bright flavor, but it may be used (and frequently is) as a foundation flavoring as well. Use it for the final sparkling touch on scrambled eggs, cooked lentils, or simply steamed vegetables, chicken, and fish.

For about ¼ cup (recipe can be doubled)

3-inch length curled cinnamon, 2 lengths if it's the thin kind, coarsely
   broken
1 teaspoon whole cloves
1 teaspoon black peppercorns
1 tablespoon plus 1 teaspoon green (white) cardamom pods
½ teaspoon whole mace or roughly broken nutmeg
1 tablespoon whole cumin seed, preferably black cumin
2 teaspoons coriander seeds

Heat a heavy, ungreased skillet over medium heat, then add the cinnamon, cloves, and peppercorns. Turn the heat to low and roast, shaking the pan frequently, about 2 minutes. Add the cardamom pods and mace or nutmeg and roast, shaking, about 2 minutes more. Now add the cumin and coriander and give the whole works a final 3 minutes or so.

The object is to toast all the spices gently without scorching any. Permit the mixture to cool, then pick out the cardamom pods, remove the seeds, and discard the husks. Grind with all the other spices in a mortar, blender, or coffee or spice grinder (a processor will not work well with such small amounts). Store airtight and away from the light in a cool place.

Murgh Massalam
(Spiced Chicken)

For 4 to 6 servings

4 tablespoons *ghee* (Indian clarified butter) or 5 tablespoons unsalted
    butter plus 2 teaspoons bland oil
1 large onion, roughly chopped, about 1½ cups
3½- to 4-pound frying chicken
½ cup whole-milk yogurt, preferably the cream-on-top kind
1-inch-square chunk peeled fresh ginger root
2 large cloves garlic
2 or 3 long hot green chilies, seeds and veins removed, sliced thin,
    about ½ cup (Include seeds if a hotter finished product is desired.)
3 tablespoons Garam Masala (see recipe on page 253)
½ cup water
⅛ to ¼ teaspoon saffron threads, soaked 5 minutes in 2 tablespoons
    warm water
Salt (optional)
2 tablespoons fresh coriander (cilantro) leaves, minced, for garnish
    (optional, do not substitute parsley)

Melt the fat over medium heat in a heavy, tight-lidded, ovenproof casserole big enough to hold the chicken. Add the onion and sauté, stirring occasionally, until it is a dark gold.

While the onion is cooking, completely skin the chicken. Cut off the wing tips and the tail and discard any pockets of removable fat. Lean on the breastbone to break it, flattening the bird. Set aside.

Remove the onion with a slotted spoon, allowing the fat to drain back into the pan, and set the pan aside. Put the yogurt in your blender or processor, then add the cooked onions, ginger, garlic, chilies, and 2 tablespoons of the Garam Masala. Blend until you have a coarse paste.

Prick the chicken all over with the tines of a fork, set it on a plate, and slather it all over with the masala paste. Rinse the grinder with the ½ cup water and set the liquid aside. Allow the chicken to marinate, uncovered, at room temperature 1 to 1½ hours. Then put the casserole, which should still have a generous layer of fat in it, over medium-high heat until the fat sizzles. Wipe off the chicken, reserving the marinade, and brown it lightly, first the breast and then the back. Remove the pan from the heat and scrape in all the reserved marinade, including everything collected on the plate. Pour the reserved masala rinse water over everything and bake in a 350°F. oven about 45 minutes, or until the chicken is tender but not falling apart.

Sprinkle the remaining tablespoon Garam Masala over the chicken and pour the saffron and water over all. Using 2 large spoons, turn the chicken over onto the breast, stirring up the sauce as you do so. Cover the casserole again, return it to the oven, and turn off the heat. Let it sit in there 15 minutes, then remove the chicken, carve into serving pieces, and assemble on a deep, heated platter. Cover the chicken with the sauce, sprinkle lightly with salt if desired, and garnish with the coriander.

Rice, especially rice with raisins, currants, or other fruit, is both delicious and traditional as an accompanying sauce mop, but baked potatoes are an attractive and easy alternative.

FURTHER CURRY CLARIFICATIONS: 1. The word comes from the Tamil *kari,* meaning sauce, and most Indian cookery experts agree that it is exactly an abundance of sauce that distinguishes a true curry. The meat or vegetable being curried is there more for flavor than bulk, the idea being to make a stewlike seasoner that will add interest to a large quantity of rice or other bland starch.

2. Yes, Virginia, there *is* such a thing as a curry leaf, according to Tom Stobart's *Herbs, Spices, and Flavorings.* Botanically *Chalcas Koenigii,* a member of the Rutaceae family, it is used especially in Madras curry powder and in south Indian vegetarian cookery.

Szechwan Shish Kebab

The seasoning is Chinese, but the method is Americanized Middle Eastern. Unlike most American shish kebabs, it is innocent of vegetables. Though good (surprise) with rice, it is even better with baked sweet potatoes, since they don't mind the fact that there is no sauce.

For 4 servings

MARINADE:
1 tablespoon Szechwan peppercorns*
2½ tablespoons tamari or other aged soy sauce
¼ cup Chinese rice wine or dry sherry
¼ cup canned hoisin sauce*
3 large cloves garlic, minced very fine
1 flower (4 to 6 seeds) star anise,* lightly crushed
2 or 3 small (2- to 3-inch) dried hot red peppers, coarsely broken

MEAT:
2 pounds lean boneless lamb, cut in 2-inch cubes
Dark sesame oil, about 2 teaspoons
Coarse salt

In a small heavy skillet over medium heat, roast peppercorns for 2 minutes or until their fragrance rises, combine the remaining marinade ingredients, add the meat, and stir and rub until all surfaces are coated. Allow to sit, covered and cool but preferably not refrigerated, at least 1 hour — 3 or 4 is better. Half a day is recommended if the only available cool place is the refrigerator.

An hour or so before you want to cook the meat, put 8 to 10 bamboo skewers to soak in cold water. Retrieve the meat, take it out of the liquid, and wipe off any large chunks of spice. Lay the pieces out on a big platter in a single layer to dry and turn them occasionally to help this happen.

Set the rack about 4 inches below the flames in the oven, as close as you think you can get the meat without burning the house down, and preheat the broiler thoroughly. String the meat, 4 or 5 cubes to the skewer, packing them touching-close but not tight. Set them under the heat and broil about 8 minutes total, turning 3 times to expose all sides. The goal is meat that is very dark, almost caramelized, on the outside but still quite rosy within. Sprinkle with sesame oil and serve at once.

---

* These items are available at gourmet, specialty, and Oriental groceries.

Meringues
Premier Pastry for the Dry Season

WINTER IS our dry season, when hair is straw, lips peel like sunburn, knuckles crack, and floorboards creak. These are the days when oils and creams, unguents and greases annoint every human surface, and carloads of vitamin E are consumed. In every home at least one heater sports an open pot of water — the world's foremost, ingeniously homemade, utterly useless humidifier. Walls as well as knuckles crack, the cat's electric, and all the beams are splitting.

But it's an ill draft that brings *no* good, friends, and the desiccating indoor atmosphere of winter is exactly the air fine meringue makers dream of.

Meringues are nothing but egg whites, sugar, and air. It's long, very slow baking that makes them so crisp and tender at the same time, and it's the nice dry environment that keeps them that way, too, for weeks and weeks and weeks on end.

When I was growing up, meringues were just meringues — star-shaped kisses of crisp sweetness flavored simply with vanilla. The next meringues were vanilla shells, their swirling sides encasing berries and cream, or ice cream. Meringues made flat and sandwiched with butter cream didn't catch up with me until college. After that came a deluge of dacquoise, and now I know a woman who puts crumbled meringue on *everything* — would probably even slap it on your oatmeal if you didn't keep a sharp eye on her. Probably be good, too.

Meringues

Meringue paste can be made different ways (see the recipes on pages 258 and 259), but all of them are baked the same way — *slowly*. If the oven is warmer than 200°F., they'll start browning before they dry out. In theory, you could make the damn things in a dehumidifier and never bake 'em at all. Commercial bakeries don't let the heat go over 125°F. Mine always come out fine, however, though my oven doesn't go that low.

If you have a pastry bag, use a wide star tube to pipe out kisses, a narrow plain one to trace flat cookies, and a narrow star to build nests with. A spoon works just as well, although the results are somewhat less decorative. Remember to keep shell shapes as thin as possible so the meringue doesn't overwhelm the filling.

Use a dab of meringue in each corner to anchor a sheet of brown paper on your flat cookie pan, then put the meringues on the paper. This is to diffuse the heat, but it also helps ease removal of the finished cookies. They don't spread, but leave enough space between them so the air can circulate.

Put the meringues in a preheated oven at the very lowest setting you trust and bake them about an hour. Check after the first 20 minutes, and if the cookies are starting to brown, turn the oven off but do not remove them. They will finish cooking in the heat left over.

They're done when a cooled one is dry clear through, though the insides of hot ones might still be sticky.

Let the cookies cool in the oven, then peel the paper from the cookies instead of lifting them therefrom. If the meringues are sticking, stroke the underside of the paper *lightly* with a dampened cloth and they'll come right off. If they don't get any more damp than that, they'll keep forever, a dubious virtue but handy.

Concerning Meringue Mushrooms

These caterers' favorites are one of the most convincing items of trompe l'oeil in the pastry cook's repertoire; they really *do* (or can) look so much like the real thing people are fooled almost until they pick one up. They are not new — there's a recipe for them in Maria Willett Howard's *Lowney's Cook Book* of 1907. Ms. Howard considered it sufficient to say, "Make a round of meringue mixture size of a quarter. Shape stems by drawing mixture upward. Sprinkle tops with cocoa. Bake in moderate oven. Remove from paper and press stems into bottom of rounds to resemble mushrooms." For those who find this recipe a bit elliptical, I can warmly recommend the excellent, exhaustively detailed instructions in *Maida Heatter's Book of Great Desserts*.

Meringue Paste 1

This is the lightest and most tender. It is also the most fragile. Do not handle it any more than you have to and get the pastries into the oven without delay.

½ **cup egg whites, usually about 4**
Pinch of salt

¼ teaspoon cream of tartar
¾ cup sifted superfine granulated sugar
⅓ cup sifted confectioners' sugar

Combine the egg whites with the salt and cream of tartar and beat with an electric mixer until they are foamy. Add the granulated sugar, 2 tablespoons at a time, gradually increasing the mixer speed as you do so. When ready the meringue should be very stiff and thick, and a bit rubbed between your fingers should be only slightly gritty. Fold in the confectioners' sugar and use the paste at once.

✳ *Meringue Paste 2*

This is also called Italian meringue. It makes a slightly tougher cookie, but that's because it's a much tougher mixture, far more tolerant of manipulation and willing to wait a bit before baking. This is the one to use when you plan to go hog-wild with the pastry points or create an elaborate meringue cake box (*vacherin glacé*) of the sort that were once so popular. A heavy-duty mixer is a necessity, by the way; those flimsy hand-held jobs haven't got the strength for this.

2 cups sugar
1 cup water
1 cup egg whites, usually about 8
¼ teaspoon salt
¼ teaspoon cream of tartar

Combine the sugar and water in a heavy saucepan and stir over medium heat until the sugar is dissolved. Cover the pan and simmer 5 minutes so the steam can wash the crystals from the sides. Uncover, raise the heat slightly, and boil, without stirring or tilting the pan, until a candy thermometer registers 238°F.

As it approaches this temperature, beat the whites with the salt and cream of tartar in a large, heatproof mixing bowl until they form stiff but still shiny peaks, aiming to have them achieve that state just when the syrup is ready.

As soon as it is, pour it in a thin stream into the egg whites as you beat them. Aim for the center of the beaters and don't stop adding or beating for an instant. Continue to beat after all the syrup is added and until the paste has cooled, or cooled to lukewarm anyway. Watch out for overheating the mixer; if yours is as elderly as mine, the motor housing'll be as hot as the syrup before you're through.

♡ Assorted Kisses

These are the classic meringue cookies of Christmas, but they're good any time of year and have the virtue of being fairly low calorie, as cookies go, because they do not contain any flour or fat. They *are* pure sugar, however, so while they're less prone to make you wide, they're not so great for your teeth. Good, though.

VANILLA KISSES

> 1 batch Meringue Paste 1 (recipe on page 257)
> ½ vanilla bean
> Some time (the bean must sit in the sugar several days)

Put the granulated sugar for the recipe in a clean jar with a tight-fitting lid. Split the vanilla bean into quarters, bury it in the sugar, and let it sit there, spreading its perfume, at least 3 days. Use a sharp, thin-bladed knife to scrape in the vanilla seeds, then sift the sugar mixture through a fine sieve. Use the flavored sugar and proceed as directed on page 257 to 258 under "Meringues."

LIME KISSES

> 1 batch Meringue Paste 1 (recipe on page 257)
> Very finely shredded zest (thin, colored outer rind) of 2 large limes, about 2 tablespoons

Make the paste, fold in the zest, and proceed as on page 257.

NUT KISSES

> ½ batch Meringue Paste 2 (recipe on page 258)
> ¼ teaspoon almond extract
> Pinch of salt
> 1 cup very finely grated blanched almonds or hazelnuts (They *must* be grated, not ground. If you do not have a nut grater and expect to use a processor, combine the nuts with 3 tablespoons sugar and resign yourself to slightly sweeter cookies. Alternatively, you can use 2 tablespoons flour and have slightly tougher cookies. One way or another, the idea is to keep the nut powder dry and floury; you're trying to avoid the release of oil.)

Make the paste as described on page 258 and beat in the extract and salt as it cools. Fold the nutmeats into the cooled paste and make kisses as described on page 257, being sure to use a wide pastry tip so the nut bits don't get hung up and drive you crazy.

*T*HE VEGETABLE REVOLUTION

WHEN YOU THINK of the revolution in the vegetable department that has occurred over the past ten years or so, chances are the first thing that comes to mind is the enormous increase in the variety of fresh plant foods available in the dead of winter. And it's not just a case of those out-of-season items such as summer squash and spring asparagus, which, though nice in their way, are not entirely satisfying. It's also the triumph of once-obscure seasonal items such as leeks, watercress, Swiss chard, and celeriac.

These are not "fancy" vegetables; country people have always grown and enjoyed them. But there was a time not long ago when only the most sophisticated of city markets carried them and everyone else had to grow their own or do without. No more. It is now quite easy not only to find these things but to find them in excellent condition, at moderate, if not, alas, low, prices. Particularly watercress, which a few pioneers are starting to grow hydroponically. Makes good sense, when you stop to think of it, the stuff being very nearly hydroponic by nature.

The artificial circumstances of the brave new watercress produce large, tender leaves and stems with plenty of flavor but none of the acrid bite sometimes found in the more conventional kind. Cleaner, too. (The disagreeable bite occasionally found in regular watercress is caused by an excess of sunlight. As an excess of sunlight also turns the leaf tips red, it always pays to taste-test any cress that looks too colorful. Happily, not all colored cress is sunburned; there's a variety that has a mahogany tinge naturally, but you might as well be sure before you buy.)

Watercress stores well. Remove any rubber bands, etc., and discard bruised leaves and stems. Set the remainder in a glass of water, stems down like a bouquet, close but not crowded. Keep in the refrigerator. You can wrap the whole works loosely in a plastic bag for a greenhouse effect that will stretch storage life even longer, if you're feeling ambitious or have gotten carried away and bought a case.

Celeriac — also known as celery root, knob celery, and *apio* — is only now beginning to be widely marketed in the United States, though it has been grown here since at least the start of the nineteenth century. Perhaps this is because celeriac, though unquestionably delicious, is not one of your lovelier vegetables. Brownish off-white, irregular, and knobby, warted with the stubs of a thousand small roots, this unprepossessing object is unlikely to attract many devotees on the strength of its looks.

Further, it is neither cheap nor all that easy to prepare. Its virtue is entirely in its fine flavor and unusual texture, the former resembling celery but stronger, the latter reminiscent of something between crisp turnips and young beets. Like these last two, celeriac is most popular in northern Europe, especially in Germany, where it is as widely grown and commonly available as the potatoes with which it is classically combined.

Shopping, Storage, and General Preparation

Celeriac is in season all winter but seems to be available irregularly. You can stock up when you find it if you have the room to store it, since celery roots are just about as durable as carrots. Store them as you would carrots, root cellar–style, in a cold, humid environment such as a perforated plastic bag in the crisper compartment of the refrigerator.

The knobs can be anywhere from the size of a small tennis ball to that of a cantaloupe, though they're never as regular in shape as those analogies imply. Where you have a choice, top-shaped yields more than broad-bottomed because the shoulders are where the meat is. Large roots, though easier to prepare, are somewhat more likely than the small ones to be woody, pithy, or both. Quality is usually pretty good because celeriac stores so well. To be sure, check that the knobs are firm, free of shrunken places and soft spots.

To prepare, begin by setting out a bowl of acidulated water (2 tablespoons lemon juice or white vinegar to ½ gallon water). Celeriac, like apples, rapidly discolors when cut unless protected, but it must be peeled, as the skin is unpleasantly tough and fibrous. Halved knobs intended for purée can be steamed in the skins and then scooped out, assuming those skins to be smooth enough to be cleanable, but as a general rule it's best to peel before you set out. For minimum waste (there's still plenty), cut the celeriac crosswise into fat slices before peeling, then use a sharp, thin-bladed paring knife to remove the irregular borders, dropping prepared slices into the acidulated water as you go. They can be left there a couple of hours if necessary, though a slight loss of flavor will result. The pre-pared slices are now ready to use as directed in your recipe, sliced thinner, cubed, julienned, etc.

Gratin of Leeks and Swiss Chard with Swiss Cheese

Though not exactly a diet delight, this is a fairly restrained main course special enough for (vegetarian) company. Preface it with a few raw vegetables, serve it with baked potatoes, and follow it with baked apples and ice cream to produce a just about effortless dinner party that, for once, contains neither pasta nor brown rice.

For 4 servings

1 large bunch leeks, enough to make 2½ to 3 cups trimmed and sliced
1½ pounds Swiss chard, about half a grocery bag, lightly piled (it shrinks)
1 large clove garlic
Butter for the pan, plus 3 tablespoons
2 cups very coarse white bread crumbs, stale but untoasted
3 ounces Swiss (Emmenthal) cheese, shredded coarse, about 1 cup
3 ounces Swiss (Gruyère) cheese, shredded coarse, about 1 cup
1 tablespoon flour
1¼ cups light cream or 1 cup half-and-half

Prepare the vegetables. Wash and trim the roots from the leeks, then slice ¼ inch thick up to the place where the leaves fall apart. About a third of your slices will have a hint of pale chartreuse and light green; as long as they're juicy-looking, they're fine. Set aside. Wash chard and spin or pat dry. Carve out the thick stems, chop into ½-inch pieces, and set aside. Shred the leaves.

Choose a shallow baking dish about 8 by 11 by 2 inches. Rub all over with the cut garlic clove, smearing out plenty of garlic juice as you go. Butter the pan and set aside.

Melt the 3 tablespoons butter in a wide skillet over low heat. Leaving a generous film in the pan, pour the remainder over the bread crumbs and toss well. Sauté the leek slices in the remaining butter over medium heat, stirring often, until they just start to soften and take color. Add the chard stems and cook, stirring often, until they are translucent.

While the vegetables are frying, combine the cheeses and the flour and toss to mix thoroughly. When the leek mixture is ready, turn it into the prepared baking pan. Crank up the heat slightly under the skillet and add the chard leaves in handfuls, stirring constantly. As they wilt, there will be room for more. Keep adding. As soon as all the chard is wilted, it's ready.

Sprinkle half the floured cheese over the leek mixture, top with the wilted chard, and sprinkle with the remaining cheese. Pour the cream over everything, crown with the bread crumbs, which should form a fairly solid-looking top crust, and bake in the upper third of a preheated 375°F. oven 30 minutes, or until the crumbs are brown and the vegetables tender. Watch out that you don't burn your mouth; that enticingly gooey cheese is *hot*.

Country-Style Soup of Watercress and Leeks

This soup has much to recommend it. It is simple to make, it uses up scraps that might otherwise be wasted, it can be cheerfully fed to vegetarians, *and* it's not full of ingredients, if you know what I mean. Simplicity itself, which could not be more welcome at this season.

For 4 appetizer or 2 main dish servings

2 tablespoons butter
2½ to 3 cups finely sliced upper green parts of leeks, about 3 medium
½ pound boiling potatoes, peeled and cubed, a heaping cup
3 cups water
2½ to 3 cups coarse, lower watercress stems, of the sort that would be
   left over from making salad, 2 large bunches worth, plus a few
   leaves if possible
Approximately ½ cup light cream, half-and-half, or milk
Salt to taste

Heat the butter in the soup pot and slowly sauté the leeks until they are translucent and soft. Stir in the potatoes, add the water, then add the watercress stems. Simmer, covered, 45 minutes, or until the potatoes are falling apart. Put the soup through a food mill or blend it and work through a fine strainer — you can't just grind it up because the leek tops are too stringy. Return the purée to the pan and add the cream until you have a smooth, fairly thin texture, thinner, for instance, than split-pea soup but not as thin as water. Add salt to taste and serve at once, garnished with the reserved watercress leaves if you have 'em, or a julienne of lettuce or a small snipping of chives if you don't. Resist the impulse to garnish with parsley; its strong flavor is obtrusive. Delicious accompanied by seriously garlicky garlic bread or freshly made corn bread and butter.

✳ Scalloped Potatoes and Celeriac with Blue Cheese

The well-loved partnership between celery and blue cheese is at work here, made subtle through the intercession of potatoes and cream. The result is filling, smooth, and rich, best served in small portions unless it's being used as a main dish, for Sunday supper, say, with the proverbial big green salad.

For 4 to 5 main dish or 6 to 8 side dish portions

Butter for the pan
1½ pounds celeriac, about 3, enough to make a scant 2 cups sliced
1½ pounds baking potatoes, about 2 large, enough to make 2 heaping cups sliced
Nutmeg
Salt
White pepper
1 heaping tablespoon flour
3 to 4 ounces crumbled Roquefort or Stilton cheese, enough to make ¾ to 1 cup
1 cup whipping cream (30% butterfat, not ultrapasteurized)
1 cup milk

Lightly butter a shallow baking pan roughly 8 inches square by 1½ inches deep and set it aside. Prepare the celeriac as described on page 262, cutting it into slices a bit less than ¼ inch thick. Peel the potatoes and slice them about ⅛ inch thick. Preheat the oven to 350°F. (put a piece of foil on the bottom to catch drips). Drain the celeriac.

Make a layer of potatoes on the bottom of the pan. Sprinkle them lightly with nutmeg, salt, and white pepper, then sprinkle on about one-fourth of the flour. Cover with a layer of celeriac, repeat the sprinklings, and top with half the cheese. Again potatoes, sprinkled, and celeriac, sprinkled and cheesed. Top with the remaining potatoes, leaving them plain. Pour the cream and milk in slowly, bathing that top layer of potatoes as you do so. Cover the pan with foil and bake 30 to 40 minutes.

Uncover and use a spatula or knife blade to press down the lid of potatoes so the sauce washes over them, then continue baking uncovered until the top is well browned and the vegetables are very tender when tested with a knife point. One or two additional pressings-down of the lid under the sauce will result in an especially gooey-crisp, heavily lacquered crust, but this refinement is by no means necessary. Let the finished scallop cool 2 to 3 minutes before serving so all the free juices will be reabsorbed by the vegetables and the whole business slices neatly.

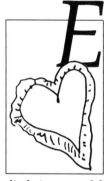

*E*DIBLE VALENTINES

THERE ARE SEVERAL ways to approach the problem. The safest and most commonly taken course is to offer one or more of the time-honored classics. Champagne comes at once to mind, also oysters, with or without caviar. Proven movers to romance supposedly include such diverse treats as truffles roasted in the ashes, candied ginger, and fillet of snake.

Alternatively, you might put out a comforting feed that will remind its consumer of the joys of domestic life — a dry martini, maybe, and a nice pot roast with plenty of gravy, mashed potatoes, and apple pie.

Or, instead of relying simply on the food itself, you might build your Valentine's Day menu around the way food is eaten. Why not do all the preparation in advance, set your table prettily with china, candles, and flowers, put out a pair of heated damp napkins, and serve a meal designed to be entirely eaten with the fingers?

Those readers who have seen the famous "eating scene" from the movie *Tom Jones* will at once recognize the possibilities. Those who have never seen the movie need only reflect for a moment on the sensual pleasure of corn on the cob, fried chicken, or barbecued ribs, on the sense of freedom from inhibition this dining style provides.

SUGGESTED MENU FOR HAND-FEEDING
Relish Tray of Assorted Crisp Vegetables
Maple-Mustard Game Hens
(see "Maple Syrup: Sweet Supreme," page 272)
Grilled Sweet Potatoes
Raspberry Fool with Fruit and Cookies

Almost all the preparation can be done the night before: the game hens split and set to marinate, the potatoes precooked, the fool concocted, and the table appointments selected. The fresh vegetables and fruit for the dessert must be dealt with at dinner time, but two servings don't take long to put together.

The contents of the relish tray will be dictated by some combination of your refrigerator and your local market, but don't forget there's more to relish than carrot and celery sticks. Green and red peppers, blades of Belgian endive, barely cooked broccoli spears, rounds or chunks of cucumber . . . at this time of year, the tomatoes are considerably more decorative than they are tasty, but wedges of tart Granny Smith apples can be used to provide the hint of juicy sweetness that tomatoes provide in the summer.

Of course, it may be that the object of your affections is too far away — physically or emotionally — for a dinner invitation to be exactly the thing. The usual response in such situations is to send chocolate, the more lavish the better, and I suppose most chocophiles will feel that solution's just fine. Personally, I prefer vanilla, for which reason I can't help suggesting sending another, even dandier candy, namely marzipan.

There could hardly be a candy more fitting. Marzipan is (or once was) reputed to be a highly effective aphrodisiac. According to the French food authority Raymond Oliver, "Maria de'Medici made great use of it." Can't ask for a better recommendation than *that*.

Although the exact recipe for Maria's marzipan was not given, it's safe to assume that while it very well may have included some strange additions of one sort or another, it did *not* include the preservatives and artificial colors that make modern commercial marzipan so repellent. If you do decide to give marzipan, you'd better make it yourself if you want to make a good impression. Fortunately, it's easy, and the homemade candy is not only far more delicious, it's a great deal cheaper, too.

♡ Red Satin Hash
(For Stick-in-the-Mud Traditionalists Who Prefer to Use Forks)

This is a somewhat lightened, decidedly romantic reworking of red flannel hash, a New England classic that combines into one comforting whole the leftover corned beef, potatoes, and beets of a traditional boiled dinner. By leaving out the potatoes and spicing things up considerably, you get a nice south of the border feeling and a simply made, inexpensive entrée perfect for a holiday supper. Round out the meal with corn bread or fresh tortillas and serve tropical fruit for dessert.

For 4 large or 6 more modest servings (or, of course, 2 servings and lots of leftovers, which can be used to good effect for baked green peppers)

1 large onion, chopped quite fine, about 1½ cups
2 tablespoons lard or vegetable oil
3 cups cooked lean beef, pork, or rich fowl such as duck or goose, chopped into roughly ¼-inch dice
3 medium-large beets, cooked, peeled, and diced slightly larger than the meat, about 3 cups
1 large clove garlic
1 to 2 tablespoons candied citron, cut into dice slightly smaller than the meat (optional)
2 teaspoons tomato paste
1 teaspoon each dried oregano and ground cumin
½ teaspoon each ground cinnamon and salt
¼ teaspoon ground cloves
1 cup beef or other broth
2 tablespoons each chopped green olives and chopped Brazil nuts or whole pine nuts
2 medium-sized fresh jalapeño peppers, seeds removed, cut into dice the same size as the citron, about 2 tablespoons, *or* 2 tablespoons minced mild green pepper plus ½ teaspoon crushed dried hot red pepper
10 to 12 pretty sprigs of fresh coriander (cilantro or Chinese parsley), or 5 to 6 inner leaves of romaine lettuce, shredded very fine

Sauté the onion in the fat over medium heat until it is golden and wilted. Stir in the meat and cook a few minutes more, until it is well impregnated with onion flavor and just starting to brown. Stir in the beets, garlic, citron, tomato paste, and spices and simmer a moment more. Pour on the broth and cook, stirring occasionally, until all the liquid has evaporated and the hash is starting to fry on the bottom.

Now add the olives, nuts, and peppers and pat the hash into a flat cake. Let it cook over slightly lowered heat about 5 minutes longer, or just until the pepper has turned bright green and the flavors have amalgamated. There being no starch, there won't be much crust, so don't wait around hoping one will form. Instead serve immediately, garnished with the fresh greenery. Coriander adds flavor, lettuce adds crunch — both are tasty. The coriander's better, but the lettuce is easier to get.

 Raspberry Fool with Fruit and Cookies

2 large or 4 small servings

1 package (10-ounces) frozen raspberries in syrup
1 teaspoon unflavored gelatin
1 tablespoon Grand Marnier or other orange liqueur
²⁄₃ cup heavy cream
1 tablespoon sugar
2 ripe Anjou or Comice pears
Thin, plain cookies, best-quality bought or homemade

Thaw and thoroughly drain the raspberries, saving the juice. Measure ½ cup plus 1 tablespoon juice into a small saucepan and sprinkle on the gelatin. When it has softened, put the pan over low heat, add the liqueur, and cook, stirring constantly, only until the gelatin is dissolved. Remove from heat, cool, then chill till the liquid becomes syrupy and sluggish, about 10 to 20 minutes.

Whip the cream, sprinkling in the sugar, until it forms stiff peaks. Beat the gelatin lightly. The resultant froth should stay put, though it won't be as stiff as the cream (rechill briefly if necessary). Fold the froth and cream together, then fold in the raspberries. Put the fool in pretty bowls or oversized wine glasses and chill, covered, at least 2 hours, as long as a day. Serve with fingers of peeled fruit and a few cookies — for dipping.

♡ Marzipan

ALMOND PASTE:
2 cups granulated sugar
1 cup water
1 pound blanched almonds, the fresher the better

MARZIPAN:
Approximately 3 egg whites
Approximately 3 cups sifted confectioners' sugar

Begin by making the almond paste. Dissolve the granulated sugar in the water in a heavy saucepan. Bring to a boil, cover the pan, and lower the heat to medium. Let the mixture cook, covered, about 4 minutes, long enough for steam to wash any sugar crystals from the sides of the pan. Uncover and boil gently, *without stirring*, until a candy thermometer registers 240°F.

While the syrup is cooking, grind the almonds until they are reduced to a smooth paste, slowly dripping in a *very small* amount (say around ½ teaspoon) cold water. The cold water helps prevent the almond oil from rising to the surface.

As soon as the syrup is ready, remove it from the heat, let it cool only a minute, then stir it into the ground almonds. You now have almond paste, useful not just for marzipan but for a number of classic pastry cook's applications. It will keep indefinitely if kept cold and tightly wrapped.

To make marzipan, measure the paste. Work in 1 egg white per 1 cup of paste. When the mixture is smooth, knead in enough confectioners' sugar to make an easily malleable but still firm dough. It usually takes about a cup of sugar per cup of paste, but this varies. The finished marzipan can be used to make little sculptures, rolled into small logs and dipped in chocolate, or rolled out between sheets of waxed paper dusted with confectioners' sugar and used to encase fruitcakes. Alternatively, you can use the marzipan ingredients and method to make the more interestingly flavored lovers' bonbons whose recipes follow.

♡ *Orange Bonbons*

For about 30 candies

1 cup Almond Paste (recipe on page 269)
1 teaspoon orange flower water
1 tablespoon finely grated orange zest (thin, colored outer rind)
1 tablespoon plus 1 teaspoon orange liqueur
3 tablespoons candied orange peel (preferably homemade), cut into
**   tiny dice**
1 egg white
Approximately 1¼ cups sifted confectioners' sugar

Combine the almond paste with the orange items, then work in the egg white and the sugar as described in the Marzipan recipe. Mold into small balls about ¾ inch in diameter. If you are feeling ambitious, shape the balls into oranges by pressing with a thumbnail at one end to make a small cross (to imitate the stem end) and cut leaves and stems from candied citron or angelica.

If you're feeling *really* ambitious, save out the candied peel when making the paste, then combine it with only about half the flavored marzipan. Roll balls of the peel-studded batch and encase them in thin skins of the lumpless one so the outsides of the "oranges" are smooth. Prick all over with the point of a toothpick to imitate orange skin; dimple and leaf as described above. I hope whoever you're making this for is worth it.

♡ *Double-Almond Bonbons*

For about 30 candies

30 large unblanched almonds, plus a few extra for testing
1 cup Almond Paste (recipe on page 269)
1 teaspoon vanilla extract
¼ teaspoon almond extract
1 tablespoon almond liqueur or cognac
1 egg white
Approximately 1 cup sifted confectioners' sugar

Spread the almonds on a flat sheet and toast them in a 325°F. oven about 12 minutes, or until a broken one is dark gold but no browner. Let them cool completely.

Combine the almond paste with everything else, moving toward marzipan as described in the marzipan recipe. Roll the finished product into heaping teaspoon-sized balls, flatten slightly, and place an almond in the center of each. Mold the paste to enclose the almond completely (unless you are going for a slightly obscene effect, in which case you can leave just a little bit of the nut peeking suggestively out).

VARIATION: If you want to make something doubly aphrodisiacal, in the Arabic style, make Double-Almond Bonbons and stuff each into a large, juicy fresh date. Heavy-duty, but not half-bad.

*M*APLE SYRUP: SWEET SUPREME

IT'S GREAT on pancakes, needless to say, also waffles, and French toast and biscuits and muffins and oatmeal and vanilla ice cream. Use it to accent citrus fruits — especially grapefruit — and to enhance apples and pears and grapes and, of course, blueberries. Maple syrup is better than honey for glazing a ham, indeed any roast pork, or giving a touch of additional sweetness to root vegetables such as carrots and beets and turnips. And it's traditional in baked beans . . . *really* traditional. The northeastern tribes were flavoring beans with bear fat and maple syrup long before the colonists got here.

In fact, they were flavoring almost everything with maple syrup. It was the Indians' principle seasoning, used as we might use salt. It was also one of their staple foods, a primary source of nourishment in the early spring season when stores were depleted and new growth had not yet started. There were special sugar camps, apart from the villages, where sap was collected in bark buckets and laboriously reduced to syrup. Having no fireproof vessels, the earliest syrup makers supposedly used red hot rocks to boil the liquid in hollowed-out logs.

Iron kettles arrived with the Europeans, but other than that, the technology didn't change much. It still hasn't. The process is simple and immutable. Wait until the first crow flies, 'long about the end of February. When warm sunny days and frosty nights follow each other week after week, bore little holes in your maple trees and collect the gallons of "sweet water" that flow from them. Process it quickly — it'll ferment if left more than a day or so. Boil it and boil it and boil it until (approximately) forty gallons of barely sweet liquid have become one gallon of maple syrup, and there you are.

Some producers are now using plastic piping to gather the sap and pumping it to the sap house instead of hauling it there. State laws govern the amount of sweetness required, and nobody is dropping hot rocks in the stuff these days. But syrup will still vary from light to dark, from smoky and rich to flowery and delicate, depending on just when and where it was made. Though maple syrup is often graded, from "A" or "AA" fancy or "light" for the palest, on down to "B" or "C" for the really dark article, this is more a reflection of color than of quality per se, since the darkest syrup has the most intense flavor.

Cooking with Maple Syrup

You can substitute it cup for cup in honey recipes, except for pastry (it is less acid and more liquid), but be careful about combining it with strong flavors such as chocolate and cinnamon. Though maple syrup's distinctive taste seems strong when you enjoy it over pancakes, that hint of the woodlands is easily overwhelmed. (The harsh flavor of fake maple products, on the other hand, annihilates all others.)

Making Sugar from Syrup

Maple syrup is all very well, but it does tend to fall off the toast. As it is much easier to find pure maple syrup than pure maple sugar, here's how to make the conversion.

Essentially, you're just boiling off more water. A candy thermometer makes things easier, but it isn't absolutely necessary. Old-timers knew the cooking was finished when they could dip a looped twig in the syrup and blow a bubble through the film of sugar that stuck to it. Use the palest syrup you can find, to minimize chances of burning, and a pan with plenty of room for it to bubble up without boiling over. Simmer over low-medium heat, stirring more and more frequently, until the temperature reaches 40°F. above the boiling point of water, or about 252°F., depending on atmospheric pressure.

If you don't have a candy thermometer, use the old-fashioned "hard-ball" test. When the syrup is thick enough to sheet from the spoon in two large drops, put a little of it into a cup of cold water. If the sugar can be gathered into a firm but pliable ball, the batch is ready.

When the syrup has reached the proper temperature, pour it into a large, clean pan and stir vigorously until it crystalizes. The stirring will get harder and harder as the sugar cools, and a point will come when you seem to be stuck with something like second-rate taffy. Persevere. The syrup will become *very* hard to stir and then it will become sugar. Transfer it to a separate container at once to finish cooling. Some will be stuck to the working pan. Put it back, briefly, over the heat, and the stuck sugar will release.

Homemade maple sugar is extremely hard, prone to pick up moisture, and inclined to be lumpy. Keep it in a cool, dry place and grind small amounts in a blender or processor as needed. If you grind the whole batch at once, be sure to store it in an airtight container. An 8-ounce bottle of syrup will make a bit less than a cup of sugar.

# Maple-Mustard Game Hens

For 2 servings

2 cornish game hens, preferably fresh ones, about 1¼ pounds each
1 tablespoon Dijon mustard
2 tablespoons lemon juice
½ cup peanut oil or other vegetable oil (not olive)
⅓ cup pure maple syrup
8 to 10 peppercorns
1 large bay leaf, crumbled
1 large clove garlic, quartered
1 bunch watercress, rinsed and picked over

Use a sharp chef's knife or kitchen shears to cut the backbone and rib cage from the birds. The bones are very soft, so it's easy to do. Turn a hen, breast side down, on the work surface. Starting just to one side of the tail piece, cut all the way to the other end, right beside the backbone. Repeat on the other side. You will now have removed the backbone in a long, even slice about ½ inch wide, and the hen will lie more or less flat. This makes it easy to see the fans of the rib bones. Remove them, too. Wipe the meat with a dampened paper towel and set the hens aside.

Put the mustard in a small bowl. Beat in the lemon juice with a wire whisk, then beat in first the oil, then the maple syrup. Sprinkle the peppercorns, bay leaf, and garlic in a shallow noncorrodible pan or bowl just large enough to hold the flattened hens in one layer. Pour in about a fourth of the marinade. Lay in the meat, cut side down, and pour the remaining marinade over it. Cover tightly and refrigerate 1 day (or at least a few hours).

Remove the meat from the refrigerator about an hour before cooking. At cooking time, move the rack so the hens will be in the upper third of the oven and preheat it to 400°F. Drain excess marinade from the hens and arrange them, cut side down, in a shallow noncorrodible roasting pan. Roast 20 minutes, baste, raise the heat to 425°F., and roast about 20 minutes more, basting once or twice if attention permits. Do not turn the meat, which should get a nice, well-browned look to it by the end of the cooking. If for some reason it's a bit pale, just run it under the broiler for a minute or two. To serve, quarter each hen and arrange on a warmed platter, garnished with the watercress.

Maple–Cream Cheese Spread

This is good on just about any bread, including bagels, and also can be used as an icing. It's particularly nice with carrot cake.

For about ¾ cup; recipe can be doubled or tripled

6 ounces cream cheese
½ cup maple syrup (The dark kind is fine.)

Let the cheese soften at room temperature. Put the syrup in a small pan and simmer, stirring occasionally, over medium-low heat, until it is thickened to the texture of heavy honey — about 235°F. on a candy thermometer. Let cool, stirring once or twice, then beat the sticky mess into the cream cheese. You must reduce the syrup before combining it with the cheese, or the mixture will curdle and separate. Store refrigerated, tightly covered, and it will keep a long time — if it lasts.

Maple-Walnut Filo Snails

For 10 large pastries

1 cup regular walnuts
1 cup black walnuts (regular walnuts can be substituted if necessary)
⅓ cup brown sugar
1 teaspoon vanilla extract
Pinch of salt
¾ cup unsalted butter
10 sheets commercial filo pastry, allow a few extras in case of tears (See "A Note about Filo Dough" on page 20.)
1¼ cups cold maple syrup
Pastry brush and clean tea towel

Grind the regular walnuts fine and set aside about ⅓ cup of them. Chop the black walnuts into coarse crumbs and combine them with the larger batch of ground nuts. Add the brown sugar, vanilla, and salt and set aside.

Melt the butter over low heat. Set out the filo sheets, flat, covered with the towel to prevent drying out. Divide the filling into ten equal portions and preheat the oven to 375°F.

Lay a sheet of filo on your work surface and use the brush to butter it lavishly with the melted butter. Arrange a portion of filling in a line about 1 inch in from a short edge of the rectangle, allowing an inch of naked pastry at both top and bottom. Fold up the long edges so the ends of the filling line are enclosed, then start with the near short edge and roll the filling into the pastry so you have a fattish snake. Curl the snake into a coil and put it seam side down on an ungreased cookie sheet.

Repeat with the remaining materials, setting each finished snail on the sheet in such a way that it will keep its neighbors from uncoiling. When all are made, brush the tops with butter and sprinkle on the reserved ground nuts.

Bake 25 minutes, then separate so the sides can brown. Bake about 10 minutes more, or until the pastries are a very dark gold. As soon as they come out of the oven, drizzle the cold syrup over them. Let them cool in the pan, then transfer to a serving platter and pour the run-off syrup on top of them.

Needless to say, these are tasty just plain, and it doesn't require any great leap of the imagination to see where vanilla ice cream might go well. For a *real* treat, try partnering the snails with small blocks of very fresh feta cheese. The salty tang is terrific against the sweetness of the maple.

COMPANY FOR BREAKFAST

WHEN THE DAWN is that cold bleak one in which late winter mornings seem to specialize, there are few comforts to equal those of a substantial breakfast, preferably a substantial breakfast that will provide not only physical nourishment but psychological uplift as well. Oatmeal, as already mentioned (page 216), can go far in this direction, but by now you have been eating oatmeal for quite a while already, and something a bit more glamorous may be necessary to achieve a similarly soothing effect. This is especially true on weekends, when the desire for differentness asserts itself most strongly. What the heck, why not make the effort? And if you are going to make the effort, why not invite a couple of friends?

The idea of breakfast as a meal suitable for socializing is one that may take some getting used to, especially if you are (as I am) the sort of person who prefers an hour of lonely communion with your coffee cup before communion with your fellow human beings. Nevertheless, it turns out that the first meal of the day is an excellent one at which to entertain, assuming, of course, the entertainees are fairly close friends.

Just think, almost none of the factors that make other party meals a bit of a production need be considered at 8 A.M. — no candles, no culinary extravaganzas, no alcohol. And no hanging around for hours. Even the most leisurely of breakfasts is unlikely to eat up a big slice of your day. Early morning visits, in other words, allow maximum at-the-table-type companionability for a minimum of hassle. Highly recommended.

Tips for Successful Breakfast Entertaining

1. Breakfast is an intimate meal, and schedules are hard to coordinate. Two or three, therefore, is about the largest appropriate number of guests.

2. Never invite anybody you feel like you have to clean up the house for — morning sunlight does tend to show the dust.

3. Do everything you can the night before. Prepare whatever can be prepared. Get the kitchen cleaned up and ready to go. Set the table and locate seldom-used ingredients like that jar of fancy homemade fruit conserve Aunt Sally sent you last Christmas.

4. Keep the menu simple, remembering that this is breakfast, not brunch, and should sit lightly upon the stomach. Something fruity, either solid or liquid, and something starchy, such as toast or pancakes, are really all that's needed, though eggs of some sort and a small amount of meat or fish are certainly on the approved list.

5. Use pretty accoutrements: cheerful place mats or tablecloth, nice china and glasses, actual napkins. A big fancy arrangement would be out of place, but a few small flowers here and there do polish up the tone.

6. The coffee and/or tea should be the best of which you are capable, freshly ground, freshly brewed, plentiful, and hot, hot, hot.

PHILOSOPHICAL NOTE: I cannot let pass this opportunity to observe that the idea of a *business* breakfast is enough to give any civilized person ulcers. If for some reason people must have business meetings that start at such unconscionable hours that guilt compels their conveners to serve coffee and Danish to those invited. I suppose it's no more than the price we must pay for the pace of modern times — but it isn't breakfast.

"No business before breakfast, Glum!" says the King. "Breakfast first, business next."   *William Makepeace Thackeray*

SUGGESTED BREAKFAST MENUS

A. Baked apples, with cream or yogurt (crisp bacon)
Assorted toasted breads or muffins
Cream cheese/fruit preserves/ butter

B. Melon wedges filled with
lightly sugared blueberries or blackberries
Cornmeal cakes with butter and maple syrup
(country sausage)

C. Southwestern Breakfast
Sober Sunrises
Breakfast Tacos
Coffee with Cinnamon and Chocolate

D. Spiced cider
(Make Mulled Cider, page 171, and chill overnight.)
Baked pears with sour cream
Hot wild rice with accompaniments —
maple syrup, butter, heavy cream, raisins . . .

Wild rice for breakfast is not so outlandish as it may sound; since the historic morning the idea first came to me, propelled of course by leftovers, the patron saint of most culinary invention, I have come to regard it as the hot cereal par excellence. Just as wild rice is usually reserved for special-occasion dinners, it is usually reserved for special-occasion breakfasts, costing as it does about ten times more than oatmeal. Oatmeal is really cheap, however, and even a big bowl of wild rice won't cost much more than a buck, even counting the maple syrup. A bargain at twice the price, especially where it really ought to be cooked in advance, since it takes so long to cook. Reheat gently in a covered double boiler, with just a few drops of water to keep it from sticking.

 A Sober Sunrise

This pretty and refreshing drink is a good choice for those who find straight fruit juice too sweet to taste right first thing in the morning.

For each drink: Put a scant tablespoon frozen orange juice concentrate in the bottom of a big (16-ounce) glass or tumbler, half-fill with club soda, and stir vigorously. The mixture will foam way up, but the foam will soon subside. As soon as there's room for it, add enough cranberry juice "cocktail" to fill the glass two-thirds full, which should bring the cap of foam right to the top. Serve at once.

 Breakfast Tacos

Breakfast Tacos are a lot less weird than they sound. Scrambled eggs go very nicely with the flour tortillas available at the supermarket, and they're delicious with fresh corn tortillas, if you're lucky enough to live where such things are available.

Plan on two 8-inch tortillas and 2 or 3 eggs per person. Assemble embellishments and give them time to come to room temperature so they don't cool off the eggs. Likely candidates include: chopped olives, shredded mild cheese, thinly sliced green onions, cubes of avocado, and bits of ham, crumbled bacon, or cooked sausage. Sour cream and Fast Blender Hot Sauce (see recipe on page 248) are good choices for toppings. Have a basket lined first with foil, then with a napkin ready to keep the tortillas warm. Warm a bowl, ideally one with a cover, for the eggs.

Wrap the tortillas in tinfoil and heat in a 350°F. oven about 20 minutes. While they are heating, very slowly scramble the eggs in plenty of butter. You want them to come out very homogenous and creamy. In fact, if you like, you can scramble in a small amount (1 tablespoon per egg) of cream or cream cheese.

To serve, just set out the warmed tortillas in the basket, the eggs in the bowl, the embellishments grouped around them. Breakfasters can assemble their own ideas of a good time — many are not too thrilled at the idea of hot sauce and onions first crack from the bag, but others, myself among them, can think of few finer ways to start a winter day.

Coffee with Cinnamon and Chocolate

Hot fresh coffee is poured simultaneously into the cups with a not too sweet or rich cocoa flavored with cinnamon. Additional cinnamon sticks in the cups are a nice touch, as is whipped cream.

For 8 to 10 large cups

CHOCOLATE MIXTURE:
4 tablespoons Dutch process cocoa
2 tablespoons sugar

¾ cup water
3-inch cinnamon stick, broken in half
1 cup cold milk

Hot coffee
Whipped cream or heated milk

Put the cocoa and sugar in a small, heavy-bottomed saucepan, then slowly add the water. Stir and mash as you add so the initially crumbly mixture becomes an absolutely smooth paste, then a thickish syrup. Insert the cinnamon stick, put the pan over very low heat, and slowly bring to a simmer, beating frequently with a wire whisk. When the syrup is hot, slowly beat in the cold milk, stirring all the while. Continue to cook, beating more and more frequently, until the mixture is almost simmering.

This makes enough chocolate to flavor 8 to 10 large cups of coffee. It will keep about a week in the refrigerator. Remove the cinnamon stick before storage so the flavor doesn't get too strong, and be sure to reheat very gently so neither milk nor chocolate scorches.

Put the hot chocolate in a warmed pot with a pouring spout — press your teapot into service if you don't happen to have a tall, graceful, nineteenth-century porcelain chocolate pot. Pour a stream of chocolate into the cups at the same time you pour in the coffee, mingling the streams and aiming for about twice as much coffee as chocolate. Garnish with a puff of whipped cream or pass a pitcher of warm milk, so drinkers can add same to taste.

❊ Lo's Cornmeal Pancakes

These are a breakfast specialty of that same Lois who's so smart about the frozen tomatoes (see "Lois's Tomato Trick," page 159), a woman who knows what's good and how to get it with the smallest possible effort.

For about 24 small cakes

1¼ cups fine stone-ground cornmeal
½ cup all-purpose flour
2 teaspoons baking powder
Pinch of salt
2 tablespoons sugar (optional)
3 eggs

2 cups milk
2 tablespoons light vegetable oil or melted butter
Grease for the griddle (may not be needed)

Combine the dry ingredients in a bowl and stir with a wire whisk until they are well combined. Put the eggs in a blender and whirl until foamy, then whirl in the milk. Dump in the dry ingredients all at once and blend, turning the machine off and on, only until they are dampened. A few lumps won't matter. The batter should be the texture of thin cream. If the blender has a good pouring spout, leave the batter where it is. Otherwise, transfer it to a pitcher.

Heat an iron or soapstone griddle over medium-high heat until a drop of water bounces. If it is well-seasoned (or covered with a genuinely nonstick coating, something I have yet to see) you won't have to grease it. As the *New England Cookbook* put it in 1905, "All new griddles are hard to manage, but as the only way to get old ones is to make them out of new ones, we are shut up to the necessity of using the new, though they do not work so well." New griddles will have to be greased, very lightly, before each batch.

To get nicely rounded cakes, hold the pitcher close to the pan as you pour. Do one test cake to start with; the batter should spread enough to make a firm-looking cake about ⅛ inch thick, with thin, almost lacy edges. Correct the batter with milk (or a few spoonfuls of flour) if necessary. Cover the griddle with cakes, being sure they don't run into each other. They're ready to turn as soon as bubbles appear and the surface looks damp but not wet. Turn them only once or they'll be tough. This batter settles very quickly; be sure to stir and recombine before each batch.

The cakes can be kept warm in a low oven so the cake maker can breakfast along with everyone else, but like every other pancake ever made, they will not be as good if you do this. Better to use a very large griddle or 2 or 3 pans and make enough for everybody all at once. Do not discard the idea of an electric skillet in the middle of the table — this is one of the very few things they are actually good for.

BLUEBERRY, OTHERBERRY, EVEN APPLE PANCAKES: This amount of batter will carry about a cup of fruit. Cut whatever it is into blueberry-sized pieces, if necessary, and toss with 1 to 3 tablespoons flour, depending on juiciness. The idea is to coat each fruit lump so it stays separate and doesn't bleed into the batter. Stir the fruit in right before making the cakes.

INDEX

Curdling, 233
Curry powder, 252–253, 255

D
Dandelion, 87–88, 90–91, 103
Dates, 221–222, 271; cutting, 222
David, Elizabeth, 31, 177–178
December, 216–241
Dictionary of American Food and Drink (Mariani), 79
Diet for a Small Planet (Lappe), 154
Dieting, 33–34
Dumas, Alexandre, Jr., 150

E
Easter, 33–43
Egg, 56, 149–150; hard-boiled, 38–39; mimosa, 39; yolks, 64. *See also* Meringue
Eggplant, 131–132, 250–251
Encyclopedia of Fish Cookery (McClane), 22
English Bread and Yeast Cookery (David), 31
Escoffier, Auguste, 177–178

F
Farmers' markets, 143–144
February, 261–281
Fenugreek, 253
Fiber, soluble, 217
Filo dough, 20, 275–276
Fish, 22, 74
Fisher, M.F.K., 109
Flour, stone-ground whole-wheat, 33
Francillon (Dumas), 150, 152
Freezing: fruit, 139; herbs, 161–162; shrimp, 243; soup, 99, 146; tomatoes, 159–160; turkey, 210; vegetables, 144–145
Fruit, 123–125, 210–211, 280–281
Frying, 24, 246–247

G
Game hen, Cornish, 274
Gardening, 45, 133–135
Garlic, 136–137, 185–186, 225–226
Gibbons, Euell, 63
Ginger, 237–239
Grain mills, 33
Greens, 97–103; warning, 103
Grigson, Jane, 88, 225

H
Halloween, 183–189
Ham, 38–41, 111–112
Hand-feeding, 266–267
Hardball testing, 273
Hazelnut, 140–142
Herbs, 126, 129, 131–132, 162; canning, 162–163; freezing, 161–162
Herbs, Spices, and Flavorings (Stobart), 255
Hess, John and Karen, 84, 109
Hibiscus flower, 129
Hints for success, 22, 277–278
Home cooking, 230–231
Howard, Maria Willett, 258

I
Ice cream, 52

J
Jane Brody's Nutrition Book (Brody), 224
January, 242–260
Jelling test, 143
Journal of Lipid Research, 104
July, 107–129
July Fourth, 107–115
Jump rope diet, 33–34
June, 86–106

K
Kale, 102–103
Kiwi, 180–181; juice, 181

L
Lamb, 15–20, 56–60, 218–219, 255–256
Lamb, Charles, 163, 165
Lappé, Frances Moore, 154
Lard, leaf, 123
Larousse Gastronomique, 38, 202
Leeks, 98–99, 104–105, 263–265
Lemon, 132–133, 140–142
Lettuce, 73. *See also* Greens
Lime, 260
Liver, chopped, 234–235
Lobster, 91–97; bodies, 92–93; summer, 92, 94; warning, 93; winter, 92, 94
Lowney's Cook Book (Howard), 258

M
Macaroon, 179–180
Maida Heatter's Book of Great Desserts (Heatter), 258

RECIPE INDEX

*Main Dishes/Assorted is a catch-all category for items that combine meat, seafood, or poultry with enough other things so a characterizing ingredient cannot readily be picked out. Those main dishes that clearly feature something are listed under their respective subheadings.

Main Dishes/Meat and Poultry

All-Purpose Low-Calorie Chicken Breast, 34
Basic Pork Scaloppini, 167
Braised Short Ribs and Apples in Cider Sauce, 173
Crisp-Skin Roast Pork, 165
Lamb Loaf with Sorrel Stuffing, 58
Lambsteak, 17
Maple-Mustard Game Hens, 274
Murgh Massalam (Spiced Chicken), 254
My Mom's Stuffed Meat Loaf, 231
Norman Rabbit, 192
Pork Sate with Peanut Sauce, 169
Pork Scaloppini Piccata, 168
Pot-Roasted Chicken, 199
Sauerbraten, 198
Scotch Collops with Spiked Onion Sauce, 218
Sort of Scandinavian Turkey, 212
Sort of Szechwan Chicken in Lettuce Leaves, 35
Szechwan Shish Kebab, 255

Main Dishes/Seafood

Carol's New Orleans–Style Barbecued Shrimp, 243
Codfish Cakes, 24
Fried Smelt, 23–24
Mussels Marinière, 88
Salmon in the Bathtub, 115

Main Dishes/Vegetable

Colache, 156
Corn Pasta with Succotash Sauce, 111
Gratin of Leeks and Swiss Chard with Swiss Cheese, 263
September Bean Stew, 155

Miscellaneous

Applesauce, 191
Cider Syrup for Pancakes and Pies, 172
Garam Masala (Hot Mixture), 253
Lobster Stock, 93
Maple–Cream Cheese Spread, 275
Maple Sugar, 273
Meringue Paste (two recipes), 258–259
Oatmeal, 216
Pizza Dough, 27
Roasted Garlic and Sesame Salt, 136

Pastry, Cakes, and Cookies

Any Fruit and Almond Kuchen, 123
Apple-Apricot Crumb Pie with Sour Cream Custard, 194
Apricot-Ginger Florentines, 238
Big Oatmeal Cookies with Dates and Nuts, 221
Boston Cream Pie (Iconoclast's Version), 80
Boston Cream Torte, 83
Cheesecake Tart, 41
Damn Fancy Chocolate Pie, 53
Deep-Dish Peach-Amaretto Pie, 122
Deep-Dish Plum and Black Cherry Pie, 121
Ginger Shortbread, 237
Intense Double-Apple Cake, 193
Intoxicating Chocolate Drops, 114
Kugelhopf, 65
Lime Kisses, 260
Maple-Walnut Filo Snails, 275
Nut Kisses, 260
Peppernuts, 239
The Quintessential Carrot Cake, 227
Vanilla Kisses, 260

Relishes and Preserves

Black and Blueberry Jam, 142
Crisp Root Relish, 212
Mustard Fruit, 210
Rose Hip Jam, 88

Sauces

All-Purpose Chocolate Sauce, 51
Basic Sorrel Purée and Sauces, 56
Browned Garlic and Pine Nut Sauce, 185
Cashew Chutney, 135
Crab Dip with Capers and Watermelon Rind, 137
Cucumber Sauce, 119
Fast Blender Hot Sauce, 248
Freezer Pesto, 162
Green Mayonnaise, 118
Herb Butters, 162
Lemon-Sesame Sauce for Grilled Vegetables, 132
Lobster Butter, 94
Pumpkin Seed Sauce for Vegetables, 207
Spiced Yogurt, 135